WOMEN IN GERMAN YEARBOOK

Volume Twenty

2004

EDITORIAL BOARD

Claudia Breger, Indiana University, 2001–2004

Gisela Brinker-Gabler, State University of New York, Binghamton, 1992–2003

Helen L. Cafferty, Bowdoin College, 1992–2003

Jeanette Clausen, Indiana University-Purdue University Fort Wayne, 1995–2004

Susan L. Cocalis, University of Massachusetts, Amherst, 1992–2003

Ruth P. Dawson, University of Hawai'i at Manoa, 2001–2004

Myra Marx Ferree, University of Wisconsin, 2001–2004

Sara Friedrichsmeyer, University of Cincinnati, 1999–2004

Katherine R. Goodman, Brown University, 2001–2004

Atina J. Grossmann, Cooper Union, 2001–2004

Patricia Herminghouse, University of Rochester, 2002–2005

Nancy Kaiser, University of Wisconsin, Madison, 1998–2003

Ruth Klüger, University of California, Irvine, 2001–2004

Barbara K. Kosta, University of Arizona, 2001–2004

Renate Möhrmann, Universität zu Köln, 1998–2003

Georgina Paul, University of Warwick, 2001–2004

PAST EDITORS

Marianne Burkhard, 1984–88
Edith Waldstein, 1984–87
Jeanette Clausen, 1987–94
Helen Cafferty, 1988–90
Sara Friedrichsmeyer, 1990–1998
Susanne Zantop, 1998–2001
Patricia Herminghouse, 1994–2002

WOMEN IN

Feminist Studies in German Literature & Culture

GERMAN

Edited by Ruth-Ellen Boetcher Joeres & Marjorie Gelus

YEARBOOK

Volume Twenty

2004

University of Nebraska Press, Lincoln and London

The German original of "Feminist Theories on the Separation of the Private and the Public: Looking Back, Looking Forward" appeared in *Feministische Studien* 21.1 (2003). The German original of "Did Women Really Read Differently? A Historical-Empirical Contribution to Gender-Oriented Reading Research" appeared in *Feministische Studien* 19.2 (2001). The English translations of the articles are printed here by the generous permission of the Lucius & Lucius Verlag, Stuttgart.

© 2004 by the Board of Regents of the University of Nebraska. All rights reserved. Manufactured in the United States of America. ∞

Published by arrangement with the Coalition of Women in German.

ISBN 0-8032-4820-2 (Cloth)
ISBN 0-8032-9845-5 (Paper)
ISSN 1058-7446

CONTENTS

Acknowledgments vii
Preface ix

**Yellowed Pages, Virtual Realities:
Publication in Women in German's Past, Present, and Future** 1
Jeannine Blackwell and Jeanette Clausen

**Traffic of Women in Germanic Literature: The Role of the Peace
Pledge in Marital Exchanges** 13
Carol Parrish Jamison

**Adam Schubart's Early Modern "Tyrant She-Man": Female
Misbehavior, Gender, and the Disciplining of Hybrid Bodies** 37
Katja Altpeter-Jones

Anna Louisa Karsch as Sappho 62
Claire Baldwin

**Scandal Writ Large in the Wake of the French Revolution:
The Case of Amalia Holst** 98
Carol Strauss Sotiropoulos

**The Hidden Face of Narcissus: Suicide as Poetic Speech
in Margarethe von Trotta's Early Films** 122
Eva Kuttenberg

**Intertextual Connections: Structures of Feminine Identification
in the Works of Karin Struck** 145
Morwenna Symons

**Neither Foreigners Nor Aliens: The Interwoven Stories of Sinti
and Roma and Black Germans** 163
Nicola Lauré al-Samarai

*   *   *

Current Feminist Work in Germany

Feminist Theories on the Separation of the Private and the Public: Looking Back, Looking Forward 184
Ulla Wischermann

**Did Women Really Read Differently?
A Historical-Empirical Contribution
to Gender-Oriented Reading Research** 198
Silke Schlichtmann

Musing Together at Year Twenty 215
Ruth-Ellen Boetcher Joeres and Marjorie Gelus

About the Contributors 232
Notice to Contributors 236

ACKNOWLEDGMENTS

The coeditors would like to thank the current Editorial Board for their welcome assistance in reviewing manuscripts, their participation in our on-line discussions, and their general support and encouragement. We also gratefully acknowledge the assistance and advice of the following individuals in reviewing manuscripts submitted for publication in the *Women in German Yearbook*.

Karen Achberger, St. Olaf College
Leslie Adelson, Cornell University
James Albisetti, University of Kentucky
Antje Ascheid, University of Georgia
Russell Berman, Stanford University
Jeannine Blackwell, University of Kentucky
Claudia Breger, Indiana University
Susan Cocalis, University of Massachusetts, Amherst
Claire Colebrook, University of Edinburgh
Glenn Cuomo, New College of Florida
Margret Eifler, Rice University
Andreas Gailus, University of Minnesota, Minneapolis
Stephen Jaeger, University of Illinois, Urbana
Lutz Koepnick, Washington University
Kader Konuk, University of Michigan, Ann Arbor
Elizabeth Krimmer, Mt. Holyoke College
Anna Kuhn, University of California, Davis
Alice Kuzniar, University of North Carolina, Chapel Hill
Helga Madland, University of Oklahoma
Michelle Mattson, Iowa State University
Charlotte Melin, University of Minnesota, Minneapolis
Sabine von Mering, Brandeis University
Marijane Osborn, University of California, Davis
Julie Prandi, Illinois Wesleyan University
Helmut Puff, University of Michigan, Ann Arbor
Jennifer Redmann, Kalamazoo College
Simon Richter, University of Pennsylvania, Philadelphia
Patricia Stanley, Florida State University, Tallahassee
Arlene Teraoka, University of Minnesota, Minneapolis
Bianca Theisen, Johns Hopkins University

Robert Tobin, Whitman College
Mara Wade, University of Illinois, Urbana

Special thanks to Victoria Hoelzer-Maddox
for manuscript preparation.

PREFACE

What does one do to celebrate a twentieth anniversary? For that is what the *Women in German Yearbook* is doing with this volume, its twentieth: celebrating a sizeable number of years of lively existence. This anniversary marks a moment in which the yearbook is approximately two-thirds as old as its parent organization, Women in German, which held its first formal meeting in 1976. The first *Yearbook,* edited by Marianne Burkhard and Edith Waldstein, appeared in 1985, with this clear statement in the editors' preface: "The *Women in German Yearbook* is a response to the growing interest in Women's Studies in German literature and culture, which has resulted in the need to disseminate relevant materials, studies, hypotheses and results" (v). Even at that early point, the broad nature of our concerns was made apparent. As the editors commented,

> [c]ertainly literary studies are a central concern, but at the same time we also feel the need to discuss notions about and attitudes toward women in contemporary society, so as to continue the all important reflection process and dialogue, which will, we hope, lead to a more accurate understanding of women's existence in all spheres of life (v).

Back to the original question: how to celebrate the twentieth occasion of a yearbook dedicated to such aims, then as well as now? In the end, we answered by concluding that this is an occasion to look not only back, but also forward. Accordingly, we have enlisted the aid of both a former editor and future president of WiG and the current president of WiG; we have assembled a group of pieces that present current feminist scholarship on the creative work of a number of German writers both present and past; we have asked a historian to provide us with a piece that in its central focus deals with an issue of concern to literary scholars as well; we have begun what we hope can be an ongoing practice of sharing the recent work of German scholars, in this case a literary scholar and a sociologist; and we editors have put down some of our own thoughts on the *Yearbook,* on WiG, and on our individual relationship to both journal and organization. We are, in other words, following past practices and at the same time, contemplating how the *Yearbook* might look in years to come.

The current volume begins with "Yellowed Pages, Virtual Realities: Publication in Women in German's Past, Present, and Future," a series of observations by Jeanette Clausen, coeditor of the *Women in German Yearbook* between 1987 and 1994 and the upcoming president of WiG, and Jeannine Blackwell, current president of WiG. Given that both of them are long-term and very active members of the organization, it struck the editors that they could comment knowledgeably on the history of WiG and its *Yearbook,* but also—as continuing, engaged members—on possible directions in which the journal might go as it moves beyond its first two decades. Their response to our request is therefore full of memories, reflections, and ruminations about what might happen: as expected, their take is both provocative and rich in ideas. What better way could there be to introduce this twentieth volume than to present an exchange that will, we hope, stimulate additional exchanges among WiG members?

In volume 19 of the *Yearbook,* we complained in the preface about the fact that none of the articles concerned pre-twentieth-century literature and culture. The response to that complaint is ample in the current volume: four of the six pieces that discuss literary and cultural questions focus on writings and cultural issues of periods before 1900. Two of those, in fact, delve back into the Germanic and early modern eras. Carol Parrish Jamison's topic may employ a phrase from a well-known 1975 article by the American anthropologist Gayle Rubin, but she uses that phrase to describe a topic in early Germanic literature. "Traffic of Women in Germanic Literature: The Role of the Peace Pledge in Marital Exchanges" examines several Germanic texts that treat the issue of so-called peace pledges, women of higher ranks who were married off to men of equal status who were perceived as threats to the peace of the women's kin. Jamison challenges the characterization of such a role of exchange as passive and concludes that early Germanic women could indeed respond actively to this supposed objectification of themselves and exert influence in both the expected role of mothers and a more public diplomatic position within their husbands' homes. Her investigation of Anglo-Saxon and Icelandic texts offers valuable comparative perspectives as well as a wealth of material that is less familiar to most of us.

Jamison's piece is followed by "Adam Schubart's Early Modern 'Tyrant She-Man': Female Misbehavior, Gender, and the Disciplining of Hybrid Bodies," Katja Alterpeter-Jones's intriguing examination of the so-called She-Man, a figure that appears in various German written texts and visual images from the late fifteenth to the early seventeenth centuries. Altpeter-Jones focuses on Adam Schubart's 1564 *Der Sieman / das ist wider den Hausteuffell* and asserts that Schubart actually presents a paradoxical image that emphasizes the centrality of gender in the social order, but also exhibits considerable discomfort around what she calls the "visibility of difference." The role of the body thus becomes paramount and extends ultimately into the traditional alignment of gender with anatomical difference and sexuality.

Claire Baldwin's "Anna Louisa Karsch as Sappho" offers a detailed and extremely interesting look at the ways in which the eighteenth-century poet both imitated and resisted her Greek literary predecessor. In the course of her discussion, Baldwin examines as well the context of the wider popular and aesthetic reception of Sappho at Karsch's time. What emerges in this combination of Karsch/Sappho and the broader reception is also a useful look at the ways in which Sappho was seen in a specifically eighteenth-century German setting that Karsch, in turn, reflected.

The final contribution to this section of literary/critical/historical pieces is Carol Strauss Sotiropoulos's "Scandal Writ Large in the Wake of the French Revolution: The Case of Amalia Holst." Here the focus is not on a poet, but on a writer of tracts concerned with education, not reflecting a tradition of poetry but rather the aftermath of the chaos of the French Revolution, especially as it affected political and social thought. Almost-contemporaries, Holst and Karsch seem in many ways like opposites. And yet practicality characterizes both of them: Karsch, with a necessary eye on the literary market and the need to sell an image of herself that would in turn lead to the sale of her books; Holst, trying, despite the reactionary period following the Revolution, to "sell" ideas concerning the need for reform in the field of girls' education. Sotiropoulos's piece is a study in accommodation: how Holst balanced her progressive views with the conservative expectations around her. What Sotiropoulos characterizes as Holst's belief in the "imperative of *Bildung* for women" was the driving force behind the treatises on education that form the basis for her discussion.

From Holst, we leap forward to the 1970s and 1980s with Eva Kuttenberg's "The Hidden Face of Narcissus: Suicide as Poetic Speech in Margarethe von Trotta's Early Films." This piece offers a compelling reading of von Trotta's representation of suicide in three of her films that blends sophisticated film analysis, psychoanalysis, and an analysis of femininity. Kuttenberg's use of Julia Kristeva as a theoretical point of departure and her inclusion of the dichotomy of male law/female self-erasure are in themselves interesting, while at the same time in her comparative approach to the films she questions dichotomies and moves instead into considerable nuances of thought.

A contemporary of von Trotta's who is a writer rather than a filmmaker is the subject of Morwenna Symons's "Intertextual Connections: Structures of Feminine Identification in the Works of Karin Struck." Although the focus is on Struck, Symons contextualizes her argument by including both Elfriede Jelinek and Ingeborg Bachmann, whose work is also read intertextually, as a contrasting picture for the primary examination of Struck's writings, from her early work of the 1970s to a later intertextual example, Struck's 1993 homage to Bachmann as she is seen within the framework of a female literary lineage and literary influence. That Struck fails, according to Symons, in terms of expanding upon her ideas of an ongoing female creativity indicates a disappointing end to a development that had begun so promisingly with Struck's clear belief in a female literary heritage.

The remaining pieces in this volume strike out in some new directions. "Neither Foreigners nor Aliens: The Interwoven Stories of Sinti and Roma and Black Germans," Nicola Lauré al-Samarai's contribution, presents the work of a historian who investigates the positions of three ethnic groups whose presence in German society is hardly a recent phenomenon, but whose impact and significance have been mostly ignored or overlooked, particularly as they might be examined within the context of Germany's colonial past. Lauré al-Samarai examines the histories of all three groups as they are specifically related to Germany, but she also moves into the present, especially as it concerns the growth of self-consciousness on the part of the Sinti, Roma, and Black Germans, but also as that development contrasts with the continuing gap in consciousness on the part of white Germans. This is a piece that not only employs the methodology of historiography but that also works above all with the analytical categories of race and ethnicity. It thereby augments feminist concerns with gender. But as Lauré al-Samarai herself implies at the end of her piece, there are many other discussions that need to take place and that would focus on other categories such as gender and sexuality. Perhaps her piece will stimulate some interesting responses that will expand upon her work.

We are pleased to present "Current Feminist Work in Germany," a new feature in the *Yearbook* that we hope will continue in future volumes. In an effort to extend our offerings of feminist work, both in the matter of discipline and national origin, we selected two particularly interesting pieces from recent volumes of *Feministische Studien,* the interdisciplinary feminist journal in Germany that, in fact, celebrated its twentieth anniversary just shortly before the *Yearbook,* in 2002.

These two contributions may represent the differing disciplines of sociology and literary criticism, but they reveal common areas of interest in their efforts to throw into question polarities and dichotomizations in gender models and in the specific concepts of public and private spheres. Ulla Wischermann's "Feminist Theories on the Separation of the Private and the Public: Looking Back, Looking Forward," offers a marvelous overview of feminist work on the public/private dichotomy, but she goes beyond that review and suggests ways in which we can and should work with the concepts in the future. She emphasizes above all the need to separate ourselves from the polarities and dichotomies that so often arise, and to focus instead on the relational aspects that characterize such a pair of terms. This stress on thinking that resembles a continuum echoes a great deal of feminist thinking in the US today, and reading about it in the context of the work of a German sociologist can be very useful to us as literary scholars.

Silke Schlichtmann's "Did Women Really Read Differently? A Historical-Empirical Contribution to Gender-Oriented Reading Research" tosses out a challenge to reading theorists (feminist and otherwise) whose practice has often been to equate "gender" with "women" and to overlook the importance of the dual-gender model in inquiries such as that concerning whether reading is a gendered activity. Using the examples of contemporary readers' responses to several of Goethe's works, Schlichtmann exposes the risk of stereotypical thinking that sees women readers as emotional, men as rational. By the use of personal narrative statements made by various readers of Goethe, she makes clear that we need to question previous gender models. And she, like Wischermann, concentrates her efforts on the breaking down of simplistic thinking that all too often hides behind a too-ready acceptance of dichotomies.

In other words, both Wischermann and Schlichtmann challenge questions and conclusions that are too simple, too facilely expressed. By presenting both pieces with their very different subject matters and methodological approaches, we hope nevertheless to point out these larger similarities and the importance of our reading across disciplines. But what we hope most of all is that this expansion of the *Yearbook*'s palette of offerings to include recent, previously published feminist work from outside the United States might continue in future volumes, thereby allowing the *Yearbook* to connect its readers with other work. And in our ongoing hope that the *Yearbook* will indeed reach a non-German-speaking feminist audience as well, we are pleased to present this work in English translation.

The final piece is not a new form for the *Yearbook*. Numbers of previous *Yearbook* editors have written joint pieces on topics of interest to our field. What is different here is that we have put together this piece with the intention of responding to the opening piece by Blackwell and Clausen by extending their observations in other directions that stem from the personal and more general impressions that each of us has concerning Women in German, primarily its *Yearbook* but also the organization itself. We felt it was time for us to speak from our experience as editors and as members of WiG, if just to present the range of issues that concern us. We speak here less as a "we," and more as two "I's," for despite our similarities, we too represent two different constituencies of the many constituencies that constitute Women in German. At the same time, in the spirit of dynamic exchange, we also respond to each other. Thus, this piece may resemble previous jointly written commentaries in the *Yearbook*, but it also has its own style and should be viewed as an encouragement to others to consider contributing jointly written pieces to the *Yearbook*.

As always, there are those whom we want to thank for their special assistance during this past year. And as always, Victoria Hoelzer-Maddox is the first on the list. Her extraordinary skills as the computer expert who formats the entire volume enable us quite literally to produce the *Yearbook*. But in addition, her extensive knowledge of copyediting and of the rules of the *MLA Handbook* keep us going and get us through. We are extremely grateful for her cheerful and welcome assistance. We want as well to thank Nicole Grewling, who has now completed her third year as Ruth-Ellen Joeres's editorial assistant in Minnesota. Nicole has been a willing and able assistant whose skills and knowledge have become ever more valuable to our work. We both want to thank our departments and colleges at Minneapolis and Sacramento for their encouragement and support, both financial and otherwise: specifically, Arlene Teraoka, Chair of the Minnesota Department of German, Scandinavian, and Dutch, and Dean Steven Rosenstone, of the College of Liberal Arts, as well as Dean William J. Sullivan, Jr., of the College of Arts and Letters at California State University at Sacramento. Because of the special nature of this twentieth volume, we also wish to thank Ilze Mueller and Sara Lennox, who willingly and with all due speed translated the German pieces by Ulla Wischermann, Silke Schlichtmann (both by Mueller), and Nicola Lauré al-Samarai (by Lennox) that are included in this volume. They are talented translators in addition to all their other skills, and we are very grateful for their assistance. And finally, there is Patricia Herminghouse, whose long term as *Yearbook* coeditor ostensibly came to an end when Marjorie

Gelus became coeditor last year. But the fact that Pat served so ably and for so many years in that position means that she remains our most valuable adviser on *Yearbook* matters. This year, in particular, when the things hammering down on the two of us threatened to bring us to a halt, Pat was there, with advice and help and wisdom. And so we thank her for yet again coming to our aid.

Speaking of thanks (Marjorie speaking here): Ruth-Ellen Joeres's three-year term as coeditor has come to an end, and she has made the difficult decision not to renew it, for professional and personal reasons. She had worked on the *Yearbook* for only a year when I came on to relieve Pat Herminghouse, and although she still felt like a beginner herself, she very ably coached me through volume 19. We have coached each other through volume 20, and we have both begun to get the hang of it now. I know that all of us Women in German are grateful to Ruth-Ellen for the skills that she has lavished on the *Yearbook*, and I will miss our close collaboration.

But I am also delighted to announce that another in a long line of talented coeditors stands ready to take up the work. Helga Kraft, of the Department of Germanic Studies at the University of Illinois at Chicago, has accepted the post. Some will also remember Helga's formidable organizing skills during the three years that our conference was held in Florida (1994–96).

Thank you, Ruth-Ellen! Welcome, Helga!

Works Cited

Women in German Yearbook 1: Feminist Studies and German Culture. Ed. Marianne Burkhard and Edith Waldstein. Lanham, NH: UP of America, 1985.

Yellowed Pages, Virtual Realities: Publication in Women in German's Past, Present, and Future

Jeannine Blackwell and Jeanette Clausen

The first two presidents of WiG reflect on the history of the organization and the *Yearbook,* take stock of the present, and speculate about the future. WiG began as a supportive community for feminist Germanists isolated in their departments from like-minded scholars. The *Yearbook* has come to embody the ethos of the organization in certain ways: feminist process and academic rigor; scholarly and creative writing side by side. Despite the high quality and rich variety of the contributions, the *Yearbook* has not yet found a substantial readership beyond WiG itself. The authors explore the promises and perils of e-publication as the likely future of the *Yearbook.* (JB and JC)

Jeanette: The editors' invitation to write a piece for this twentieth volume of the *WiG Yearbook* was an opportunity to reflect on where we began and how far we've come, as well as to project some ideas for the future. Women in German as an organization goes back to 1974. Our first annual conference took place in 1976 and the first volume of the *Yearbook* was published in 1985.[1] Back then, the camera-ready copy was prepared on typewriters. Today it appears that journals published as bound volumes may soon go the way of carbon copies and mimeographed newsletters. It is important for WiG to engage in reflection and planning not only to keep pace with change, but also to become a more vital force in the profession. What does the future hold for our organization and for the *Yearbook*? How, to use a cliché from strategic planning, can we take WiG to "the next level"? The climate for feminism, higher education in general, and German Studies is much different than twenty years ago.

How the *Yearbook* Got Legs

Jeannine: The *Yearbook* grew out of a need to find venues for feminist publications, and it emerged at a time when some academic feminist groups were experiencing a crisis in growth and development. American feminism had survived a struggle over separatism and other issues that divided or mortally wounded many feminist collectives and coalitions. Academic feminists were trying to decide if and how much they had sold out to the establishment. Amazingly enough, the Coalition of Women in German survived the troubled waters of early feminism, partially because of long-term and long-distance friendships nurtured by the organization and its annual conference. But it survived as well because the members, isolated in small, beleaguered German departments strewn across America, needed WiG to recharge and reconnect. Women who had edited free feminist circulars and newspapers found themselves finished with graduate school and landing in the academy. But what would their next feminist writings look like? We knew we could produce a lively, important, witty newsletter. We knew we could create a collaborative, spontaneous hilarious artwork known as the WiG Cabaret. Could we carry that verve and vitality into different forms?

Jeanette: What we began with was mostly enthusiasm and a sense of urgency: where were we going to publish our work if we didn't have our own journal? The first issues of the *Yearbook* were modeled in part on the volumes produced every year by the GDR Symposium in Conway, NH. Published by the University Press of America, each volume contained a selection of papers from the previous year's symposium. WiG, we thought, could pull together papers from our annual sessions at AATG, MLA, and, of course, the WiG conference. However, we quickly saw the need to cast a wider net and in fact to solicit contributions from feminist scholars who probably wouldn't have sent their work to WiG at the time.

Jeannine: We knew how great the papers were in the WiG sessions at the various conferences—I am thinking about the double session on Romantic women at the MLA in 1985, for example—and we wanted to capture this energy to show what the organization's members were really doing. Another source of inspiration was the first conference of *Frauen in der Literaturwissenschaft* (Women in Literary Scholarship) in Hamburg in 1983, organized primarily by Inge Stephan and Sigrid Weigel. Several of us attended that conference and presented papers there. Even though the West German feminists had organized much later than we, and their group was much smaller and localized, they were preparing a conference volume right then and there. WiG had to get moving! Their first conference volume, *Feministische Literaturwissenschaft: Dokumentation der Tagung in Hamburg im Mai 1983* (Feminist Literary Scholarship: A Documentation of the Conference in Hamburg in May 1983; Berlin 1984) came out before the first *WiG Yearbook,* and their second conference volume, *Frauen-Weiblichkeit-Schrift* (Women—Femininity—Writing), appeared in 1985, the same year as the first *WiG Yearbook.* Several of us published there as well. It was a shock to see how fast they moved papers into print. WiG was a larger and more grassroots organization, but we needed their impetus and example to move into more structured venues in the profession.

One of the issues back in the 1980s was whether feminism in the university was selling out. As Women's Studies programs became established, more feminist scholars got tenure, and specializations developed, many of us were uncertain about how "professionalized" we wanted to become. Were we becoming institutionalized and losing our cutting edge? I recall that this was part of our concern as WiG discussed the possibility of a journal or yearbook. Were we going to wind up rejecting people's work as the big boys did? How were we going to make sure we had feminist process as we moved toward a national voice in German Studies?

Feminist Process in WiG, Feminist Mentoring in the *Yearbook*

Jeanette: I believe that WiG as an organization was and is more committed to a feminist process than many feminist associations—those four-hour business meetings at our conferences and WiG's long-standing resistance to any kind of governance structure that smacked of a hierarchy are proof of that. WiG's decision at the fall 1999 conference to elect a president and vice president was not made lightly, but only after much debate over the seemingly conflicting values of democratic decision-making and efficiency, or at least chaos-reduction. WiG's egalitarianism is also rooted in its beginning as a group of graduate students and (mostly) untenured assistant professors. In those early days, Wiggies helped each other negotiate job searches, publication, and eventually promotion and tenure. And today, helping feminist students and faculty succeed in the profession continues to be one of our major priorities.

Those two commitments—to feminist process and to supporting WiG members in the early stages of their careers—are reflected in the *Yearbook,* which has from the beginning had a strong mentoring component. Every refereed journal has a review process and provides some feedback to authors about the work they submit, but blind review is no guarantee of a fair or thoughtful reading of papers—even by WiG members. That's why the *WiG Yearbook* editors are proactive in terms of mediating reviewers' comments in a supportive and constructive manner so that the author is not overwhelmed by criticisms but can actually make use of them. In this way, the editorial process comes to embody a feminist approach to reviewing and revising papers submitted for publication, and to fostering the authors' scholarly and professional development. It parallels the mentoring that WiG provides in other ways, for example, in the practice of assigning the organizing of conference sessions to teams consisting of one experienced individual and one with less or no experience, or in the principle that the WiG Steering Committee membership should include graduate students as well as professors. It is exhilarating and gratifying to see the cutting-edge scholarship and dynamic leadership that these arrangements often produce. It turns out that academic rigor and feminist process are not an oxymoron, but a creative fusion that WiG can be proud of, and a tradition we should continue.

Jeannine: I experienced that mentoring first hand in that first issue of the *WiG Yearbook*. I was transforming a WiG conference presentation into a paper called "Anonym, verschollen, trivial: Methodological Hindrances in Researching German Women's Literature." My anonymous readers gently but firmly showed me how to remove the colloquialisms and undergird my arguments about unknown women writers. I had to rewrite only twice before they and the editors were satisfied. It was as rigorous as a *PMLA* editorial board reader report I received the same year, but not half so terrifying.

On the other hand...

Jeanette: Other lessons learned from twenty years of the *WiG Yearbook* may also be relevant here. For example, you can't escape the double-bind factor. People are reluctant to publish in a journal without an established reputation, but it's impossible to establish a reputation without good articles by up-and-coming scholars.

Jeannine: That's why the editors often encouraged members with some name recognition to submit work to the *Yearbook*. If recognized names appeared, we thought, the stigma of being marginalized would be partially erased. This action takes active recruitment, as editors have learned. It can also lead, however, to having a reputation of publishing the Old Girls, whose scholarship and topics may not be cutting-edge. I think we have struck a good balance here. And sometimes, editors have been stung by ambitious scholars who have submitted or promised their work, then turned around and pulled it for a more prestigious publishing venue. This can be an embittering experience for editors who so value the feminist mentoring process and have learned another lesson the hard way: not all women are self-sacrificing, fair, and generous. It is, however, part of the maturation process both in feminism and in Women in German, as we move from the dominance of one generation of scholars to the next.

Feminist Activism and Feminist Theory

Jeanette: Like many feminist organizations that began in the 1970s, WiG members were vocal in espousing activism—in fact, some of our earliest publications, such as the WiG reviews of German language textbooks, were much-needed activist interventions in the profession at the time. Activism was a value that we wanted and needed to maintain, although some feared that it would be at the expense of theory. The *Yearbook* had an important role to play in mediating the *Theoriedebatten* that took place within the organization, especially at the annual conferences. When the *Yearbook* began publication, there was still something of a bias against feminist work in our field as not being theoretically grounded—in part for good reason, since many early feminist analyses were uneven at best and lacked a theoretical framework more often than not. So, an early goal was to insist that papers published in the *Yearbook* should make use of relevant theoretical work—a self-evident reality today, but an uncomfortable topic for WiG at the time. Helen Cafferty and I struggled to articulate a responsible and yet balanced editorial policy on the issue in our postscript to *Yearbook 5*, "Who's Afraid of Feminist Theory?"[2] As WiG made progress on this front, we also hoped to participate in feminist discourses on a wider scale, to add the voices of German Studies to those that continue to shape feminist theory and criticism nationally and internationally.

Jeannine: We failed miserably at theorizing in the first decade of WiG as an organization (1975-1985). With the advent of the *Yearbook*, our lack of structure and theory in dealing with German culture became palpable. We wanted to participate in relevant debates, but the *Yearbook* came on the scene just as a variety of French feminisms dominated the landscape. Many of us found much of this feminist theory to be too apolitical, even reactionary, to use. Many of us were grappling with the politics of a divided Germany and its impact on women, and could not find a theory that incorporated all the praxis of women's lives and cultural production. We kept discovering women writers who needed a good positivist write-up before we were ready to move on to theorizing about them. And so we kept off the track of theory for much too long. We periodically chided ourselves for this absence or explained ourselves to each other in the *Yearbook*. The editors gave postscripts and commentaries on this problem, as well as on other hot spots in feminist studies, such as the language of feminism, New Historicism, and the future of Germanistik in America. Only when we turned to film, film theory, and cultural criticism did the *Yearbook* really accomplish its goal of integrating our discoveries with a plan and an explanation. And the *Wende* (fall of the Berlin wall) was part of that change: we were desperately in need of a theory of culture that could explain the turns of desire and politics in a changed, no longer Eurocentric world. We needed theory to explain our own role as practitioners in a national literature, an antiquated, contradictory, but nevertheless useful artifact. We are somewhat better at creating and using theory now, much of this expertise generated by younger WiG members, not us old-timers.

Of course the *Yearbook* is not just about theory. It has a wonderful range of genres: poetry, theory, and history written by the artists and poets themselves, translations, interviews, bibliographies, the occasional diatribe, new discoveries, humor, and satire.

Creative Scholarship and Translation

Jeannine: WiG generates a kind of bravery by association in its *Yearbook* composition and its conference. Getting to know our guests at the WiG Conference, such as Barbara Frischmuth, Margot Schroeder, Luise Pusch, Jeanette Lander, and Herta Mueller, we were able to relax and enjoy them as authors and acquaintances. We found that we could actually talk with writers on a very personal level. Then Barbara Frischmuth volunteered to give us a short work or two to include in the second *Yearbook* volume (1986). Suddenly, we graduate students and assistant professors were published next to great writers, who had become our friends! For some of us, this was an incredibly empowering juxtaposition. It allowed us to make our own writing more creative. Some of us translated their works for publication in the *Yearbook,* others interviewed them for *Yearbook* introductions. Not only did these texts generate wonderful reading for our own use, they brought us self-confidence about our own abilities. For the organizers of the speaker tours, it brought us organizational skills that we have used to run universities. It gave an American venue and an audience to some great German-speaking writers, filmmakers, and critics.

The range of creative essays—from opinion pieces to critical theory and politics, and retrospectives on our past—makes the *Yearbook*'s composition much freer than standard journals in German literature and culture. I am thinking about essays by Helga Königsdorf, Ruth Klüger, Luise Pusch, Sara Lennox, and Jutta Brückner. There is a flow from editors' frame to creative work, creative translation, scholarly article, critical politics or theory, and the editors' postscript or retrospective. I have learned to appreciate that feminist refashioning of the scholarly text in WiG.

Jeanette: The range of work published in the *Yearbook* marks another way in which the journal embodies the ethos of the organization: to combine serious feminist academic writing and scholarship with creativity, humor, and spontaneity, just as we do at our conferences. It is a quality that makes us unique and one that I, at least, would not want the journal to lose as we continue to mature as an organization. So, with all these positive qualities, why isn't the *WiG Yearbook* on the required reading list of every scholar in the field?

The Profession's Best-Kept Secret?

Jeanette: The quality of work published in the *WiG Yearbook* is easily on a par with that of other journals in the field of German Studies. Yet the *Yearbook* appears not to be widely read or cited by scholars outside of WiG itself. In part, this may simply reflect the fact that we are our primary audience, not yet mainstreamed into German Studies as a whole—which is itself a relatively small field. To make the *Yearbook*'s content accessible to an audience beyond German Studies, the WiG editors made a policy decision several years ago that all articles would be published in English. Articles submitted in German are translated into English after having been reviewed, revised, and accepted. But while the English-only policy has made the articles accessible to readers who don't know German, the *Yearbook* probably is still physically inaccessible to feminist scholars in other fields, in large part because a yearbook is a peculiar genre that falls somewhere between an anthology and a journal. A yearbook doesn't necessarily pop up on the radar screens of librarians responsible for serials subscriptions; thus, even if a scholar in another discipline should happen to read a review of a recent *Yearbook* volume or find a reference she wants to follow up on, she is not likely to find the *Yearbook* in her library and will probably have to wait several weeks to receive it through interlibrary loan.

The problem of getting the *Yearbook* onto library shelves is especially acute in the current era of budget cuts for libraries and university presses that have contributed to the much-discussed crisis in scholarly publishing, direly proclaimed by Stephen Greenblatt in a May 2002 memo to the MLA membership and analyzed in an article by the MLA Ad Hoc Committee on the Future of Scholarly Publishing.[3] *PMLA* editor Carlos J. Alonso recently reported anecdotal evidence of tenure and promotion files having been forwarded to school- and campus-level committees with a copy of Greenblatt's memo attached.[4] Surely this crisis is another force helping to keep the *WiG Yearbook* one of the profession's best-kept secrets. It was inevitable that budget cutbacks combined with an unrelenting pressure on faculty to publish in order to achieve tenure and promotion would create a severe supply/demand imbalance: the demand by faculty and future faculty for publication outlets continues unabated, but there is no matching demand by faculty or libraries to purchase scholarly books and journal subscriptions. Who can afford them? And who has the time to read them anyway?

These are some of the issues that WiG must face head-on if we are to make the *Yearbook* into a must-read publication. The solution that the current editors have proposed—to rename the *Yearbook* and turn it into a "real" journal that appears two or more times a year—is an attractive option but out of reach for WiG financially at this point. Our relationship with the University of Nebraska Press is good, but each year the treasurer holds her breath until the cost of purchasing copies of the *Yearbook* and mailing them to WiG members has been paid in installments over several months.

Jeannine: Mailing costs, paper publication costs, lengthy time to publication—all of these factors increase the price we have to pay. I think it is time to consider an on-line journal in place of a *Yearbook*. It would give us the flexibility to experiment with new forms of writing; we could incorporate book reviews that would be extremely current; we could innovate with feminist dialogue in the electronic environment. We could add color in text and image, film clips, historical portraits, art work, concrete poetry, and voiceovers.

Jeanette: Journals like that are already beginning to appear. Here is a quote from the press release announcing *Innovate: journal of online education*:

> *Innovate* is dedicated to presenting articles via the most dynamic, interactive technology that is available. For each article, the journal provides an online discussion forum, an interactive web cast that connects authors and readers, and a "read-related" feature that links visitors to articles on similar topics. A multimedia classifieds section and journal editions in multiple languages are both in the planning stages.[5]

Doesn't this sound exactly like the kind of journal you have in mind? But we'll need electronic seven-league boots to catch up from where we are now, I think.

WiG's First E-Steps

Jeanette: WiG has been inching toward electronic publication for a while. The WiG web site, created in the mid-nineties by Brenda Bethman and others at the University of Massachusetts, Amherst, and maintained on the UMass server for several years, has had its own domain name and web space since early in 2002. The web site made the move to electronic registration for the 2004 WiG conference a logical next step (with the option for members who prefer paper to register by snail mail).

Jeannine: Much earlier, the Berkeley collective set up the WIG-L listserv. That was our first live, interactive communication. And although it does not officially belong to WiG, I want us to remember Michelle Stott James's magnificent website sponsored by Brigham Young University, *The Sophie Project, A Digital Library of Works by German-Speaking Women* at <http://sophie.byu.edu/>. It has been endorsed by Women in German and has many collaborators and contributors from the WiG membership. Michelle is attempting to launch an on-line journal there named, appropriately enough, *Sophie*. The site has had more than 33,000 hits, and that bodes well for German feminism on the web.

Jeanette: But the really big step was the *WiG Newsletter*. In the fall of 2003, after more than a year of planning, the *Newsletter* went electronic, posted on the web site in a password-protected file. An email announcement with the password and login procedure was sent to all WiG members—and the *Newsletter* editors promptly found their mailboxes overflowing with scores of returned emails to members whose accounts had changed or whose mailboxes were full—or maybe their universities' servers were reading the *WiG Newsletter* message as SPAM. This early experience with the E-Newsletter highlights an important issue: if we want the *Yearbook,* in a new online incarnation, to be a benefit of membership, we will have to solve the problem of reliably notifying members that it is available. An alternative to password-protected publication would be to make the online journal free to anyone who happened upon it—but then, what would be the motivation to join WiG? This is a thorny issue with major financial implications, since membership income has always been our primary (and only reliable) source of funding. And it appears that the WiG membership has begun to dwindle in the last couple of years—since the most recent dues increase, actually.

Jeannine: The Steering Committee and the Editorial Board have grappled with these issues and problems without being ready to take the big leap yet. But each step brings us closer to electronic ability and accuracy. What will put this new, sleek, renamed *Yearbook* on the map will be absolutely current reviews of new feminist books and possibly films on things German. If we can offer that, we will be the first German academic journal to do so. Readers will beat a path to the website if we can deliver that timely information in a multimedia environment.

Jeanette: The publication of book reviews is another area where supply and demand are at odds. Everyone loves to read book reviews, but hardly anyone wants to write them, because they don't count much toward promotion or tenure and writing them takes time away from "real" scholarship. Could the multimedia environment transform the lowly book review into a new genre that counts as serious academic work?

The Promises and Perils of Electronic Publication

Jeanette: Another lesson that WiG perhaps still needs to learn is that feminist vision is not enough. I believe WiG had a kind of vision of what the *Yearbook* might become, but what we haven't had is a plan, beyond just getting the next volume together. If the *Yearbook* is going to survive and grow, we need to develop a strategic plan to guide us. Having used the organizational skills we learned in WiG to move into leadership positions in our universities, we must now use the long-range planning skills we've learned in those jobs to lead WiG into the electronic future.

Jeannine: We need to lay out a vision at the annual conference about the intellectual and cultural problems we want to see addressed. The *Yearbook,* or an on-line publication that replaces it, should then bear down on that area. I think we used to do this: remember the discussions that emerged at conferences and then became thematized in our research?—on lesbianism and German Studies, fascism and speaking German, historical witchcraft, eroticism and feminist film, for example. My vision is an on-line journal with a clever, easily recognizable name. It will capture the attention of the media, for we consistently address one pressing multinational cultural issue after the next. People hold their breath, waiting to see what intellectual pronouncements will emerge from the bad girls (and boys) at Women in German. Scholars in German as well as in other fields will hope (or fear) that their names will be bandied about in the next issue.

Jeanette: Before we commit to moving the *Yearbook* to an electronic format, we need a solid grasp of the potential benefits and costs of online publication. Here are a few questions.

1. How do we get a handle on what the possibilities are for electronic publication, specifically for a small organization like WiG? Recently, the MLA has been considering various alternatives for dealing with the crisis in scholarly publishing, including the possibility of becoming an electronic repository of manuscripts. Alonso cited the successful National Academy Press, created to publish books in the fields of science, engineering, and health, as a possible model for such an initiative (< http://www.nap.edu/ > ; 222). What should or could be the relationship of WiG to such ventures by the MLA or other associations?

2. What are the hidden costs and pitfalls of electronic publication? The article by the MLA Ad Hoc Committee on Scholarly Publishing cites several: the costs of the editing process; the lack of standardization of software programs for reading electronic documents; uncertainty as to how permanent electronic publication will be, since digital storage systems continue to undergo changes; and the possibility that large conglomerates could eventually control access to electronic sources, which would be the kiss of death for humanities scholars (*Profession 2002*, 180). Recently, some journals have opted to publish simultaneously in a print version and electronically. Jennifer L. Holberg and Marcy Taylor, the editors of *Pedagogy,* caution that even package electronic subscriptions, such as Duke University Press's Project Muse, may not protect journals from extinction, for if libraries cancel their print subscriptions in favor of electronic collections, there will not be enough income to support the journals.[6]

At first glance, it might seem that the concerns enumerated above don't apply to WiG—what editorial costs? Our *Yearbook* editors, like all the editors and officers of WiG, are not paid. We have relied on their commitment to WiG and to feminist scholarship to carry out their editing responsibilities (usually with modest support from their chair or dean for a student assistant and access to a phone line) and pass the finished articles on to the redoubtable Victoria Hoelzer-Maddox, who hasn't raised her prices in years for word-processing services to WiG. At present, the major cost of the *WIG Yearbook* is purchasing the copies for our members from the University of Nebraska Press. If we can't find WiG members who can provide the kinds of electronic editing services needed for a high-quality online journal, can we afford to outsource those services? Can we afford the kind of editing and tech support that will make our journal accessible to the audiences we want to reach? No matter how exciting the content, if our e-journal is not easily accessible to scholars with varying levels of access to the internet and to tech support, it will not be successful.

3. How do we find the answers to these questions? Laying out a vision at the annual WiG conference is a start. Probably we'll also need a task force of some kind to look at other electronic journals—what kinds of infrastructure do they have, what are their sources of funding, what are the logistics of producing them? I think we need that information in order to identify the best model for WiG. And, to understand both the access issues and the true potential of online publication better, maybe our next step should be an international WiG conference held online, so that more of our international members could participate in the discussion. Are we ready for this?

Jeannine: We're ready. We have to be, if WiG is to thrive in the twenty-first century. Appointing that task force will be your first job as the second president of Women in German.

Notes

[1] The *Yearbook* was published by the University Press of America from 1985 to 1991 and by the University of Nebraska Press since 1991. The coeditors have included Edith Waldstein, Marianne Burkhard, Jeanette Clausen, Helen Cafferty, Sara Friedrichsmeyer, Pat Herminghouse, Susanne Zantop, Ruth-Ellen B. Joeres, Marjorie Gelus, and Helga Kraft. Each volume is ably formatted by Victoria Hoelzer-Maddox. It is circulated to all members.

[2] *Women in German Yearbook 5: Feminist Studies and German Culture.* Ed. Jeanette Clausen and Helen Cafferty. Lanham: UP of America, 1989. 131-35.

[3] "The Future of Scholarly Publishing." *Profession 2002*: 172-86.

[4] "Having a Spine: Facing the Crisis in Scholarly Publishing." *PMLA* 118.2 (Mar. 2003): 217-23.

[5] <http://www.uliveandlearn.com/marketing/innovate.cfm>

[6] Editors' Introduction: "Getting the Profession We Want, or A Few Thoughts on the Crisis in Scholarly Publication." *Pedagogy: Critical Approaches to Teaching Literature, Language, Composition, and Culture* 4.1 (Winter 2004): 1-7.

Traffic of Women in Germanic Literature: The Role of the Peace Pledge in Marital Exchanges

Carol Parrish Jamison

In order to bind men together and ensure peace, Germanic women of the highest rank sometimes served as peace pledges and were trafficked in marital exchange. Analysis of the women in *The Wife's Lament, Wulf and Eadwacer, Beowulf,* and *Volsungasaga* elucidates the political implications of such exchanges. This essay answers anthropologist Gayle Rubin's call for further exploration of traffic in women in her 1975 article "The Traffic in Women: Notes on the 'Political Economy' of Sex" and also acknowledges Karen Newman's challenge that feminists expand Rubin's paradigm to consider how women might function beyond the role of object. In fact, Germanic women had a number of possible responses to marital exchanges and could find ways to assert their influence as mothers and diplomats by king-making, or king-breaking, in their new husbands' homes. (CPJ)

In her 1975 article "The Traffic in Women: Notes on the 'Political Economy' of Sex," anthropologist Gayle Rubin explores the role of women across various cultures and times as objects of marital exchange. "The result of a gift of women is more profound than the result of other gift transactions," writes Rubin, "because the relationship thus established is not just one of reciprocity, but one of kinship" (173). Paving the way for subsequent research on the topic, Rubin concludes her work by requesting "a search...which might demonstrate how marriage systems intersect with large-scale political processes like state-making" (209). This request has been granted by numerous scholars, notably Karen Newman, whose 1990 article, "Directing Traffic: Subjects, Objects, and the Politics of Exchange," challenges the acceptance of women as "objects only" and adds to Rubin's discussion several queries that "feminist criticism [using] the 'traffic in women' paradigm rarely address" (52n). Specifically, Newman objects to the fact that "analyses of women as objects of exchange...too often participate in a discourse of oppression that produces women as victims" (50).

Both Rubin's and Newman's discussions are directly relevant to studies of the female characters in a wide range of Germanic literature, both in time and geographic origin, who are trafficked in marital exchange. In order to bind men together and ensure peace, Germanic women of the highest rank sometimes served as peace pledges. Usually the daughter of an important warrior or king, the peace pledge would be married off to a man of high status who might be perceived as a potential threat to her kin in hopes of forming an alliance, or at least preventing conflict. Tom Shippey describes the strategies governing such marital arrangements: "Queens could be used to set up a future alliance with strangers."[1] The union might be more tightly sealed if the bride's son were sent back to her own people to be raised by his maternal uncles and to live among maternal cousins. This marital arrangement fits Rubin's description of traffic as a gift transaction in which women, and sometimes sons, are exchanged to forge unions and prevent hostilities. The woman could become, in the best of situations, a sort of diplomat, participating actively in marital arrangements, advising her husband, and engaging, to some extent, in the negotiations of the mead hall. However, in a society that valued warfare, marrying off women as a means to ensure peace could turn out badly, in such cases emphasizing the woman's unfortunate plight as object of male exchange.

The Germanic woman who acts as peace pledge might contend with her situation in various ways, some of which open up Rubin's original queries about state making and confirm Newman's call for feminists to consider women beyond the role of "object, inert, passive, bearer of meaning" (49): (1) she may succumb to the role of an object and acquiesce to a marriage she does not desire; (2) she may be seen as a threat by her husband's family and find herself (and any sons from the marriage[2]) in a precarious position; (3) she may establish herself in her new husband's home and become a king maker, balancing her loyalties and using her diplomatic skills to forge peace; or (4) she may even rebel against the system of exchange, refusing to assume a diplomatic role in her new husband's home and seeking vengeance on him by allying herself with her own kin.

Although the practice of exchanging certain upper-class women for peace is documented in historical accounts, the focus in this essay is upon literary portrayals of trafficking.[3] Such portrayals feature prominently in the following works: *The Wife's Lament* and *Wulf and Eadwacer,* both elegies that are preserved in the ninth-century Anglo-Saxon

Exeter Book; *Beowulf,* composed some time between the middle of the seventh and the end of the tenth century; and *Volsungasaga,* an Icelandic text recorded in the thirteenth century but concerned with material substantially older, some of which is preserved in the Old Norse Poetic Edda.

These works are recorded in different centuries and *Volsungasaga* in a different country, yet all reflect the shared literary legacy and common culture of the Teutonic people. The inclusion of *Volsungasaga* might appear to be a temporal stretch, yet the *Beowulf* poet himself shows knowledge of this saga in the episode commonly referred to as "the Sigmund digression" (874–97). Furthermore, a number of scholars have noted striking similarities between the Danish and Anglo-Saxon traditions. For instance, both Helen Damico in *Beowulf's Wealtheow and the Valkyrie Tradition* and Robert Luyster in "*The Wife's Lament* in the Context of Scandinavian Myth and Ritual" base their studies on similarities between Icelandic and Anglo-Saxon portrayals of women. Exploring similarities between Hildeburh in *Beowulf* and Signy in the *Saga,* Robert A. Albano writes that

> although the tale of Sigmund [in *Volsungasaga*] was written in a later century and at a different location, both it and the tale of Finn [in *Beowulf*] deal with Germanic tribes sharing similar cultural attitudes and beliefs; and, if one considers the oral tradition of both tales, the actual dates of their origins may be fairly contemporaneous (1).

Similarly, Anne Klinck finds between the Old English elegies and the Old Norse tradition "a shared heritage—in the narrow context Germanic, but in a broader frame of reference universal" (*Old English Elegies* 239). With this comment, Klinck affirms Newman's thesis that traffic in women is universal, but she also acknowledges the shared heritage of Icelandic and Anglo-Saxon literature and invites a closer look at the particular manifestations of traffic of women in Germanic literature.

The works discussed in this essay invite comparison for several other reasons, as some links can be found among them. For example, *Beowulf* shares with *Volsungasaga* a Scandinavian setting, and Klinck proposes that it is "not impossible" that *Wulf and Eadwacer,* because of its strophic structure, may have been influenced by Old Norse, "although the dates of the poems make direct influence improbable" (*Old English Elegies* 239). Further, a portion of *Volsungasaga* is retold in *Beowulf,* and both *Volsungasaga* and *Wulf and Eadwacer* draw heavily upon wolf imagery. Although the female characters who act as peace pledges in *Volsungasaga* are often described as having more personal agency than their Anglo-Saxon counterparts, their inclusion is crucial to this discussion, for which a primary goal is to explore the less obvious autonomy and sometimes subtle rebellion of the women in the Anglo-Saxon texts. Thus, I have chosen these particular texts for their shared depictions of traffic in early Germanic women, for their potential to elucidate the political implications of such exchanges, and, most importantly, for their portrayal of an array of options and actions available to the women acting as peace pledges.

The two elegies, *Wulf and Eadwacer* and *The Wife's Lament,* feature women who each grieve for the absence of a particular man. As I shall demonstrate, a plausible scenario is that their grief could stem from their roles in peace exchanges. Both poems are preserved in the *Exeter Book* and are unique in being the only Anglo-Saxon works narrated by women. Classified as elegies because of their plaintive tone and somber mood, they are commonly considered alongside four other poems in the *Exeter Book* of similar mood. The narrator of *The Wife's Lament* seems to be a peace pledge whose husband has left his homeland, perhaps exiled for some undisclosed crime, or perhaps to lead his men in battle. The narrator notes that she has searched for her husband earlier, but the poem itself describes her enclosure in an earth cave (something scholars have struggled to define). Although the narrator's specific situation cannot be determined from the text, her confinement to the earth cave may hinge on her earlier status as a peace pledge. Perhaps she is a foreign bride who is perceived as a threat by her husband's kin: "heht mec mon wunian on wuda bearwe, / under actreo in þam eorþscræfe"[4] (someone sent me to dwell in the woods under an oak tree in an earth cave; 27–28). Upon her husband's departure, his kin apparently turn on her, refusing to integrate her into their family and plotting against her: "Ongunnon þæt þæs monnes magas hycgan / þurh dyrne geþoht" (that man's kinsmen began to contemplate by means of secret thought; 11–12). Much of the poem reflects the narrator's grief as she is separated not only from her own kin, in the way that the marital exchange would necessitate, but from her new husband and his kin as well.

The enclosure of the female narrator is further emphasized when the work is considered in conjunction with another elegy, *The Husband's Message,* sometimes interpreted as its companion piece. There is no convincing evidence that the two poems are necessarily companion pieces beyond their inclusion in the same manuscript. Nonetheless, a consideration of the two together is useful for contrasting the enclosed, static female with her wandering male counterpart who successfully finds a new lord and establishes a position in a new home. *The Husband's Message* takes the form of a message written in runes by a husband who urges his wife to join him in his new home. But the narrative also emphasizes that the husband has made *himself* an object of traffic. In a society in which fighting and loyalty are exchanged for wealth, he has successfully exchanged his services, likely as warrior, for a position in a new lord's home. On the other hand, the female in *The Wife's Lament* is desolate and isolated. She complains, "Þær ic sittan mot sumorlangne dæg / þær ic wepan mæg mine wræcsiþas" (There I must sit through the long summer's day; There I must weep my exile; 37-38). Stripped of hope, deprived of mobility, and apparently rejected by her in-laws, she sits in her earth cave and grieves.

The wife appears passive throughout most of the poem, an object of exchange stripped of value when her husband and his kin reject her. However, one need not leave the poem with the impression that she is inert. The final lines of the poem, often interpreted as mournful, may in fact be an active gesture made by a frustrated woman who acts as peace pledge. About Anglo-Saxon women, Bernice Kliman writes, "if [she] may not fight, she can speak" (35), and perhaps the narrator of this elegy attempts to exert some power through language. In her article "Women's Words as Weapons," Barrie Ruth Straus posits that the narrator's speech itself is an active gesture culminating in a curse upon those who have caused her suffering. And in his recent article "The Problem of the Ending of *The Wife's Lament*," John D. Niles agrees that the final lines, although intentionally ambiguous, are, in fact, an attempt on the narrator's behalf to bring about vengeance in the form of a curse. The passage with Niles' translation follows:

> A scyle geong mon   wesan geomormod,
> heard heortan geþoht,   swylce habban sceal
> bliþe gebæro,   eac þon breostceare,
> sinsorgna gedreag,   sy æt him sylfum gelong,
> eal his worulde wyn,   sy ful wide fah
> Feorres folclondes,   Þæt min freond siteð
> under stanhliþe   storme behrimed
> wine werigmod,   wætre beflowen,
> on dreorsele.   Dreogeð se min wine
> micle modceare—he gemon to oft
> wynlicran wic.   Wa bið þam þe sceal
> of langoþe   leofes abidan (42-53).

Ever may a young person [of that treacherous kind] be wretched; ever may the thoughts of his heart be bitter! In like manner, may he who maintains a blithe demeanor also experience grief that cuts to the heart, a tumult of constant sorrows. May all his worldly joy depend on himself alone! May he be hated far and wide in some distant land, so that my lover, my "protector," will sit beaten by an icy storm under a stony slope, desolate, drenched with rain in a dreary dwelling place. My lord will come to know great trouble in mind. Too often he will recall a happier home. Sad is the lot of those who must wait in longing for a loved one![5]

Niles provides ample textual evidence of Germanic cursing in both Biblical and pre-Christian contexts, concluding that "[t]he mental world of the people in that era must have been permeated by the notion that people were capable of doing harm to others through the power of their words" (1133). In Niles' reading, the wife resorts in her isolation to a curse, the sole option available for vengeance against the husband who has betrayed her. Isolated and unable to seek the assistance of her kin, she may rely upon language as her sole means to comment on a peace exchange gone bad.

The second of the elegies, the enigmatic *Wulf and Eadwacer,* has been variously interpreted, although most scholars now concur that the poem is a reflection of female grief. *Hapex legomena* and ambiguous language make the source of the narrator's grief difficult to pinpoint, but the most viable reading, in my view, is that her grief is primarily for her child.[6] If a peace exchange is not successful, the son, once given to his mother's kin, could become estranged from her and even endangered. This reading of the elegy was made legitimate by Marijane Osborn in her article entitled "The Text and Context of *Wulf and Eadwacer.*" Osborn explains that the narrator's grief "[suggests] the apprehension that such a mother as 'peace-weaver' might well feel when sending her son away to fulfill his destiny in her native land" (187). The narrator's actions and language indicate that she may be in this situation: a peace pledge whose exchange in marriage has unhappy consequences for herself and her son.

In my reading, this elegy concerns three characters: the narrator, a woman who acts as a peace pledge; her husband, Eadwacer; and their son, Wulf.[7] Like the female in *The Wife's Lament,* this narrator is also confined; she sits apart and grieves, perhaps for impending enmity between her husband's kin and her own: "þonne hit wæs renig weder, ond ic reotogu sæt" (Then it was rainy weather, and I sat weeping; 10).[8] But she makes an active gesture, urging Eadwacer to hear her pleas: "Gehyrest þu, Eadwacer?" (Do you hear, Eadwacer?; 16). By asserting herself, cajoling Eadwacer to take some action, she renders herself more than mere object. Her imploring speech indicates that she has something important to say, and she expects to be heard. The direct address to Eadwacer sets this woman apart from the narrator of *The Wife's Lament,* whose final words are, whether curse or lamentation, solitary. In *Wulf and Eadwacer,* the words of the narrator are diplomatic rather than vengeful, persuasive rather than hopeless. She intends for Eadwacer to hear and heed her message.

Osborn explains that

> It was a Germanic custom to try to ensure peace between feuding tribes, to "settle the feud," by arranging a marriage between the daughter of one ruler and the son of the other; when a son was born of that union he would be sent at about the age of seven to be brought up by the mother's people ("Text and Context" 187).

The importance of such exchanges is implied by Shippey, who suggests that "Perhaps the vital relationship was not between husband and wife, nor parents and children, but between the children of the next generation: the male maternal cousins who could be expected to be on friendly and non-competitive terms." As Newman suggested might be the case, the situation of the son in my reading of this elegy indicates that men, too, could be objects of traffic in marital exchanges. For the narrator of *Wulf and Eadwacer,* the exchange of the son is no source of comfort. Shippey explains that sending the son to live with his maternal kin might ensure future peace among the woman's relatives back home, yet the narrator of this elegy seems preoccupied with the possibility that the exchange will not bring peace to her husband's kin and her own. About the consequences of exchanges involving sons, Osborn writes, "Sometimes this worked, but often it did not, and the mother involved would be helpless as the tragedy folded in upon her" ("Text and Context" 187). Perhaps this is the situation for the narrator of this elegy: she fears that her marriage has not formed an alliance that can maintain peace between her own and her husband's kin.

The narrator's concern about the exchange of her son in such a situation may be evident from the first line of the poem in the term "lac," which has been translated variously as "battle," "sacrifice," "gift," and "message." Considered in the context of the worried yet hopeful narrator, the term embraces all of these contents. If the "lac" given to the narrator's people is her own son, he could either be a "gift," a "message" of peace or, if her marriage has not promoted peace, an assurance of impending battle in which her son might be pitted against his father. Thus, the narrator worries about her son who may be, as the term "lac" so vividly implies, either gift or prey. Thus, the first line contains a deliberate pun: "It is to my people as if one might give gift/battle/sacrifice."[9]

The second line continues the punning. The term *apecgan* has been translated variously with meanings ranging from "taken in" and "receive" to "consume" and "devour." Fiona and Richard Gameson explain that this term occurs only twice in Old English. "Judging from its other appearance and from related compound forms," they write, "it would seem to mean 'to serve, minister to, give food to.' It has been suggested that it could also mean 'kill,' because of its use in the phrase *ecgum ofpegde* 'served with swords' (*Genesis A* 2002b)" (458). Again, the ambiguities of this term may reflect the situation of the narrator and her son. The narrator's kin might receive her son as a symbol of peace who could prevent hostilities abroad. If peace does not ensue between the foreign tribes despite the traffic of mother and son, the son may be killed in imminent battle, metaphorically speaking, "devoured" by the political upheaval that could erupt as a consequence of an unsuccessful marital exchange. Arguing that the term *apecgan* implies being "taken as if he were some kind of object," Klinck explains that "[h]e is presented as an object to be used or consumed, not as a guest to be welcomed" ("Animal Imagery" 6). Thus, both the woman and her son may be treated as objects of exchange; both are at risk when the traffic of mother and, subsequently, of son fails to bring about peace.

The narrator's concern for her son's safety is reiterated in line 5, in which she says, "secure is that island, surrounded by fens." Yet she also refers to *wealreow weras,* or "slaughter-cruel men" in line 6, and in line 11, she refers to the *beaducafa,* or the "battle-quick" one. These lines provide further evidence that the narrator may have been trafficked in a foreign marital exchange and that she fears enmity between her "slaughter-cruel" kin and the "battle-quick" Eadwacer, whom I believe to be her husband. The narrator's conflicted emotions toward Eadwacer are another source of debate. He has been described as a rapist (Mitchell and Robinson 298), a tyrant, an abusive ward, and a resentful cuckold, and the narrator has been described as "impotently trapped within a relationship she resents or hates" (Gameson and Gameson 63). Such readings overemphasize the pain the narrator feels in Eadwacer's embrace, and neglect or gloss over the pleasure which, as the poem reads, is foremost of her emotions: "wæs me wyn to þon wæs me hwæþre eac laþ" (that was a pleasure to me then, but also pain; 12). I see her ambivalence as a consequence of her position as peace pledge. The narrator has mixed feelings about her husband's embrace, perhaps the natural response of the trafficked woman whose loyalties should be divided between her own and her husband's kin to promote peace.

The narrator seems fearful of enmity and particularly concerned for the safety of her son, Wulf, to whom she makes frequent reference.[10]

The name "Wulf" would have special meaning for an Anglo-Saxon audience and particularly within the context of this poem. The connotations of this name may be indicative of the son's own ambiguous role in the peace exchange, for the wolf is both warrior (apparent in the frequent use of the term as a warrior's name and the ferocious characteristics associated with the animal) and common prey. Wolf imagery is woven throughout the poem and occurs again in line 9: "Wulfes ic mines widlastum / wenum dogode" (I pursue like a dog my Wulf's journey with expectations). Although the verb at the end of this line is a *hapax legomenon* and is sometimes glossed as *hogode,* Osborn effectively argues that the term *dogode* is deliberate, and that "to change it is to subvert the poet's meaning" ("Dogode" 175). Likewise, Gameson and Gameson explain that "converting an *h* to a *d* would not be an obvious transcriptional error" (459). In her discussion of animal imagery in the poem, Klinck says that as a verb, it is a "nonce-word and would mean 'pursued like a dog'" ("Animal Imagery" 8). As Klinck describes the distraught narrator, "She resembles a mere dog.... And her son is a wretched animal" ("Animal Imagery" 11). Actively involved in the political matters that involve her son, the narrator "dogs," or follows, the trafficking of her son in her mind and then voices her frustration over the exchange.

The narrator's concern for her son is nowhere more clear than in her direct address to Eadwacer, but the lines following this address are perhaps the poem's most difficult: "Uncerne earne hwelp / bireþ Wulf to wuda" (our wretched whelp Wulf bears to the woods; 16–17). For the problematic and frequently emended "earne," I adopt the popular translation "wretched," an apt description of the son's role as peace pledge. In Osborn's reading, the "whelp" is a second child who is carried off by an older brother. "The awakening of her *murnende mod* is sudden and sharp," Osborn writes, "as she discovers that Wulf has returned after all, to no good purpose" ("Text and Context" 186). But the fact that the narrator mourns for Wulf throughout the poem makes the sudden change of heart toward him seem unlikely. Rather, it seems logical that the "whelp" in these lines is synonymous with the "Wulf" addressed earlier. Perhaps these final lines refer to a different "Wulf," a blood relative. Although Osborn does not discuss this possibility, her idea that the poem concerns brothers fits Shippey's description of a foreign marriage in which an older brother, perhaps an older stepbrother, sees the narrator's son as a threat and seeks to eliminate him. The "Wulf" in line 17 might also be a maternal relative, such as an uncle, who is assuming his responsibility of raising his sister's son. In this scenario, the narrator fears separation from her son because her marriage has not brought peace.

Bruce Mitchell and Fred Robinson describe the difficult social predicament of the peace pledge, who was "given in marriage...to patch up a blood feud [and thus] was involved in...conflict between loyalty to her lord, her husband, on the one hand, and her family on the other" (137). The intentionally ambiguous language of the narrator seems to portray the conflicted loyalties of a peace pledge. The narrator of *Wulf and Eadwacer* laments her situation and then assumes a more active role as she pleads, perhaps with her husband, to preserve a precarious peace and thereby save their son, who may himself be an object of exchange. Although she does not rebel against the marital exchange, as do the women in some of the following examples, she does not accept her predicament passively.

The full gamut of reactions and situations of the peace pledge can be found in *Beowulf*. Her crucial role in this best known of all Anglo-Saxon texts has been described by Jane Chance as "[dependent] upon peace making, either biologically through her marital ties with foreign kinds as a peace pledge or mother of sons, or socially and psychologically as a cup-passing and peace-weaving queen within a hall" (98). The first female introduced is Wealtheow, a successful peace pledge whose marriage has, apparently, brought peace between her husband's tribe and her own. She has, it seems, balanced or shifted her loyalties and assumes an important role in her husband's hall, distributing mead and gold rings to her husband's thanes and actively participating in forging political alliances. Her actions in the mead hall enable her to empower her husband's men, for those she serves first seem placed in a position of privilege. Wealtheow's "presence and actions help the lord at his task" of preserving peace, explains L. John Sklute. "If [her role] reflects anything of the social system of the Anglo-Saxons," he writes, "it is that of the diplomat" (539). It is difficult to perceive Wealtheow as an object: she has established a new identity in her husband's hall, occupying a position that enables her to participate in king-making decisions.

Hygd, Hygelac's young wife, also moves beyond the role of object after her marriage to Hygelac and seems successful at establishing herself as diplomat. The narrator describes her thus:

Hygd swiþe geong,
wis, wel-þungen, þeah þe wintre lyt
under burh-locan gebiden hæbbe
Hæreþes dohter; næs hio hnah swa þeah
 ne to gneaþ gifa Geata leodum
 maþm-gestreona.[11]

Hygd, very young, wise, accomplished, though [she] has lived few
years under castle enclosure, Hæreth's daughter; she was not niggardly, however, nor too stingy with gifts to Geatish people
(1925–31).

Not unlike the exiled male in *The Husband's Message,* who assumes an important place in his lord's home, both Wealtheow and Hygd find new lands and prestige in their new homes. Both Hygd and Wealtheow participate in negotiations in the mead hall, not hesitating to intervene in matters concerning the futures of their sons as kings. Wealtheow demonstrates diplomacy in her words to Hrothgar as she urges him not to neglect his sons by favoring Beowulf above them. Hygd, too, is concerned with her son, offering the throne to Beowulf when her son is in his minority. Not merely protective, loving mothers, Hygd, Wealtheow, and the narrator of *Wulf and Eadwacer* all seem to recognize the important role of their sons to the bonds of the *comitatus,* and all use the mother/son relationship to exert some influence.

But Hygd and Wealtheow's appearances in *Beowulf* are surrounded by, and probably intended to contrast with, the narratives of less successful women who have been exchanged in marital agreements and are consequently rendered powerless. The Finn digression, for example, is noted for its portrayal of the unhappy Hildeburh, about whom Shari Horner writes, "It is obviously [Hildeburh's] story, and she frames the digression. At the same time, she is framed by it [for].... Her story is...enclosed by two appearances of Wealtheow" (70). The references to Wealtheow, she adds,"overlap with and guide our interpretation of Hildeburh's story" (71). The Anglo-Saxon reader would surely contrast the situations of the two women: Wealtheow, who, according to Horner, "surmount[s] the passive peaceweaver role in order to influence political and dynastic decisions" (77), and Hildeburh, who endures great loss and exerts little influence in her husband's hall. Married off to Finn, Hildeburh is visited by her brother, Hnæf. Hildeburh's marriage has not brought peace between her husband's tribe and her own, for her brother is attacked and killed during the night by her husband's men. She loses her son, too, in this battle, who, like Wulf in my reading of *Wulf and Eadwacer,* may have been exchanged and is fighting alongside his uncle.

When traffic in women fails to preserve peace, another of the women's duties is to grieve over the destruction. Thus, Hildeburh orders a funeral pyre, upon which are placed together the corpses of her son and brother. Horner explains,

Though we do not hear her voice, and though many critics have
found her to be hopelessly passive throughout the episode, the

moment at which she orders the funeral pyre is, rather, a moment of intense narrative, textual, and sensory power. She orders a visual symbol of destroyed peace accord (71).

Horner adds that "the pyre serves as her commentary or gloss on a peace-weaving system that is...destined to self-destruct" (73). *Beowulf* includes a similar scene in which a woman grieves by a pyre upon the hero's death. In this passage, the female mourns, along with Beowulf's men, not only Beowulf's demise, but also the destruction of his kingdom. Although we do not hear the actual words of this Geatish woman, perhaps it is not insignificant that, near the conclusion of *Beowulf,* the poet includes the lamentations of a female before a pyre. In the case of Hildeburh, however, the narrative of the female does not end with the description of her mourning before the pyre. Along with the return of jewels and gold, Hildeburh is returned to her kin, as if she were, indeed, mere object.

Hrothgar's daughter, Freawaru, is another example of an exchange that is doomed to fail. Beowulf predicts that Freawaru's new husband's kin will resent the young bride. Her situation is poignantly described by the narrator: "Oft seldan hwær / æfter leodhryre lytle hwile / bongar bugeþ, þeah seo bryd duge!" (Very seldom after the fall of a prince for a short while does the deadly spear rest, although the bride is good; 2029–31). This passage illustrates vividly the helpless situation of the peace pledge whose marriage may not prevent war. In a discussion of the traffic of women in the Big Man systems of Highland, New Guinea, Rubin writes that the "weight of the entire system may come to rest on one woman kept in a miserable marriage" (207). Similarly, Germanic society depended upon marital arrangements involving peace pledges that, as evidenced by Freawaru, Hildeburh, and the female narrators of the elegies, were sometimes unsuccessful. In the cases of these Germanic characters, however, the misery of the marriage culminates in bloodshed and violence. Christopher Fee sums up the "fundamental flaw" of exchanging women as peace pledges: "the social cohesion [it provides] is only effective in situations where such cohesion is necessary in the first place" (291).

Unless one reads Hildeburh's request for the funeral pyre as a symbolic action, both Hildeburh and Freawaru seem helpless and silenced. However, *Beowulf* includes examples of peace pledges who blatantly rebel against the process. The first of these is Thryth, who initially puts to death those men who dare to look at her. Introduced most likely as a foil to the obedient Hygd, Thryth performs "firen ondrysne" (terrible crimes; 1932). Her very name, if one accepts the popular reading that the description *mod þryðo* includes her name, has been interpreted to mean "arrogance" (Wrenn 299). Another popular reading is that Thryth is first depicted as an unmarried woman who is not willing to participate in a peace exchange. She puts to death potential suitors as an act of rebellion. Shippey, citing the occurrence of such terms as *sinfrea* and *cwenlic,* argues convincingly that Thryth is already a married queen when her narrative begins, and that the narrative indicates two marriages. Thus he contends that, in her first marriage, she is a "morally dubious" queen whose refusal to participate in the activities of her husband's mead hall results in violence.[12] In either scenario, her misbehavior could be read as a rebellion against the peace exchange: she is either an unmarried woman refusing to participate in a marital exchange by killing would-be suitors or a married queen rebelling against the peace exchange *post facto* by refusing to participate in her husband's hall.

Thryth acquiesces to her role as peace pledge only after her marriage to Offa. Someone, likely her father, advises her to go "ofer fealone flod" (overseas; 1950) to Offa's court where she becomes an exemplary queen. A renowned warrior, Offa surely would have made a formidable enemy to Thryth's kin, and so her conformity in this marriage (whether it is her first or second) benefits both her own kin and her new husband. This "before and after" behavior demonstrates that the success of marital exchanges depends upon the willingness and capability of the woman to assume a diplomatic position in her husband's court. Osborn explores Thryth's narrative as one that Hygd has seriously considered: "She weighed contrasting stories about Thryth's character... and chose the better side of her predecessor" ("Two Women" 61). Osborn reads the narrative of Thryth as a comment on Hygd's autonomy. The placement of the narrative about Thryth directly after the description of Hygd is meaningful. It indicates that Hygd has considered Thryth's actions, rejecting the early misbehavior and instead modeling herself on Thryth's ultimate diplomacy.

Thryth's early penchant for destruction makes her comparable to Grendel's mother, whose own monstrous behavior and appearance classify her as only marginally human. Even more isolated than the unsuccessful peace pledge, Grendel's mother is utterly excluded from human society. Whereas Horner describes her as "undoubtedly the least enclosed woman in Old English literature" (81) because of her masculine actions, Jane Chance describes her as a "tribeless queen or lady" (102). Chance explains that she is an "antitype of the peace-weaving queen [who] behaves like a king, using the sword to rid her halls of intruders or unwanted 'hall guests'" (106). Sharing something in common with the women who lose their sons as part of a peace exchange, Grendel's mother, too, grieves for her son. When Beowulf fatally wounds her son, she exchanges violence for violence. Such aggressive behavior, deemed masculine, largely contributes to Grendel's mother's status as "monster," setting her apart from, and in contrast to, the women who act as peace pledges in the text. But the monster-mother's vengeance is not such exceptional female behavior if one adopts Niles' reading of *The Wife's Lament,* in which the narrator "has only words with which to strike out at the object of her anger" (1141), and if one considers the initial wrath of Thryth and the wrath of some of the women in the Icelandic tradition.

The women of *Volsungasaga* are generally more aggressive than their Anglo-Saxon counterparts and are often empowered by their abilities as soothsayers. Although their voices are typically loud and their actions demonstrative, they also act as peace pledges, and an examination of their reactions to the peace exchange can help modern readers to "hear" the sometimes softer voices of women in Anglo-Saxon texts. For example, whereas Beowulf reports that Freawaru's marriage will end unhappily, the text of *Beowulf* itself, by recording neither Freawaru's thoughts nor words, portrays her as a passive object of exchange. On the other hand, in *Volsungasaga,* Signy openly expresses to her father her dissatisfaction with his choice of her husband. She freely states her unwillingness to act as a peace pledge in marriage to Siggeir: "Þessu tali tekr konungr vel ok svá synir hans, en hon sjálf var þessa ófús, biðr þó feðr sinn ráðá sem oðru því sem til hennar tœki"[13] (The king was favorably disposed to the idea, as were his sons, but she herself was against it, although she asked her father to decide about this as he did about other matters concerning her; 4). Signy makes clear her objections to the marriage: "Eigi vilda ek á brott fara með Siggeiri, of eigi gerir hugr minn hlæja við honum" (I don't want to go away with Siggeir, nor do I feel at all warmly towards him; 5). She relents when her father is insistent, but refuses to be integrated into her in-laws' clan. In fact, she plots against her new husband.

When Signy's father (King Volsung) and his sons come to visit, she urges them to go home and muster forces. As she has predicted, her marriage does not bring peace; her new husband slays her father. Consequently, Signy sides with her brother, Sigemund, and is instrumental in bringing about her husband's death. She sends her sons to Sigemund, but her intent is not to seal the peace exchange. Rather, her motive is vengeance. When her sons prove unimpressive warriors, she callously has them killed. Signy so hates her new husband's tribe that she resorts to mating with her brother Sigemund to produce a formidable rival against her husband. Thus, Signy assumes an active, aggressive role in king-breaking as she plots her husband's death. Signy's vendetta might be compared to the initial violent behavior of Thryth and to the vengeance of the narrator of *The Wife's Lament,* who, according to Niles,

> remains embedded in a nexus of social relationships, and what she has suffered is a social crime and not just a personal injury. In the eyes of a sympathetic party, any action that she takes in response to her suffering...could be regarded as a defense of the honor of her kin as a whole (1143).

Similarly, Signy's actions indicate her sole concern of protecting the honor of her father and brothers.

In fact, the son of her incestuous relationship with Sigemund does kill Signy's husband, leaving Signy free, one would imagine, to return to her own people. However, once Signy has been married off by her father, she does not return home as the symbol of a failed peace exchange. Rather, she willingly steps into the funeral pyre, choosing death at the side of the husband she so begrudgingly married:

> Hefi ek þar til unit alla hluti at Siggeirr konungr skyldi bana fá. Hefi ek of svá mikit til unnit at fram kœmisk hefndin, at mér er meðengnum kosti líft. Skal ek nú deyja með Siggeiri konungi lostig er ek átta hann nauðig.

> Everything that I have done has been to bring about King Siggeir's death. And I have done so much to achieve vengeance that to go on living is out of the question. I shall now gladly die with King Siggeir, reluctant though I was to marry him (14).

As with the funeral pyres in *Beowulf,* this funeral pyre might also be interpreted symbolically, and Signy's decision to join her husband in the pyre may be her final statement on the devastation wrought by a marriage she vehemently opposed.

The responses of women in *Volsungasaga* to marital exchanges are varied. Whereas Signy is not given a choice by her father and must unwillingly marry, King Eylimi's daughter, Hjordis, is allowed to choose between two men, Sigmund or Lyngvi. Her father tells her, "Þú ert vitr kona, en ek hefi þat mælt at þu skalt þér mann kjósa. Kjós nú um tvá konunga, ok er þat mitt ráð hér um sem þitt er" (You are an intelligent woman and I say that you should choose your own husband. So choose between the two kings, and your decision in the matter will be mine, too; 19). Hjordis chooses Sigmund in a diplomatically wise move that is reminiscent of Hygd's decision to offer the throne to

Beowulf rather than her own sons. Although Sigmund is advanced in age, Hjordis realizes that he has greater renown, and she chooses him for the political advantages offered to her own people by such a union.

In the case of Sigrun, another of the *Volsungasaga* women who act as peace pledge, the family's wishes are ignored. Sigrun defies her father, King Hogni, who has promised her in marriage to Hoddbrodd. She takes action to prevent the marriage, asking Helgi to fight against Hoddbrodd. Helgi does so, and she rewards him by marrying him and making him king. But not all of the women in *Volsungasaga* are given an opportunity to express their opinions or the power to manipulate events. Gudrun's daughter Svanhild is never allowed a voice in the text. She is married off to a foreign king, Jormunrek. A victim of conflict within her prospective husband's home, she is killed by the aging king to whom she is betrothed when he suspects that she is in love with his son.

The women of *Volsungasaga* seem aware that men depend upon traffic in women, and they are often an active part of marital negotiations. King Gjuki's wife, Grimhild, instigates the marriage of her stepdaughter, Gudrun. A sorceress, Grimhild uses her magical abilities to bring about a marital arrangement that promises to empower her husband. She is fully aware of the potential advantages in a marriage between her stepdaughter, Gudrun, and Sigurd: "sá at engi mátti við hann jafnask, sá ok hvert traust at honum var, ok hafði ofr fjár, miklu meira en menn vissi dœmi til" (she saw how no one could claim to be his equal, and what an asset he was, having immense wealth, far greater than any heard of before; 47). She urges her husband:

> Hér er nú kominn inn mesti kappi er finnask mun í veroldu. Væri at honum mikit traust. Gipt honum dóttur þína með miklu fé ok slíku ríki sem hann vill, ok mætti hann hér ynði nema.

> The greatest champion to be found anywhere in the world is here with us now. He would prove a great asset. Give him your daughter in marriage, a large sum of money and whatever dignities he would like, and perhaps he will live here happily (47).

The plot is complicated by the fact that another powerful woman, Brynhild, has already claimed Sigurd but is tricked into marrying Gudrun's brother, Gunnar, for whom she has no love. Once she learns that she has been tricked, Brynhild refuses to assume her role in Gunnar's hall: "því at aldri sér þú mik glaða siðan í þinni holl eða drekka né tefla né hugat mæla né gulli leggja góðklæði né yðr ráðgefa" (you'll never again see me happy in your hall, neither drinking, nor playing at chequers, nor speaking in a friendly tone, nor working fine materials in gold, nor giving you advice; 54). She is aware that her husband depends on her diplomacy in the mead hall and will be politically damaged without her participation. Further, she tells her husband that he must kill Sigurd or "Þú skalt láta bæði ríkit ok féit, lífit ok mik, ok skal ek fara heim til frænda minna ok sitja þar hrygg, nema þú drepir Sigurð ok son hans" (You'll lose both power and wealth, your life and me, and I shall go back to my family and live there sorrowfully, if you don't kill Sigurd and his son; 57). Brynhild is a soothsayer, and her words are prophetic, but they are equally vengeful. She is keenly aware that her husband's kin depend on the alliance with Sigurd, whose marriage to Gudrun has proved a valuable asset. Like Thryth, who initially reacts with violence in her first husband's or her father's hall, Brynhild is intent on king-breaking. She is determined to have Sigurd killed, not simply because she believes he has rebuffed her, but because she is keenly aware that his death will wreak havoc among her husband's kin.

Gunnar's family recognizes the importance of their alliance with Sigurd. Although Gunnar agrees to kill Sigurd at his wife's insistence, he is urged by another brother, Hogni, not to commit this act. Hogni explains that the family depends upon the alliance formed by Sigurd's marriage to their sister:

> Eru engir konungar oss jafnir ef sjá inn hýnski konungr lifir, of slíkan mág fám vér aldri, ok hygg et hversu gott væri ef vér ættim slíkan mág ok systursonu, ok sé is hversu þetta stenz af.

> No kings are a match for us if this Hunnish king is alive, and never again shall we get a brother-in-law like him, and think how fine it would be if we had a brother-in-law like him and nephews, too (57).

The reference to nephews provides further evidence that marital alliances might be sealed when sons from arranged marriages align themselves with maternal kin. The exchange of sons is important to the political situations described in *Volsungasaga* and is first emphasized when Signy decides to send her sons to her brother Sigmund. Sigmund is unaware that the only son who passes his tests is in fact his own rather than Siggeir's child. He obviously depends upon the alliance with his nephew and makes an effort to ensure that the boy will ally himself with his mother's kin by reminding the boy of the wrongs performed by Siggeir. Hogni's comments indicate that Gudrun's family also recognizes the value of such an alliance with a nephew and will regret the death of Sigurd all the more if he is killed before nephews are born.[14]

Gudrun realizes the importance of her own role in the peace exchange and her family's dependence on her marriage to Sigurd. She chastises her brother for killing Sigurd and makes clear to him the consequence of his actions. With Sigurd's death and without a son from the union between Sigurd and Gudrun, her family has forfeited a valuable alliance. Although Gudrun is offered recompense for the murder of her husband in the form of gold, any autonomy provided by the wealth is cut off as she subsequently acts as peace pledge again, but without success. The stepmother Grimhild once more arranges the marriage, this time to the wealthy King Atli. When it becomes apparent that this marital arrangement will not form a peaceful alliance, Gudrun remains loyal to her family. After the marriage, Gudrun tries to warn her brothers against visiting when she realizes that her husband intends an attack against them. Upon their arrival, she tries to mediate, asking if there is any chance for reconciliation. When she hears that there is not, she fights alongside her brothers and, once her brothers are slain, seeks vengeance on King Atli by feeding him the hearts of their children.

R.G. Finch writes that in *Volsungasaga,* "blood ties mean more than marriage and clan solidarity enjoins acquiescence in the murder of one husband and the vengeful destruction of another" (xvi). Both Gudrun and Signy take clan solidarity to an extreme by sacrificing their own children to enact vengeance on their husbands. Certainly their actions are more demonstrative, or at least easier to interpret, than the actions of some of their Anglo-Saxon counterparts who may also act out of vengeance—the narrator of *The Wife's Lament* who possibly curses her husband, Hildeburh whose ordering of a funeral pyre may be a symbolic statement, Thryth who initially reacts to men with violence, and even Grendel's mother, who grapples with Beowulf to avenge her son's death. Yet the women who act as peace pledge in the Anglo-Saxon texts and in *Volsungasaga* contend with many of the same dilemmas: balancing loyalties between their new husband's kin and their own, finding ways to participate in marriage negotiations, parting with sons as part of the exchange, and enacting vengeance when marriages fail.

A study of these Germanic women who act as peace pledges answers Rubin's call for further exploration of traffic in women, and at the same time acknowledges Newman's response that feminists should move beyond Rubin's groundbreaking paradigm. According to Rubin, "kinship and marriage are always parts of total social systems, and are always tied into economic and political arrangements" (201), and, in many respects, these arrangements were oppressive to Germanic women, who sometimes had no voice in marital decisions and could end up in unhappy and even disastrous unions. Nonetheless, as Karen Newman posits, "woman as object is only one dimension of the force field that figures a sex/gender system" (49). Early Germanic women had, in fact, a number of possible responses to marital exchanges and could find ways to move well beyond the role of object, asserting their influence as mothers and diplomats by king-making, or king-breaking, in their new husbands' homes.

Notes

[1] In "Wicked Queens and Cousin Strategies in *Beowulf,*" Shippey uses historical accounts as a means of discussing the character Thryth in *Beowulf*. In addition to foreign marriages, Shippey also describes domestic marriages between paternal cousins that were "designed to ward off the kind of trouble which paternal cousins could be expected to provide" in competing for the throne.

[2] As will be discussed in the text of this essay, sons were sometimes sent back to maternal kin to be raised by their uncles. If peace did not ensue, the son might be pitted against his father's kin. Sons might also have been vulnerable from birth, especially if the mother acts as peace pledge and is a second wife. Any offspring from the first marriage might see the son as a threat.

[3] Pauline Stafford's *Queens, Concubines, and Dowagers: The King's Wife in the Early Middle Age* is especially useful for its discussion of historical accounts of trafficking. Stafford notes that "marriages between dynasties were common in the sixth, seventh, and eighth centuries in the endless war- and peacemaking among the emergent Germanic kingdoms" (44). She also recognizes that, while the purpose of exchanging women in marriage was to keep peace, "their presence at a foreign court generated tensions that could end in tragedy" (44).

[4] Passages from the elegies are based upon editions of the poems in Anne Klinck's *The Old English Elegies: A Critical Edition and Genre Study*. All translations of elegies are mine unless otherwise indicated. References are to line numbers.

[5] The crux of Niles's argument hinges on his translation of certain present tense verbs as indicative of future time, a practice in keeping with other Anglo-Saxon poems. He describes this translation as "a modern English paraphrase" rather than a literal translation, which would be, he claims, difficult because of the highly ambiguous language of the poem (1145).

[6] Although a popular reading is that the narrator mourns a lost lover, I concur with J.A. Tasioulis and Marijane Osborn that such a reading is unlikely. Tasioulis writes that "[t]he interpretation of the poem does not stand or fall on what can be assumed to be typical or atypical situations in

Old English literature, but it is still worth noting that grieving mothers far outnumber adulterous or lovelorn wives" (2). Osborn agrees that interpreting the narrator to be an unhappy lover is unlikely "because most OE loyalty crises occur within the family group" (183). Another scholar who effectively argues that the narrator mourns the loss of a child is Dolorous Warwick Frese in "*Wulf and Eadwacer*: The Adulterous Woman Reconsidered."

[7] My own argument for the narrator's role as peace pledge closely mirrors Osborn's, although she reaches different conclusions about the ultimate emotions of the narrator by arguing for four characters: the narrator, her husband Eadwacer, her son Wulf, and a second son, the "whelp" in line 16 of the poem. My original ideas about this elegy are in my article "*Wulf and Eadwacer*: A Mother's Lament for her Son." I revisited this topic in a presentation entitled "Wolves and Peaceweavers" at the International Medieval Congress at Western Michigan University in May 2002.

[8] In "The Ambiguity of *Wulf and Eadwacer*," Peter S. Baker notes that the term *reotugu* does not translate as quiet grieving, but refers to wild lamentation and wailing. He points to two other Anglo-Saxon occurrences of the term as a referent to a mother grieving for her son. In the *Fortunes of Men* (46), *reotan* describes the lamentations of a woman standing beside her son's funeral pyre, and in *Beowulf*, the term describes the thundering heavens as Grendel's mother laments the death of her monstrous son (48). In both instances, the term refers to violence and implies active rather than subdued grieving. Whereas Osborn notes the stasis of the narrator as opposed to the wanderings and movement of Wulf ("The Text and Context of *Wulf and Eadwacer*" 181), I maintain that the narrator's lament itself—violent weeping and imploring speech—is active.

[9] Peter S. Baker argues that "gift" is the most likely reading, although I am convinced that the other readings should not be eliminated. Some critics, including JaneMarie Luecke and J. Tasioulas, have argued that the child is literally abandoned or sacrificed. I argue that the sacrifice is metaphoric, a consequence of the traffic in sons of peace pledges.

[10] In line 9, the narrator states that Wulf is the source of her sorrow. Wulf, if one takes it to be a name, has led a number of scholars to conclude that the poem is about outlawry, although E.G. Stanley effectively dismantles this notion, concluding that "there is no evidence for believing that...the monothematic name *Wulf* would have suggested to the Anglo-Saxons, as it has to generations of Anglo-Saxonists, that Wulf is an outlaw" (53).

[11] All passages from *Beowulf* are from Fr. Klaeber's third edition of *Beowulf and the Fight at Finnsburg*. Translations are my own. References are to line numbers.

[12] Friedrich Klaeber is one of several scholars who argue that Thryth is unmarried at the beginning of the narrative. Disagreeing with this reading, Shippey contends, "If Klaeber's view were accepted, we would have a Beowulfian version of *The Taming of the Shrew,* with Offa taking the role of Petruchio." Such a reading diminishes Thryth's automony, according to Shippey.

[13] All passages and translations from *Volsungasaga* are from R.G. Finch's edition with facing-page translation. References are to page numbers.

[14] In addition to the exchange of nephews, the sons of wealthy and noble families in Icelandic tradition were usually in fosterage outside of the family nexus. Although my purpose is to discuss the traffic of women and their sons solely in marital exchanges, one of Jenny Jochens' reasons for fosterage elucidates the role of the nephew who is fostered by his mother's kin. In "Old Norse Motherhood," Jochens explains: "In addition to economic security, fosterage also provided ties as binding as blood relations. In this way the sons obtained new networks of kin relations" (207).

Works Cited

Aertsen, Henk. "*Wulf and Eadwacer*: A Woman's *Cri de Coeur*—For Whom? For What?" *Companion to Old English Poetry.* Ed. Henk Aertsen and Rolf H. Bremmer, Jr. Amsterdam: Vrije UP, 1994. 119-44.

Albano, Robert A. "The Role of Women in Anglo-Saxon Culture: Hildeburh in *Beowulf* and a Curious Counterpart in the *Volsunga Saga.*" *English Language Notes* 32.1 (Sept. 1994): 1-10.

Anderson, James E. "*Deor, Wulf and Eadwacer,* and *The Soul's Address*: How and Where the Old English Exeter Book Riddles Begin." *The Old English Elegies: New Essays in Criticism and Research.* Ed. Martin Green. London: Fairleigh Dickinson UP, 1983. 204-30.

Baker, Peter S. "The Ambiguity of *Wulf and Eadwacer.*" *Studies in Philology* 78.5 (1981): 39-51.

Bessai, Frank. "Comitatus and Exile in Old English Poetry." *Culture* 25 (1964): 130-44.

Brady, Caroline. "Warriors in *Beowulf*: An Analysis of the Nominal Compounds and an Evaluation of the Poet's Use of Them." *Anglo-Saxon England* 11 (1983): 199-246.

Chance, Jane. *Woman as Hero in Old English Literature.* New York: Syracuse UP, 1986.

Damico, Helen. *Beowulf's Wealtheow and the Valkyrie Tradition*. New York: St. Martin's Press, 1984.

Damico, Helen, and Alexandra Hennessey Olsen. *New Readings on Women in Old English Literature*. Bloomington: Indiana UP, 1990.

Desmond, Marilynn. "The Voice of Exile." *Critical Inquiry* 16.3 (Spring 1990): 572-90.

Enright, Michael. "Lady with a Mead-Cup: Ritual, Group Cohesion, and Hierarchy in the Germanic Warband." *Frühmittelalterliche Studien* 22 (1988): 170-203.

Fee, Christopher. "'Beag' and 'Beaghroden' in *Beowulf*." *Neophilologische Mitteilungen* 97.3 (1996): 285-94.

Finch, R.G., ed. and trans. *The Saga of the Volsungs*. London: Thomas Nelson and Sons, Ltd., 1965.

Frese, Dolores Warwick. "*Wulf and Eadwacer*: The Adulterous Woman Reconsidered." *Religion and Literature* 15.1 (Winter 1983): 1-22.

Fry, Donald K. "*Wulf and Eadwacer*: A Wen Charm." *Chaucer Review* 5 (Spring 1971): 247-63.

Gameson, Fiona, and Richard Gameson. "*Wulf and Eadwacer, The Wife's Lament*, and the Discovery of the Individual in Old English Verse." *Studies in English Language and Literature: "Doubt Wisely." Papers in Honour of E.G. Stanley*. Ed. M.J. Toswell and E.M. Tyler. New York: Routledge, 1996. 457-74.

Horner, Shari. *The Discourse of Enclosure: Representing Women in Old English Literature*. New York: State U of New York P, 2001.

Jamison, Carol Parrish. "*Wulf and Eadwacer*: A Mother's Lament for her Son." *Publications of the Mississippi Philological Association* (1990): 88-95.

Jochens, Jenny. "Old Norse Motherhood." *Medieval Mothering*. Ed. John Carmi Parsons and Bonnie Wheeler. New York: Garland, 1996. 210-22.

_____. *Women in Old Norse Society*. Ithaca: Cornell UP, 1995.

Klaeber, Fr. *Beowulf and the Fight at Finnsburg*. 3rd ed. Boston: D. C. Heath and Company, 1950.

Kliman, Bernice W. "Women in Early English Literature, 'Beowulf' to the 'Ancrene Wisse.'" *The Nottingham Mediaeval Studies* 21 (1997): 32-49.

Klinck, Anne L. "Animal Imagery in *Wulf and Eadwacer* and the Possibilities of Interpretation." *Papers on Language and Literature* 23.1 (Winter 1987): 3-13.

_____. *The Old English Elegies: A Critical Edition and Genre Study*. Buffalo: McGill-Queen's UP, 1992.

Luecke, Janemarie. "*Wulf and Eadwacer*: Hints for Reading from *Beowulf* and Anthropology." *The Old English Elegies: New Essays in Criticism*

and Research. Ed. Martin Green. Rutherford: Fairleigh Dickinson UP, 1983. 190–203.
Luyster, Robert. "*The Wife's Lament* in the Context of Scandinavian Myth and Ritual." *Philological Quarterly* 77.3 (Summer 1998): 243–70.
Mitchell, Bruce, and Fred C. Robinson. *A Guide to Old English*. 6th ed. Cambridge: Blackwell, 2001.
Newman, Karen. "Directing Traffic: Subjects, Objects, and the Politics of Exchange." *Differences: A Journal of Feminist Cultural Studies* 2.2 (Summer 1990): 41–54.
Niles, John D. "The Problem of the Ending of *The Wife's Lament*." *Speculum* 78.4 (Oct. 2003): 1107–50.
Osborn, Marijane. "Dogode in *Wulf and Eadwacer* and King Alfred's Hunting Metaphors." *ANQ: A Quarterly Journal of Short Articles, Notes, and Reviews* 13.4 (Fall 2000): 3-9.
_____. "The Text and Context of *Wulf and Eadwacer*." *The Old English Elegies: New Essays in Criticism and Research*. Ed. Martin Green. Rutherford: Fairleigh Dickinson UP, 1983. 174–89.
_____. "'The Wealth They Left Us': Two Women Author Themselves through Others' Lives in *Beowulf*." *Philological Quarterly* 78 (Winter 1999): 49–75.
Renoir, Alain. "A Reading of *The Wife's Lament*." *English Studies* 58 (1977): 4–19.
_____. "*Wulf and Eadwacer*: A Non-Interpretation." *Franciplegus: Medieval and Linguistic Studies in Honor of Francis Peabody Magoun, Jr.* Ed. Jess B. Bessinger and Robert P. Creed. New York: New York UP, 1965. 147–63.
Rubin, Gayle. "The Traffic in Women: Notes on the 'Political Economy' of Sex." *Toward an Anthropology of Women*. Ed. Raya R. Reiter. New York: Monthly Review Press, 1975. 157–210.
Shippey, Tom. "Wicked Queens and Cousin Strategies in *Beowulf* and Elsewhere." *The Heroic Age: A Journal of Early Medieval Northwestern Europe* 5 (Summer 2001) <http://www.mun.ca/mst/heroicage/issues/5/Shippey1.html>
Sklute, L. John. "'Freoþuwebbe' in Old English Poetry." *Neophilologische Mitteilungen* 71 (1970): 534-54.
Stafford, Pauline. *Queens, Concubines, and Dowagers: The King's Wife in the Early Middle Ages*. Athens: U of Georgia P, 1983.
Stanley, E. G. "Wolf, My Wolf!" *Old English and New: Studies in Language and Linguistics in Honor of Frederick G. Cassidy*. Ed. Joan Hall et al. New York: Garland, 1992. 46–62.

Straus, Barrie Ruth. "Women's Words as Weapons: Speech as Action in *The Wife's Lament*." *Texas Studies in Language and Literature* 23 (1981): 268–85.

Tasioulis, J.A. "The Mother's Lament: *Wulf and Eadwacer* Reconsidered." *Medium Ævum* 65.1 (1996): 1–15.

Tupper, Frederick. "The Cynewulfian Runes of the First Riddle." *Modern Language Notes* 25 (Dec. 1910): 235–41.

Wrenn, C.L., ed. *Beowulf*. London: Harrap, 1973.

Adam Schubart's Early Modern "Tyrant She-Man": Female Misbehavior, Gender, and the Disciplining of Hybrid Bodies

Katja Altpeter-Jones

Herr Sieman, the ambiguously gendered figure of the She-Man that finds representation in texts and images from the late fifteenth through the early seventeenth century, has received scant attention by literary scholars and has typically been read as a metaphor for imperious wives who wish to rule over husbands and households. In this article, I offer a reading of the early modern She-Man as an allegory of gender. Focusing on Adam Schubart's *Der Sieman / das ist wider den Hausteuffell* (The She-Man / this is against the house-devil) of 1564, I demonstrate that the author, in fashioning the figure of the She-Man, privileges gender as a category guaranteeing social order. At the same time, however, Schubart's text bespeaks a deep anxiety around the issue of visibility of difference. I argue that in negotiating this anxiety and in pointing toward the body and to sexuality as the loci on which gender difference can and must be inscribed, Schubart performs the quintessentially modern gesture of relating gender to anatomical difference and sexuality. (KAJ)

In a recent article on ideals of femininity and masculinity in German didactic literature of the Middle Ages, Ingrid Bennewitz and Ruth Weichselbaumer draw attention to Thomasin of Zerclaere's early-thirteenth-century directive that a courtly lady ideally ought to have just enough intelligence and spirit "that she may act in a courteous and well-mannered way and show an agreeable disposition through delightful speech and a chaste state of mind." If a courtly lady has more than this required amount of intelligence and knowledge, however, Thomasin advises her to display it sparingly lest she appear to be outwitting the men around her: "If, in addition, she also possesses reason and education, she ought to have enough decency and be sufficiently cultured that she will not reveal how much reason she has: after all, one would not want her as authority."[1]

This issue of *Obrigkeit,* of authority, as it plays out in gender relationships, is present in medieval articulations of the roles of men and women in society. But oftentimes it is present implicitly only, and rarely is it addressed as explicitly as in the text passage quoted above. However, by the fifteenth century the question of "who is on top" in gender relations becomes an issue of primary concern to the writers of conduct literature and satire, as well as to the publishers of broadsheet prints and pamphlet literature. Certainly, the Middle Ages has its stories of Phyllis riding Aristotle and of imperious wives attempting to subvert their husbands' authority.[2] But it is the early modern printing revolution that makes possible the seemingly limitless multiplication and wide distribution of texts and images that depict a gendered world turned upside down. During this time of enormous upheaval—spiritual, political, and social—images and texts that portray the world out of joint seem both to speak to as well as rouse people's anxieties about the tenuously stable world in which they live, and disorderly women who defy their husbands' authority frequently function as symbols of a world turned upside down.

It is precisely during this time that *Herr Sieman* or Master She-Man—a term most commonly read as designating the married woman who assumes more power in the household than she is entitled to—enters the scene and becomes a presence in a number of satirical and didactic texts as well as in the visual culture of early modern Germany.[3] *Herr Sieman* attains his/her most prominent position in an eponymous and ostensibly popular text by the otherwise little known Lutheran minister Adam Schubart.[4] In his *Der Sieman / das ist wider den Hausteuffell* (The She-Man / this is against the house-devil), Schubart writes: "The powerful tyrant She-Man is now attacking our country. Comes marching along with the power of armies and wants to prove his dominance. He wants to conquer all countries and presses for all men to be first and foremost obedient to their wives" (252; lines 57–64).[5]

It is Schubart's portrayal of this female oddity of the She-Man that will occupy me in this article. In exploring this exceptional she-male, I will proceed in two steps. I wish to examine, first, the different modes of transgression associated with the figure of the She-Man. In many respects the She-Man's transgressions resemble those acts of misbehavior ascribed also to women in the medieval satirical and didactic tradition, and in various genres and media contemporaneous with Schubart's text. However, in contrast to the medieval didactic tradition in which an excessively vocal woman simply betrays bad manners and a lack of social decorum—see Thomasin's exhortations quoted at the beginning of this article—and in contrast also to contemporaneous, that is, other early modern texts and images in which a vociferous wife or an unruly woman is a challenge primarily to husbands and fathers, the early modern figure of the She-Man is conceived, as I will demonstrate here, as a socially and politically disruptive force that respects no boundaries. She-Man rules at home and in public, invades the homes of the pauper and the nobleman, conquers foreign lands, and disrupts the operations of civic institutions. What emanates from Schubart's text and its depiction of Master She-Man's limitless incursions into all aspects of public and private life is, I will argue, a deep skepticism regarding the effectiveness of several of the most fundamental principles guaranteeing order in early modern society.

But what is even more exceptional about the sixteenth-century figure of the She-Man is the fact that the subversion of social norms by a woman is conceived here explicitly as an act of gender transgression. For in Schubart's text, the woman who oversteps the boundaries of proper wifely behavior by acquiring and wielding excessive domestic and public power becomes a man, of some sorts at least: a She-Man. I argue that in fashioning the hybrid figure of the she-male Schubart shifts emphasis: his text is no longer simply an examination of proper wifely conduct but offers in addition a contemplation of the difference between men and women. Schubart's text is, as I conclude at the end of part one, first and foremost an exploration of the concept of gender. This first section of the paper is therefore labeled "Privileging Gender."

In part two of this article, I note a paradox. While the text privileges the category of gender, it simultaneously points to the difficulty in upholding and ascertaining gender difference. In examining this paradox, I analyze a passage that describes a fight between the narrator and Master She-Man and that places the body at the center of the struggle over dominance. I argue that the text manages to redraw the boundaries of gender difference only by referring, although not without hesitation, to the body and to sexuality as the loci on which gender difference can and must be inscribed.

Schubart's text consists of three distinct parts. It starts out with a brief and rather perfunctory reference to the devil who, Schubart declares, has selected the divinely ordained estate of marriage as a primary object of attack in his struggle to ruin Christianity. The house-devil, that is, the devil responsible for anything that is awry in the household, seeks to ruin marriages and the estate of marriage in general by creating discord and animosity between spouses. Interestingly, Schubart quickly discards the model of the traditional *Teufelbuch*[6] and, instead of detailing the work of the devil with regard to marriage and the domestic sphere, zooms in on what seems to concern him most: the issue of a wife's refusal to show obedience toward her husband. As the generally conceived topic of marital strife with a focus on the roles of both marital partners gives way to a discussion of the issue of female insubordination, the figure of the house-devil steps into the background and a new culprit is conjured up: the She-Man.[7] At this point, too, the narrative style changes, and Schubart concludes what up to this point reads as a piece of marital advice literature.

The second part introduces a male narrator who tells the audience of two encounters he has had. He recounts how he first met another man who told him about the havoc Master She-Man is wreaking everywhere in the country and how later, on returning home, he promptly encountered Master She-Man in person in his own home where the unruly she-male quickly began to torment the narrator with the same acts of brutality earlier described by the narrator's informant. However, we learn that in the end the narrator remains victorious and ends Master She-Man's rebellion by killing him/her. In its crude humor, detailed descriptions of acts of physical violence, and depictions of uncouth behavior by all involved, this part of Schubart's text uses topoi from short narrative genres such as *Märe* and *Schwank*.[8]

Part three cleverly presents itself as a sermon written by the narrator himself who, moved by his frightful encounter with Master She-Man described in part two, has proceeded to write an exhortation to spouses regarding proper marital comportment. Like part two, this third passage is composed in rhymed couplets. Its style is quite different, however. Referring to the Bible, texts from the Graeco-Roman classical tradition, and contemporary folklore, and repeatedly addressing the audience directly, the text here presents an exhortation on proper marital conduct, with a pronounced focus on wifely and female obedience. Although the wiles of Master She-Man are presented in greatest detail in part two, *Herr Sieman* effectively replaces the house-devil in all three parts of Schubart's text.

Privileging Gender

In describing Master She-Man's conduct, Schubart repeatedly avails himself of the imagery of gender inversion that figures prominently and enjoys great popularity in medieval and early modern literary, visual, and performative culture.[9] Many of Master She-Man's transgressions invert traditional gender norms and put men into the position of women and vice versa: where *Sieman* claims power and mastery, he/she turns the husband (i.e., him who is supposed to be master) into a servant (255; 151–54). The husband is shown taking care of women's business (he goes to the market [257; 237–41] and spins wool [302; 1776–77]). And he displays various forms of behavior typically ascribed to women (he complains, cries, and curses excessively [256; 178–80] and is frivolous with the money Master She-Man has saved [258; 248–49]). Analogously, the imperious wife claims mastery in areas traditionally reserved for men (by consuming alcohol excessively [258; 268–75], and by threatening physical violence [254; 121–22]).[10] In addition, Master She-Man transgresses by speaking immodestly or aggressively (254; 119–20)[11] and by claiming mastery over financial matters (268; 248–49).[12] On the most fundamental level, Master She-Man's transgression is his/her refusal to be subject to a husband's authority. The She-Man thus displays the same behavioral patterns that Brietzmann has identified as characteristic of the "evil woman" in much of medieval and early modern German literature.[13] Schubart explicitly refers to Master She-Man's incursions as attempts to invert a divinely ordained social order,[14] and the didactic superstructure of this text suggests to audiences that *Der Sieman* is primarily concerned with reassigning women to their proper roles.[15] Neither the depiction of the misbehaving and scandalous wife, nor the representation of a woman who usurps male power and inverts a proper gender order by moving into spheres of male dominance is thus particularly novel. One may therefore be tempted to read Master She-Man as just another, albeit more fanciful, approach to representing the imperious wife.

In a number of ways, however, *Herr Sieman* outdoes his/her counterparts in medieval and contemporaneous (i.e., other early modern) texts, for She-Man's threats go far beyond the sphere of home and family. While She-Man's origins lie in the home—identified in the following passage specifically as the realm of the kitchen—*Herr Sieman* is spreading his/her realm geographically far. "And quite a few places are now almost famous," writes Schubart, "for the fact that Master She-Man has entered them with many thousand horses and has set up camp there. And may God mercifully prevent the sparks from She-Man's kitchen from flying uncontrollably and from setting things on fire" (244). This passage—the first in Schubart's text to describe Master She-Man and his/her actions in any detail—works on several levels. First, it substantiates the image of *Sieman* as a symbol of inversion: originally introduced as desiring to upset the hierarchy of husband and wife by seeking to rule over her husband, Master She-Man further upsets an order understood as natural by infringing on what is considered male territory (i.e., warfare). Secondly, these acts of inversion are associated with extreme disorder, as *Sieman's* acts are likened to the chaos and lawlessness of war and destruction.[16] What particularly interests me in this passage, however, is the reference to Master She-Man's ubiquitous presence. As in the text passage quoted earlier in this article, in which She-Man attacks the entire country and—indifferent to the concept of national sovereignty—desires to bring all countries under his/her control, so here, too, *Sieman* is described as attacking and conquering several geographical locations simultaneously.[17]

Disrespectful of geographical distance and national or cultural distinctness, She-Man shows irreverence also toward social distinctions. For *Sieman* does not recognize social hierarchies and their concomitant exclusivities and instead attacks on all social levels.[18] She-Man assaults the peasant as well as the priest, and harasses the urban burgher as well as the nobleman at his courtly residence. Thus the narrator is told by his informant: "I was staying at a peasant's house. He was not a happy fellow. He had at home an evil dragon [later identified as *Herr Sieman*] who was immobile like a church steeple" (254; 107–10). The narrator speculates that surely in urban areas, Master She-Man encounters resistance from the cities' burghers: "There is resistance in the cities," he ventures, "the citizens are putting up a fight. They remain masters over the She-Man, so that he cannot overcome the city walls" (257; 218–21). The narrator's companion replies that, unfortunately, the contrary is the case and adds that even noble lords are no match for Master She-Man: "Do you think that the nobility has it easy all the time and never suffers hardship? The She-Man regularly wants to rule there. Yes, princes and great lords are almost defenseless against him" (260; 319–25). Similarly, the narrator's companion informs him that priests are not immune to *Herr Sieman's* attacks: "The She-Man frequently comes riding into their homes. They have to be his hostages. He torments and mistreats them as he pleases. And they are expected to suffer all this silently" (262; 404–07). In other words, *Sieman's* conquests reach geographically far and transcend boundaries of social status and profession. Peasants cannot defend themselves, and neither can burghers, representatives of the nobility, princes, and "great lords." Priests as well as laymen suffer Master She-Man's attacks, and the countryside as well as cities and courts fall victim to the incursions of *Herr Sieman*.

In addition, the she-male's power of influence extends over all significant civic places and institutions. "Master She-Man rules in the city, in the house, on the marketplace, and in the city council," the narrator is told (257; 234–35). And when a little later he encounters *Sieman* in his own house, he is warned by him/her: "I want to rule everywhere: in the house, the kitchen, the storage rooms, and in the assembly hall" (264; 457-58). Not to be contained geographically or to be reined in by the classificatory powers of social status and profession, She-Man also rules both inside and outside the house, and dominates public places and civic institutions. In other words, *Sieman* respects no boundaries whatsoever—geographical, national, social, professional, and institutional. In his/her indomitable quest for dominance and power, *Sieman* means the ruin of both "POLYTIA und OECONOMIA" (246), the former referring to the public sphere and the state, the latter to the domestic sphere of home and family.

The acts of Schubart's *Sieman* go beyond those of unruly females typically portrayed in medieval or early modern texts and images. His/her acts of insurgence by far exceed those of the medieval courtly lady who may overstep the boundaries of propriety by speaking too much or too freely, or that of the satirical figure of the wife riding her husband, who constitutes a threat to her marital partner.[19] *Herr Sieman's* attacks are, in contrast, systematic and sweeping: they are portrayed as acts of warfare that threaten not only an individual husband or *Hausvater* and his household but endanger the power of men of all professions and of any social status. They threaten the proper operations of households, civic institutions, political bodies, and nations.

In his/her systematic attack on all areas of public and private life, his/her disrespect for geographical and national boundaries, and irreverence for distinctions of social and professional status, Schubart's she-male systematically undermines the effectiveness of some of the most significant boundaries that constitute lines of demarcation within sixteenth-century social hierarchies: geographical and national demarcations and the distinctness of professional and social affiliations all dwindle in the face of She-Man's ambitious attacks. The figure of *Herr Sieman,* I argue, thus marks not simply a world "turned upside down." For if something is upside down, it means only that roles are inverted, but that rules and categories remain intact. The figure of the She-Man, however, signals a world in which previously solid boundaries and clearly legible signifiers of order and hierarchy, of inclusion and exclusion, have lost their meaning. Roles are not simply turned on their heads, but completely dismantled. This is a world in disarray.

Herr Sieman effects the destabilization of precisely those institutions and boundaries that are presented as vulnerable, fragile, and tenuous in a great number of sixteenth-century texts and images that articulate anxieties around threats of disorder. In a culture in which disorder—whether real, rhetorical, or imagined—figures prominently,[20] the disorder caused by Master She-Man would thus not have been without referential potential, and the image of the freely roaming She-Man would have been open to multiple interpretations and associations. The lack of imperial strength and cultural cohesion of a ceremoniously named Holy Roman Empire (Puff 19);[21] increasing poverty that caused large numbers of the poor and unemployed to roam the countryside in search of employment and money; the hopes and fears related to increased upward and downward social mobility and shifts in social stratifications;[22] the Peasants' War and other forms of rebellion that in reality brought violence and bloodshed to many parts of the empire and undermined traditional social hierarchies;[23] challenges to religious orthodoxy[24] and, in Lutheran theology, the leveling of differences between laypeople and priests: the figure of Master She-Man mobilizes many of these amorphous, interwoven, and anxious fantasies simultaneously.[25]

And I think it is in this light that we have to read the figure of the early modern She-Man. For it is precisely against the backdrop of the inflationary dynamics that in the fifteenth and sixteenth centuries mark so many of the recognized taxonomies and hierarchies—of nationality, religion, profession, and social status—that the figure of *Herr Sieman* stands out as particularly striking. For where Schubart portrays the vulnerability and instability of these taxonomies and of their respective means of organizing society, he clearly foregrounds—as an alternative means of classification, it would appear—the category of gender and its organizational potential. In Schubart's text, the battle against disorder is clearly articulated as a contest over the validity of the concept of gender, and gender becomes the salient category for creating order and for making sense of the world.

At a time when many other seemingly stable methods for ordering and understanding the world undergo destabilization and dismissal, the category of gender, the text seems to indicate, becomes increasingly important as a signifier of exclusion and inclusion and as a potential guarantor of order in an ever more volatile social formation. In privileging the category of gender, Schubart's text thus mirrors and draws attention to a decisive shift that feminist historians have discerned as constitutive of early modern society and culture: the more systematic exclusion of women from positions of power and influence, the increased monitoring of gender difference, and, concomitantly, the essentializing of the category of gender itself.[26] It is especially in the discourse on marriage that this privileging of the category "gender" and of its classificatory potential is most evident.

Scholars have long acknowledged the importance of marriage reform within the larger project of sixteenth-century social and religious reform. At the end of the nineteenth century, Kawerau points to the centrality of marriage to the Reformation project and notes that many reformers recognized matrimony's key role in the enforcement of social order. In his "Sermon on the Estate of Marriage" of 1550, Erasmus Alberus, for example, names as the third reason why matrimony is a laudable institution the fact that among all estates that God instituted and ordered, matrimony is the very first and the one from which all other estates derive.[27] In this model, marital, social, and divine order are to be imagined as concentric circles. The innermost circle is matrimony. If matrimony is properly ordered, then order will radiate out from it, ensuring in turn the proper order of society and divine creation.[28] "Compared with the dramatic religious and political transformations of the times," writes Harrington, from whom I borrow the image of the three concentric circles (42), "marriage reform might be assumed a peripheral concern among secular and religious authorities. In fact, it stood by implication at the heart of almost every major legal, religious, and social reform of the period" (26). "Paternal authority" constituted the epicenter of this concentric model in which

> the well-known head of the household, or *Hausvater,* was joined in sixteenth-century rhetoric by two other paternal authority figures—the *Landesvater* (political ruler) and the *Gottesvater* (God the Father)—thus representing what Luther and other Protestant reformers considered "the three orders of Christian society": *ecclesia* (Church), *politia* (State), and *oeconomia* (household) (Harrington 40).

This model suggests that if marital order is the foundation of all order, then marital disorder is the root cause of social disorder. At the same time, the order that defines marital relationships—a hierarchical arrangement based on distinct and complementary roles for men and women; we might call it "gender" for short—becomes the ordering principle of society and the divine order. Furthermore, if in reformed thinking matrimony is considered the only acceptable form of adult living and "an order for all humankind" (Puff 149), then matrimony as the epicenter of social, political, and divine order provides the model for proper social roles for all male and female individuals in all imaginable social contexts. Within the reformed tradition—and Schubart certainly belongs here—the relationship of husband and wife thus becomes paradigmatic for all men and women at all levels of social and political organization. And the difference between husbands and wives, men and women, in short, a binary and hierarchically organized gender model with clear separations of male and female behavior, becomes the decisive moment in the constitution and preservation of the three concentric levels of order.

In fashioning the figure of the She-Man, I contend, Schubart performs exactly this gesture of abstraction—of shifting emphasis from an exploration of individual marital behavior (here especially: wifely misconduct) to a contemplation of the concept of gender (as the foundation of all order)—that is at work also where reformers relate the concrete behavior of men and women in marriage to the foundational principles of all social order. Master She-Man, then—though ostensibly a metaphor for female insubordination—becomes a kind of allegory for gender itself. We see this clearly also if we take a closer look at the figure of the She-Man. For *Herr Sieman* is not simply a wife who wishes to be husband or a woman who behaves like a man. *Herr Sieman*, I believe, signifies something more, and it is a contemplation of the issue of inversion that makes it possible to locate this "something more."

Schubart does not present a straightforward case of gender-role inversion, because in his text the woman who oversteps the boundaries of proper wifely behavior by acquiring and wielding excessive domestic and public power becomes not a man, but a she-male. It is by undoing the image of the She-Man, and by asking which positive might inform the formation of the negative *Sieman,* that we see what Master She-Man represents. By inverting the inversion presented in Schubart's text, we do not arrive at "woman/wife" (for might we not just as well arrive at "man/husband"?). Rather, by restoring a putative positive to the inverted *Sieman,* we arrive at *sie* and *man*. *Herr Sieman,* then, is not a case of female-to-male inversion, but emerges instead as the inversion of the concept of difference between "she" and "man." As such, the term signals the amalgamation of something that ought to be separate and can therefore be interpreted as the inversion to the concept of gender difference. Read in this way, *Herr Sieman* becomes a cipher for the concept of gender and the question of difference.

Inscribing Difference

But obviously there is a significant problem with Schubart's explicit privileging of the category of gender as the taxonomic model for organizing all men and women at all social levels and for guaranteeing social order. Schubart's impetus is primarily didactic. He fashions the figure of *Herr Sieman* as a warning to both women and men. Dedicating his book "to all dear brothers and sisters in the estate of marriage" (242), he indicates his hope "that it may guide wives to obedience" (248). And approximately half of his text is—as he puts it—"an exhortation...on how spouses ought to behave with each other" (271). Where Schubart portrays a world in disarray, he does so precisely in hopes of upholding in real life a properly ordered gendered world and the social order it promises. In light of inoperative social, professional, and geographical distinctions and hierarchies, Schubart seems to suggest, gender promises distinctions, hierarchies, and order.

Paradoxically, however, although the text stresses the importance of a clear distinction of gendered behavior, it ends up portraying gender as just as volatile and problematic a category as the other categories of social demarcation it depicts as defunct. For any woman may at any point cease to be a real woman and turn into something manlike. The text's ambiguity on this point, on gender's ability to constitute the taxonomy that guarantees social order in light of other defunct ordering mechanisms, is echoed in an interesting way by another kind of ambiguity: that of the hybrid She-Man figure itself.

She-Man comes into being when a wife refuses properly wifely comportment, takes up the accoutrements of male conduct, and invades the spheres of male dominance. In many places, the text marks this transition clearly by letting "she" become "he." Thus, masculine personal and possessive pronouns are used consistently in reference to Master She-Man in the following passage:

> The powerful tyrant She-Man is now attacking our country. Comes marching along with the power of armies and wants to prove his dominance. He wants to conquer all countries and presses for all men to be first and foremost obedient to their wives (252; 57–64).

In another passage, however, the text wavers in its assignment of a grammatical gender in reference to the She-Man. The boundaries between "he" and "she" are ill-defined, for example, where the narrator recounts his personal encounter with Master She-Man. First described as "a woman of stern looks" (263; 449) and grammatically marked as "she" (263; 450), this figure then identifies herself/himself as *Sieman*. "I bid her welcome," the narrator reports, "and soon brought out a jug of wine. She did not want to accept it and said 'I am Master She-Man'" (263–64; 451–54). Yet, despite the fact that the woman has at this point identified herself/himself as *Sieman* and despite the fact that the narrator, too, has addressed her/him as such (264; 465), the narrator continues to refer to her/him as "she" (264; 479, 484). The gender confusion is pronounced also during the ensuing fight that eventually results in Master She-Man's death. Here the narrator switches to the masculine personal pronoun,[29] then—only three lines further down—back to the feminine pronoun,[30] only to switch back again after another four lines.[31] After this point and throughout the increasingly brutal clash, the exclusive use of the masculine personal pronoun continues. Only after Master She-Man has been killed do feminine personal and relative pronouns slip back into the narrator's account. Even though these pronouns now refer to the feminine noun "hautt"—She-Man is here described as "böse hautt," as "evil skin"—they also obstinately refer the reader back to the gender ambiguity inherent in the image of the She-Man and to the fact that *Herr Sieman* is both male and female.

Of course, the fashioning of the figure "She-Man" is in itself profoundly ambiguous. For *Sieman,* although he/she ceases to be a woman, never fully becomes a man either. Instead, the term She-Man marks a hybrid, even monstrous, in-between. Like the hermaphrodite who in much of Renaissance literature appears as a monstrous creation, *Herr Sieman* is fashioned as an abnormality, as a monstrosity not only in spirit and behavior but also in body.[32] When, for example, the text's narrator encounters Master She-Man in his own house, he beats him/her repeatedly. Three times, the narrator believes that he has killed Master She-Man, but each time the creature comes back to life after a short period of time. In this context, the narrator refers to *Sieman* as "evil dragon" (266; 539) and "that animal" (268; 605), and the undertaker refuses to bury Master She-Man, claiming that the creature is "not human" (266; 541).

While Schubart thus points to the singular importance of the category of gender within sixteenth-century German social order, he acknowledges that, although order on all concentric levels relies on it, it is a slippery thing. Gender conformity, and particularly women's gender conformity, needs to be closely monitored, he suggests, especially because non-conformity comes in degrees, and almost imperceptible first steps in this direction may quickly lead to complete gender disorder in which monstrous gender-hybrids rule the world. The ambiguity of the animal-like She-Man and the text's own uncertainty regarding the possibility of preventing the generation of such hybrid aberrations both bespeak a deep anxiety vis-à-vis the concept of gender. How then are we to read this profound and double ambiguity in the presentation of the She-Man: the privileging of the category of gender, yet the text's simultaneous portrayal of this order as volatile and slippery; and the wish to uphold the difference between men and women, yet parallel to this, the depiction of how easily and effortlessly difference can be undermined?

In his article on "The 'Other' in the Age of the Reformation," Hans Hillerbrand writes: "the societal identification of the Other always includes not only the declaration of a social norm but also the concomitant effort to make the Other *visible*" (251; my emphasis). What makes the She-Man truly frightening is, I believe, the fact that one cannot identify him/her readily. Any woman may at any given point turn into a She-Man. And once she has become a She-Man, she/he cannot be recognized as such and as being different from other "normal" women. There is, in other words, a problem of visibility. One should be able to identify a She-Man. But even more importantly, there should be a reliable means for identifying and guaranteeing difference. Behavior, it appears, should be anchored to something fixed, dependable, and clearly identifiable that guarantees difference and makes possible the monitoring of gender conformity. More than anything, Schubart's hesitation and ambiguity with regard to gender seem to veil an anxiety around the issue of the visibility of difference. For the She-Man looks just like a woman, yet behaves like a man.

I am aware of only one visual representation of *Herr Sieman*.[33] In it, Master She-Man cannot be distinguished from a woman proper. He/she has female physiognomy and is dressed like a woman. Similarly, the oft-depicted woman who assumes an excessive amount of power in the household looks just like a "normal" woman, except that she has equipped herself with the insignia of power. Clothing often functions as the principal signifier that marks a woman as properly or improperly gendered. According to this taxonomy, the woman with excessive ambitions of power might be portrayed wearing pants or as desiring her husband's trousers. The focus on clothing and on the accoutrements of domestic power certainly suggests an interest in identifying visual manifestations of difference that clearly mark transgression and the Otherness of the transgressor. At the same time, clothing is obviously a rather superficial and volatile means of making gender visible. One may mislead by dressing up in gender-inappropriate attire, and clothing can be changed at will. It is, in other words, unreliable as a signifier of difference and as a guarantor of the visibility of Otherness.[34]

"Sometime in the eighteenth century," writes Thomas Laqueur, "sex as we know it was invented" (*Making Sex* 149). Until then, he argues, a "one-sex" model prevailed in which men and women were seen to be physiologically and anatomically more or less identical, with the woman being considered a less well-formed version of the male whose genitalia were that of a man, only inverted and turned inward.[35] Within this "one-sex" model, it was not impossible for individuals to change their sex, even rather spontaneously. In women, physical exertion, abrupt movements, or a particularly wide spreading of the legs while jumping over a creek might cause the female genitals to drop out, thus turning a woman into a man.[36] Concurring with Laqueur's analysis of major shifts in the understanding of sexual difference in the eighteenth century, Londa Schiebinger writes:

> Laqueur has focused primarily on changing views of male and female sexual organs, but the [eighteenth-century] revolution in sexual science was more fundamental, marked by a methodological rupture in explanations of sexual difference. At long last, ancient theories of sexuality—the Aristotelian/Galenic theory of humors and biblical accounts—were overturned by modern materialistic theories that grounded sexual difference in the *fabric of the body* (37–38; my emphasis).

Schubart's text makes no explicit reference to the physiological or anatomical differences between men and women, although his text clearly operates under the premise that men and women are and should be of a different kind. Yet the body is by no means absent from his text. Indeed, in Schubart's *Sieman*, as in many medieval and early modern texts that describe with striking explicitness and brutality a husband's beating of his wife's several disobedient "skins," the numerous attempts at resistance launched by various men against Master She-Man always appear as acts of physical violence.

Notably, the most violent attacks on She-Man's body occur in those text passages where his/her gender identity appears most indeterminate. Thus it is in the passages in which the narrator wavers in his use of masculine or feminine pronouns that references to Master She-Man's body are most numerous and that the disciplining of the ambiguously gendered creature's body is depicted most vividly. "Be quiet and peaceful and don't be proud. Do you see that large piece of wood? I'll tan your hide with it," threatens the narrator (264; 469–71). Similarly he reports: "That made me take up weapons all the more. I took a sharp halberd and—enraged—I hit the She-Man violently" (264; 496–98). And after another brief reference to beating (265; 506), the text continues with the following graphic description: "I hit She-Man over the head and threw him on the floor like a pot. He was lying stretched out in front of me. I covered him with blows, instantly struck him, and beat him black and blue from head to toe. I beat his loins, back and belly, and also his thighs" (266; 527–34).

The violent attacks on *Sieman's* body continue, and blood starts flowing, until finally Master She-Man lies half-dead and the narrator has "tanned his hide to pieces" (268; 596). At this point the narrator hires four lansquenets and encourages them to "beat this animal black and blue once or three times or four [and] smash its arms and legs to pieces" (268; 604–07). They in turn dutifully "beat the She-Man so violently on his head and entire body that he lay dead right away" (268; 610–12).

Ostensibly an instance of spousal punishment for wifely insubordination, the disciplining of Master She-Man's body reads differently if one chooses to interpret Schubart's *Sieman* as a cipher of gender and difference. In this case, the punishment is directed not at an unruly woman but at the body that fails to perform proper gender conformity and on which difference collapses. Read in this way, it is as though the text, in its search for a visible marker of gender difference, focuses on the body as that element that deserves punishment for failing to do its job of properly marking and upholding difference.

However, equally significant is that in these passages gender appears linked not only to the body but also to sexuality. For what is at issue here and what ultimately determines the outcome of the fight between the narrator and *Herr Sieman* are the presence or absence of and the power to wield specific male or female body parts, here metaphorically represented by the weapons used in the fight: among them a large piece of wood (264; 470), a sharp halberd (265; 497), a sharp sword (267; 585), and an iron flail (266; 524). Weaponry and various household objects frequently function as metaphors for male and female genitalia, and the use of the imagery of warfare is commonplace for describing sex acts, especially in carnival plays.[37] To a sixteenth-century audience, the reference to sex and to male and female sexual organs in this passage would have been quite obvious.

Perhaps not surprisingly, *Herr Sieman*—by picking up a spear (265; 517) and a sharp knife (267; 589)—makes use of the same phallic weapons that the narrator uses. But the text also refers to female anatomy and physiology. This is the case where it describes the objects that receive blows from the various phallic weapons described. There is, for example, the threat "I will beat you on your shield and helmet" (264; 482). And being attacked by a phallic weapon is described as resulting in a serious wound (267; 590) and severe bleeding (267; 579).[38] Surprisingly, even though the narrator's arsenal of penetrating weapons is much larger than Master She-Man's, the narrator appears twice as the sexually receptive side—his shield is beaten and he receives a gash—whereas Master She-Man is portrayed as sexually receptive only once (the red blood is his/hers).

In the end, however, the narrator emerges victorious: his arsenal of weapons of attack is larger than Master She-Man's, he ultimately gains the upper hand in the fight, and he disciplines the She-Man until the latter ceases to exist. Yet it is only by means of a rather drawn-out and violent struggle that the narrator remains victorious, and the fact that a fight is necessary suggests that the issue is by no means predetermined. Furthermore, we may suspect that in order to end the reign of *Herr Sieman*—to redraw the boundaries of gender difference clearly—the narrator needs to ensure that he is the one who commands the weapons of attack and who comes out on top in the brawl. If the narrator can be victorious in the end, it is only because he manages to assert the full meaning of difference by connecting gender with the body and sexuality, and by proving clearly who is anatomically equipped and has the power to penetrate. Upholding difference and, by extension, social order, the text implies, is possible only where gender takes recourse to anatomy and sexuality.

If we read gender not only as encompassing the "differences and similarities between men and women" but also as a negotiation of the "norms marking the boundaries between the sexes" (Wunder 39), then Master She-Man becomes a kind of allegory for gender itself and for the various thorny issues related to this concept and to the question of difference. Where does one sex/gender end and the other begin?[39] How does difference manifest itself, and how and where can it be securely and permanently inscribed? Read in this way, the physical struggles described at length in Schubart's text are a reminder "that gender difference and hierarchy had to be produced and secured," and that "[k]eeping that hierarchy in place was an ongoing struggle" that demanded "enormous cultural labor" (Howard 423).

Laqueur writes that "[i]deology, not accuracy of observation, determined how [the anatomical differences between man and woman] were seen and which differences would matter" (*Making Sex* 88). He concludes that only in the eighteenth century did ideology make possible and necessary the inscription of gender on bodies that were visibly and unmistakably sexed either male or female. Yet Schubart's sixteenth-century text, by insistently pointing to the body as a site for the inscription of difference, seems to tell a different story. We can only speculate whether texts such as Schubart's, which point to the importance of gender difference in an orderly world but reveal such deep anxieties about the ability to uphold and defend those same differences, may have precipitated the push toward the making visible of difference and may have provided the impetus not only for a complete demise of a Galenic model of isomorphic male and female anatomy,[40] but also for the consolidation of a two-body model with its potential for the concrete physiological and anatomical inscription of gender difference.

Further exploration of the numerous other texts that feature Master She-Man and of various examples from the large body of marital advice and conduct literature that like Schubart's text fuse the thinking about social order with a focus on the body and its disciplining might substantiate what the examination of one particularly striking textual example can at this point only state as a hypothesis: that in the sixteenth century, conduct and marital advice literature signals shifts in the conceptualization of gender, long before they articulate themselves explicitly in the authoritative discourses of eighteenth-century science, medicine, law, and politics.

Notes

All translations of primary and secondary sources are my own, unless otherwise indicated.

[1] This is my own translation of two text passages from Thomasin's *Welscher Gast* (qtd. in Bennewitz and Weichselbaumer, 45).

[2] See, for example, Brinker-von der Heyde.

[3] Bolte observes that the figure of *Herr Sieman* denotes either an effeminate man, especially a subordinate husband, or a wife who rules instead of and over her husband. He adds that the figure of the She-Man can, thirdly, represent the personification of female rule and dominance. Most frequently, however, he concludes, the terms *Herr Sieman* or *Doktor Sieman* designate an insubordinate wife (296). Compare also Kawerau (773). On the various meanings and uses of the term *Sieman* see also the entry "Siemann" in *Deutsches Sprichwörter-Lexikon*. Where Adam Schubart conjures up the figure of *Herr Sieman,* he represents precisely this kind of unruly and rebellious wife. At the very beginning of his text, where he lets the book address the audience in its own voice, Schubart writes: "My name derives from the She-Man. I speak of unruly wives" (241).

[4] For specific, albeit scant, information on Schubart, see "Schubart, Adam," *Deutsches Literatur-Lexikon*; "Schubart, Adam S.," *Allgemeine deutsche Biographie*; and Stambaugh (2: 441–42). It is difficult to assess with accuracy the role played by the early modern figure of the She-Man in the literary imagination of the fifteenth and sixteenth centuries. Wiltenburg writes: "[M]any contemporary references show that the figure of She-Man [Siemann] was well known" (*Women in Early Modern Germany* 14). Bolte references numerous texts from the late fifteenth through the early seventeenth century that feature Master She-Man. Thus *Herr Sieman* appears in the writings of some of the most prominent literary voices of the time: Martin Luther, Hans Sachs, Georg Wickram, Burkhard Waldis, and Andreas Musculus all refer to Master She-Man in their works (296–97). And *Herr Sieman* is a familiar figure also in sixteenth-century drama (see Price, esp. 152–58). Kawerau notes, however, that Schubart's depiction of the She-Man may well be the most popular one among the numerous texts that make reference to this unruly she-male (777). Schubart's text first appeared in print in 1564 and was reprinted at least three times in 1565, 1568, and 1569, respectively (see "Schubart, Adam," *Deutsches Literatur-Lexikon*).

The fact that the text was printed and then reprinted three times in five years may give some indication of its popularity.

   [5] Schubart's text in Stambaugh (2: 237-307). The complete title is *Der Sieman das ist wider den Hausteuffell. Wie die bösen Weiber jhre frome Menner und wie die bösen leichtfertigen Buben jhre frome Weiber plagen, Sampt einer Vemanung aus H. Schriefft und schönen Historien, wie sich frome Eheleutt gegen einander verhalten sollen...* (The She-Man, this is against the house-devil. How the evil wives torment their pious husbands, and how the evil, careless fellows torment their pious wives. Including an exhortation from Holy Scripture and pleasant stories on how pious spouses ought to behave with each other).

   [6] Literally meaning "devil-book," the term *Teufelbuch* is used to label texts of various lengths that either satirize or vilify certain forms of socially unacceptable behavior by making a specific devil responsible for the maligned transgression. There are, for example, dance-, drinking-, and gambling-devils, house- and marriage-devils, cursing-devils, and "whoring"-devils. *Teufelbücher* were written mainly by Protestant authors, and their purpose was primarily didactic. The genre enjoyed great popularity especially during the second half of the sixteenth century. For an excellent introduction to the *Teufelbuch*-genre and its popularity in the sixteenth century, see Bebermeyer's entry on "Teufelliteratur" in *Reallexikon der deutschen Literaturgeschichte* (esp. 382-92). Also of relevance are Osborn, Grimm, Ohse, Roos, and the epilogue provided in each of the five volumes edited by Stambaugh.

   [7] Typically, *Teufelbücher* that focus on marital conduct elaborate on the behavior of both spouses and on a variety of related issues (economics, the raising of children, the disciplining of servants, the relationship of family and household to the public). See, for example, Nicolaus Schmidt's *Zehn Teufel* (1557; in Stambaugh, 2: 309-56) and Andreas Musculus' *Eheteufel* (1556; in Stambaugh, 4: 83-132). In contrast, Schubart—although the title of his text suggests otherwise—focuses narrowly on female conduct and specifically on wifely insubordination.

   [8] The entry on "Schubart, Adam" in *Allgemeine deutsche Biographie* points to parallels between Schubart's text and medieval and late-medieval *Mären*.

   [9] For a discussion of gender inversion in early modern culture, see especially Davis, Kunzle, Stallybrass, and Underdown.

   [10] Davis writes of parades and festivities in which wives, as part of a carnivalesque inversion of gender roles, "were shown hitting their husbands with distaffs, tripe, sticks, trenchers, water pots; throwing stones at them; pulling their beards; or kicking them in the genitalia" (169).

[11] In medieval as well as in early modern representations of disorderly females, women who defy their husbands' authority typically first make use of what is portrayed as their most effective weapon: their tongue (Wiltenburg, *Disorderly Women* 97). "The overall picture presented to German audiences was one in which good wives kept silent" (Wiltenburg, *Disorderly Women* 95).

[12] In visual representations, the economically powerful wife equips herself with the accoutrements of power and influence—a purse with money, for example, and the keys to the household's storage rooms. Price identifies "pants, purse, and sword" as the symbols of the imperious wife's domestic power (152-53). In a woodcut by Hans Schäufelein entitled "The Subservient Husband" (1536), the large and imposing figure of the insubordinate wife is portrayed holding a stick in her left hand. With it, she is threatening her husband, who is shown hunched over, obediently doing laundry. The wife's right hand rests close to her waist where she wears a large purse and an impressive key ring. Reproduced in Geisberg (3: 1056).

[13] Throughout Brietzmann's study, failure to obey her husband appears as a key characteristic of the "evil wife." Other common characteristics highlighted in this exploration of "evil wives" are infidelity, pride, stinginess, sloth, verbal and physical aggressiveness, alcoholism, and vanity.

[14] The verb used is *verke(h)ren* as in the following passages: "Gott wird dadurch sein ordnung verkert" ("God's order is thereby being inverted;" 260; 336); "Ich wiell dier alles verkehren" ("I will invert everything for you;" 264; 460); and as a final exhortation toward the end of the text: "Dem Weibe zu einem Herrn / Dies soll man nit lassen verkern" ("Turning a wife into a master: one must not tolerate this inversion;" 299; 1664-65).

[15] "Symbolic inversion," defined as "any act of expressive behavior which inverts, contradicts, abrogates, or in some fashion presents an alternative to commonly held cultural codes, values, and norms be they linguistic, literary or artistic, religious or social and political," can, of course, serve a number of often conflicting purposes (Babcock 14). It may free culture from "the limitations of 'thou shalt not's'" (Babcock 21), or function as "means for letting off steam" by protesting an established order while ultimately preserving and strengthening it (Babcock 22, paraphrasing Heinrich Schurtz). Or it may constitute a form of play through which "social threat can paradoxically be expressed without threatening" (Babcock 25) and through which cultural crises can be abstracted and comprehended by "casting them in the form of ludic antitheses" (Babcock 25; the quotation is Brian Sutton-Smith's). "[I]nversions," Babcock writes, "may operate as a means of social control, of social protest, of social change, and of social deviance" (30). Inversion's potential for stimulating social change is emphasized by Davis.

[16] Kunzle (49), Davis (160), and Stallybrass (204) note the use of representations of women engaged in warfare and conquest as images of disorder and gender inversion in early modern visual culture.

[17] An anonymous broadsheet print from approximately 1525 with the title "Docktor Syman" uses the same militaristic metaphors to describe the She-Man's entrance into an innkeeper's house. Here, as in Schubart's text, Master She-Man shows irreverence for national and geographical boundaries, for *Docktor Syman's* presence has grown significantly and is felt "everywhere in the world" (my translation of the original text passage as it appears in Bolte 301). The broadsheet, consisting of image and text, is reproduced in Geisberg (4: 1306) and Bolte (300). Wiltenburg offers the German text with English translation (*Women in Early Modern Germany* 14–23). I discuss this visual representation of Master She-Man in part two of this article ("Inscribing Difference").

[18] Kawerau notes Master She-Man's disregard for distinctions of social status (779).

[19] In the three early-thirteenth-century *Mären* discussed by Brinker-von der Heyde (Stricker's "Das wilde Ross," Sibote's "Frouwenzuht," and an anonymous version of "Aristoteles und Phyllis"), female insubordination appears, at least on the textual level, as first and foremost a domestic problem affecting individual men.

[20] Robisheaux points out that in the pamphlet literature of sixteenth-century Germany, "one theme often stood out above all others: the fear of social, political, and religious disorder, the perception that the underpinnings of the whole social order were dangerously unstable, uncertain, continually in flux. That many pamphleteers still held up for their readers the social values of a society of orders—hierarchy, social harmony, religious unity, corporate solidarity, the common good, deference, obedience—could only have intensified the feeling for many that society had become unstable. For those ideals bore even less resemblance to social reality in 1550 than they had fifty years before" (95). Similarly, Maria E. Müller takes note of the "massive growth of the literature of order during the early modern period that suggests a high need for regulation in all areas of public and increasingly also of private life" (17).

[21] Kunzle relates the reality of an "extraordinary agglomeration of petty states in a constant state of political flux" to the sensitivity among the early modern German middle classes "to concepts of social mutability and reversibility" (77).

[22] For England, Amussen relates perceptions of disorder to increased vagrancy as well as to increased mobility, both social and physical (see esp. 175).

[23] See, for example, Blickle's study of rural and urban rebellions.

[24] Robisheaux refers to the loss of religious unity as one of the factors contributing to a pervasive "sense of unease, and at times desperation, that reached into every princely and peasant household" (10).

[25] Schubart uses very few specific references to current or historical events, and his gestures toward the tenuous status of certain means of organizing society and experience are oblique. The full referential potential inherent in Schubart's description of the dysfunctional nature of such categories as profession or status becomes apparent in a comparison with another *Teufelbuch* that concerns itself with questions of marital conduct. Andreas Musculus's *Eheteufel,* although less focused on the issue of female insubordination than Schubart's text, also features the figure of *Doctor Simon*. Musculus, however, relates his discussion of Doctor She-Man's rule directly to an actual historical event—the Peasants' War—and thus points to a very real dissolution of order, which he in turn links to Doctor She-Man's appearance and to the issue of female disorder (in Stambaugh, 4: 126). In Musculus's interpretation, female insubordination is analogous to the peasants' rebellion because both attempt the inversion of the seemingly natural hierarchy between master and servant. In contrast to Schubart, however, Musculus does not privilege the category of gender over other means of classification.

[26] Wiesner writes: "The early modern period appears, then, to be a time of continual reinforcement of gender hierarchies and patriarchal structures, which we can trace in court records, marriage manuals, dramas, paintings, songs, sermons, and a variety of other sources" (311). In her analysis of gender and class dynamics in early modern England, Susan Amussen demonstrates that gender emerges as a privileged category in debates on the nature of order and disorder and as the key battleground in the establishment of social order. She argues that gender functions as a rallying point especially in the battle against disorder within a class system (182). Rublack notes a similar focus on gender in the German territories where "fears about loss of control were mapped on to gendered as well as class-related images" (6). Roper refers to the increased focus on gender conformity in Reformation Augsburg as a "theology of gender" (1). Just why women were increasingly excluded from positions of influence and power and why gender conformity becomes an issue of primary concern is a question of such complexity that it cannot be dealt with adequately here. For a brief yet comprehensive and nuanced account of factors determining attitudes toward the role of women and men and toward gender in early modern Germany, see Wunder.

[27] The German title is "Predigt vom Ehestand, über das Evangelium, Es war ein Hochzeit zu Cana." See Kawerau (770).

[28] For similar early modern articulations of the centrality of matrimony in an ordered society see Harrington (esp. 25–47).

[29] "Enraged, I hit the She-Man violently and threw him on the floor" (265; 498-99).

[30] "Thus she says, 'you poor devil'" (265; 502).

[31] "I thought in truth that he was dead" (265; 507).

[32] "Hermaphrodites are...firmly placed in the category of monsters by Renaissance physiologists" (Maclean 12). Puff quotes a short passage from Martin Luther's *Against the Roman Papacy, an Institution of the Devil* (1545). In this text, Luther refers to those at the top of the Church hierarchy as "*hermaphrodites,* androgynes, catamites [*cynaedi*], buttfuckers [*pedicones*], and similar *monsters of nature*" (qtd. in Puff 142; my emphasis).

[33] See note 17.

[34] The donning of men's clothes is typically the first step taken by women who wish to pass as male, either temporarily during charivaris and carnival (Davis 160), or more permanently, as described in the case of "Maiden Heinrich" (Lindemann 131) or Catalina de Erauso (Perry 127ff.), who both lived as men over a period of several years. Wiesner depicts the public outrage when early in the seventeenth century a few women in London began dressing in "slightly masculine dress." She describes the public's fear that "such dress would lead to a breakdown in distinctions of social class as well as gender" (307). Howard refers to the same case of "women dressing mannishly in the streets of London" around 1620 and notes that these instances of female crossdressing were understood as "transgressing both class and gender boundaries" (420). Howard's insightful discussion of the public reaction to female crossdressing in early modern England attests to the fact that the "semiotics of dress" (421) was a key battleground in the struggle to enforce properly gendered behavior and to identify a basis for the proper differentiation of men's and women's roles. On the importance of clothing for the enforcement of proper gender roles, see also Wunder (44).

[35] In his focus on anatomical discourses and specifically on Galenic models of anatomy that continued to circulate throughout the early modern period, Laqueur presents an oversimplified picture of early modern approaches to sex difference. In contrast, Cadden demonstrates that medicine and science had means of thinking about sex difference that were very much in line with what appeared as an unquestionable social reality: that men and women were different. Through a meticulous analysis of the various ancient and medieval discourses that concerned themselves with the differences between men and women, Cadden thus relativizes Laqueur's claims, arguing that the one-sex model was only one among numerous competing models (Cadden 3).

[36] See Laqueur (*Making Sex* 7, 126-28; "Orgasm" 122). On the "mutability of genitalia and the symmetry of male and female bodies" (Rublack 12), see also Lindeman.

[37] Johannes Müller discusses the use of images of warfare to represent sex acts (146-51) and of penis metaphors (79-87) in fifteenth-century carnival plays.

[38] For the use of the shield- and wound-metaphor to represent female sexual organs, see Müller (56-58).

[39] Davis suggests that this question, among others, should inform the further study of early modern rituals of gender inversion (177).

[40] For a discussion of Galen's predominantly isomorphic model of female and male anatomy, see Cadden (30-37).

Works Cited

Amussen, Susan Dwyer. *An Ordered Society: Gender and Class in Early Modern England*. Oxford: Blackwell, 1988.

Babcock, Barbara A. "Introduction." *The Reversible World: Symbolic Inversion in Art and Society*. Ed. Barbara A. Babcock. Ithaca: Cornell UP, 1978. 13-38.

Bebermeyer, Gustav. "Teufelliteratur." *Reallexikon der deutschen Literaturgeschichte*. 2nd ed. Vol. 4. Berlin: de Gruyter, 1984. 367-403.

Bennewitz, Ingrid, and Ruth Weichselbaumer. "Erziehung zur Differenz: Entwürfe idealer Weiblichkeit und Männlichkeit in der didaktischen Literatur des Mittelalters." *Deutschunterricht* 55.1 (2003): 43-50.

Blickle, Peter. *Unruhen in der ständischen Gesellschaft 1300-1800*. Enzyklopädie Deutscher Geschichte 1. München: Oldenbourg, 1988.

Bolte, Johannes. "Doktor Siemann und Doktor Kolbmann, zwei Bilderbogen des 16. Jahrhunderts." *Zeitschrift des Vereins für Volkskunde* 12 (1902): 296-307.

Brietzmann, Franz. *Die böse Frau in der deutschen Litteratur des Mittelalters*. 1912. 2nd ed. Berlin: Mayer & Müller, 1967.

Brinker-von der Heyde, Claudia. "Weiber-Herrschaft oder: Wer reitet wen? Zur Konstruktion und Symbolik der Geschlechterbeziehung." *Manlîchiu wîp, wîplîch man: Zur Konstruktion der Kategorien Körper und "Geschlecht" in der deutschen Literatur des Mittelalters*. Ed. Ingrid Bennewitz and Helmut Tervooren. Berlin: Schmidt, 1999. 47-66.

Cadden, Joan. *Meanings of Sex Difference in the Middle Ages: Medicine, Science, and Culture*. Cambridge: Cambridge UP, 1993.

Davis, Natalie Zemon. "Women on Top." 1965. *Feminism & Renaissance Studies*. Ed. Lorna Hutson. Oxford: Oxford UP, 1999. 156-85.

Geisberg, Max. *The German Single-Leaf Woodcut: 1500-1550*. Rev. and ed. Walter L. Strauss. 4 vols. New York: Hacker, 1974.

Grimm, Heinrich. *Die deutschen "Teufelbücher" des 16. Jahrhunderts: Ihre Rolle im Buchwesen und ihre Bedeutung*. Frankfurt a.M.: Buchhändler-Vereinigung, 1959.

Harrington, Joel F. *Reordering Marriage and Society in Reformation Germany*. Cambridge: Cambridge UP, 1995.

Hillerbrand, Hans J. "The 'Other' in the Age of the Reformation: Reflections of Social Control and Deviance in the Sixteenth Century." *Infinite Boundaries: Order, Disorder and Reorder in Early Modern German Culture*. Ed. Max Reinhart. Kirksville: Sixteenth Century Journal Publishers, 1998. 245-69.

Howard, Jean E. "Crossdressing, the Theatre, and Gender Struggle in Early Modern England." *Shakespeare Quarterly* 39.4 (1988): 418-40.

Kawerau, Waldemar. "Lob und Schimpf des Ehestandes in der Litteratur des sechzehnten Jahrhunderts." *Preussische Jahrbücher* 69 (1892): 760-81.

Kunzle, David. "World Upside Down: The Iconography of a European Broadsheet Type." *The Reversible World: Symbolic Inversion in Art and Society*. Ed. Barbara A. Babcock. Ithaca: Cornell UP, 1978. 39-94.

Laqueur, Thomas. *Making Sex: Body and Gender from the Greeks to Freud*. Cambridge: Harvard UP, 1990.

———. "Orgasm, Generation, and the Politics of Reproductive Biology." *Gender and History in Western Europe*. Ed. Robert Shoemaker and Mary Vincent. London: Arnold, 1998. 111-48.

Lindemann, Mary. "Gender Tales: The Multiple Identities of Maiden Heinrich, Hamburg 1700." *Gender in Early Modern German History*. Ed. Ulinka Rublack. Cambridge: Cambridge UP, 2002. 131-51.

Maclean, Ian. *The Renaissance Notion of Woman: A Study in the Fortunes of Scholasticism and Medical Science in European Intellectual Life*. Cambridge: Cambridge UP, 1980.

Müller, Johannes. *Schwert und Scheide: Der sexuelle und skatologische Wortschatz im Nürnberger Fastnachtspiel des 15. Jahrhunderts*. Deutsche Literatur von den Anfängen bis 1700 2. Frankfurt a.M.: Peter Lang, 1988.

Müller, Maria E. "Naturwesen Mann: Zur Dialektik von Herrschaft und Knechtschaft in Ehelehren der Frühen Neuzeit." *Wandel der Geschlechterbeziehungen zu Beginn der Neuzeit*. Ed. Heide Wunder und Christina Vanja. Frankfurt a.M.: Suhrkamp, 1991. 43-68.

Ohse, Bernhard. *Die Teufelliteratur zwischen Brant und Luther*. Diss. Freie U Berlin, 1961. Berlin: Ernst-Reuter-Gesellschaft, 1961.

Osborn, Max. *Die Teufelliteratur des 16. Jahrhunderts*. Hildesheim: Olms, 1965.

Perry, Mary Elizabeth. *Gender and Disorder in Early Modern Seville*. Princeton: Princeton UP, 1990.
Price, David. "When Women Would Rule: Reversal of Gender Hierarchy in Sixteenth-Century German Drama." *Daphnis* 20 (1991): 147-66.
Puff, Helmut. *Sodomy in Reformation Germany and Switzerland, 1400-1600*. Chicago: U of Chicago P, 2003.
Robisheaux, Thomas. *Rural Society and the Search for Order in Early Modern Germany*. Cambridge: Cambridge UP, 1989.
Roos, Keith L. *The Devil in 16th Century German Literature: The Teufelsbücher*. Frankfurt a.M.: Peter Lang, 1972.
Roper, Lyndal. *The Holy Household: Women and Morals in Reformation Augsburg*. Oxford: Clarendon, 1989.
Rublack, Ulinka, ed. *Gender in Early Modern German History*. Cambridge: Cambridge UP, 2002.
Schiebinger, Londa. *Nature's Body: Gender in the Making of Modern Science*. Boston: Beacon, 1993.
"Schubart, Adam." *Deutsches Literatur-Lexikon: biographisch-bibliographisches Handbuch*. 3rd rev. ed. Vol. 16. Bern: Francke, 1996. 399.
"Schubart: Adam S." *Allgemeine Deutsche Biographie*. Vol. 32. Leipzig: Duncker & Humblot, 1891. 587-88.
"Siemann." *Deutsches Sprichwörter-Lexikon: Ein Hausschatz für das deutsche Volk*. Vol. 4. Leipzig: Brockhaus, 1876. 560-61.
Stallybrass, Peter. "The World Turned Upside Down: Inversion, Gender and the State." *The Matter of Difference: Materialist Feminist Criticism of Shakespeare*. Ed. Valerie Wayne. Ithaca: Cornell UP, 1991. 201-20.
Stambaugh, Ria. *Teufelbücher in Auswahl*. 5 vols. Berlin: de Gruyter, 1972.
Underdown, David E. "The Taming of the Scold: The Enforcement of Patriarchal Authority in Early Modern England." *Order and Disorder in Early Modern England*. Ed. Anthony Fletcher and John Stevenson. Cambridge: Cambridge UP, 1985. 116-36.
Wiesner, Merry E. *Women and Gender in Early Modern Europe*. 2nd ed. Cambridge: Cambridge UP, 2000.
Wiltenburg, Joy. *Disorderly Women and Female Power in the Street Literature of Early Modern England and Germany*. Charlottesville: UP of Virginia, 1992.
―――. *Women in Early Modern Germany: An Anthology of Popular Texts*. Tempe: Arizona Center for Medieval and Renaissance Studies, 2002.
Wunder, Heide. "Gender Norms and Their Enforcement in Early Modern Germany." *Gender Relations in German History*. Ed. Lynn Abrams and Elizabeth Harvey. London: U College P, 1996. 39-56.

Anna Louisa Karsch as Sappho

Claire Baldwin

Anna Louisa Karsch became known as "the German Sappho" in the early 1760s and she performed this social and poetic role self-consciously to develop and market her public literary persona. In poems written for the public, Karsch performs the role of Sappho to position herself aesthetically as a female poet of tender sentiment and natural genius. She strives to balance an embrace of Sappho as poetic ancestor with an assertion of difference and independence from her, pointedly distancing herself from the image of the female poet inspired by passionate love. The specific German "fictions of Sappho" of the mid-eighteenth century—namely, her image in the popular imagination, the philological consideration of her fragments, and the interpretation of Sappho in vying aesthetic theories—provide an important context for the dimension that the Sappho-persona brings to Karsch's poetic self-fashioning. (CB)

Anna Louisa Karsch (1722–1791) has been known as "the German Sappho" since 1761, when her friend and literary advisor Johann Wilhelm Ludwig Gleim complimented her poetic skills by likening her to that famous poet from Lesbos, "the mother goddess of poetry."[1] Karsch willingly took on this role and engaged the name of Sappho in both her published poems and her unpublished letters, especially in those to Gleim himself. In her first years after moving to Berlin in 1761, she was celebrated as a poetic sensation and natural talent, paraded and published, but also criticized, not least because of her adoption of "Sappho" as a poetic alias.

What representations of Sappho were predominant around 1760 and how did Karsch define and employ the role of Sappho to fashion her public persona? In what follows I will present the over-determined image of Sappho current in the German cultural imagination of the mid-eighteenth century and argue that it offers an important framework of interpretation for both Karsch's poetic self-understanding and the reception of her writing. As Joan DeJean has shown, the "fictions of Sappho" that hold sway in a particular historical moment and place can reveal much about that culture's attitudes toward creative women. Most of Karsch's published poetry in which she alludes to Sappho, including those poems collected in the posthumously published *Gedichte* (Poems) of 1792,[2] dates from the early 1760s, the period in which she first adopts the name Sappho as a social and a poetic role. Karsch draws on the popular, philological, and poetic reception of Sappho of the time to stage her public persona through her poetry. In doing so, I argue, she strives to balance an embrace of Sappho as poetic ancestor with an assertion of her difference from Sappho, and she even distances herself from what is arguably the primary association with Sappho's poetry, the image of the female poet inspired by love.

A closer look at Karsch's public performance of Sappho in her poetry contributes to the current scholarly investigations of Karsch's poetic adoption of first-person roles, which have centered on the nexus of her biography and her poetic persona. Critics have illuminated how Karsch's effective stylization of details in her biography supports the image of herself as poet that she wished to convey (Becker-Cantarino; Barndt, "Mein Dasein"; Schaffers). Her life was circumscribed by hardship: she suffered under extreme poverty as a member of the fourth estate, her family relationships were difficult, as a child she had but a brief reprieve from toil followed by her return to work for her mother, she endured two marriages to abusive husbands, she faced difficulties as a single, impoverished mother disgraced by divorce. To increase her earnings, Karsch composed occasional verse and encomiums celebrating the battles of Friedrich II. The attention this poetry received eventually led to her change of fortunes and brought her to Berlin.

From these biographical facts, Karsch and others constructed a story of literary virtue rewarded that illustrated the redeeming power of literature and the indomitable strength of Karsch's poetic, religious, and patriotic inspiration that gave rise to her natural poetic expression. In her letters to Johann Georg Sulzer, but also in biographical details incorporated into her poetry, Karsch directed her audience to view her as an untutored poetic talent. Karsch's enactment of this role in her poetry and in her letters reflects theoretical poetic concerns of the mid-eighteenth century, and her position within these aesthetic currents has also been a subject of debate in scholarship. In casting herself as a singer of the people, Karsch appealed to the desire of Storm and Stress aesthetics for an original voice and identified herself with a poetics that took its guidance from native genius and nature, conceived of as a realm free from constricting conventions and rules. Karsch augmented her biographical self-stylization through her identificatory performance of the role of Sappho to position herself aesthetically as a female poet of natural genius and tender sentiment. The specific German fictions of Sappho of the mid-eighteenth century provide an important context for interpreting the dimension that the Sappho-persona brings to Karsch's poetic self-fashioning.

German "Fictions of Sappho"

In her day, Karsch was by no means unique in being associated with Sappho. As the only classical female model available for a modern female poet, such honorific usage of Sappho's name to recognize a woman's literary achievements and to provide women writers with cultural authority was widespread across Europe, for example in France and England, as well as in the German states.[3] Yet the role of Sappho did not always imply approbation. It could also be used to isolate a creative woman and mark her as eccentric, an exception to the rule of the male artist. In seventeenth-century Germany, for example, Sappho was employed as a negative example in bitter satires against women writers in order to deter them from their literary endeavors (Rüdiger, *Sappho* 36). In the struggle "between women who would like to bear the name of a latter-day Sappho and men bent on reproving her—and, by implication, them" (Reynolds 102), the name "Sappho" could be employed to malign women writers by associating them with the scandalous aspects of Sappho's reputation that had accompanied the figure since antiquity.[4] Divergent interpretations of Sappho's texts and life had long circulated through commentaries and lexicons, translations and imitations of her verse, and even pure fictions.[5] Common to all, however, was the importance of the link between Sappho's poetry and her passion, however diversely that passion was described. In some stories, Sappho's poetic strength was a sign—and a consequence—of the strength of her desire, while in others, she was punished for her transgressive passions by a loss of her poetic creativity. Thus from early on, Sappho became the icon of female poetic achievement and the "original poet of female desire" (DeJean 6), and her poetic power was said to be lost and gained in conjunction with her amorous affairs.

In mid-eighteenth-century German culture, the nexus between Sappho's passion and her art was construed differently depending on which of three perspectives on the figure was paramount for the interpreter: the popular image of Sappho, the philological interest in her verse, or the theoretical assessment of her poetic style. The first rested on fascination with an exceptional and scandalously passionate woman—the collective popular imagination created and perpetuated myths about the artist's life for entertainment and excitement. The second sought to collect, edit, translate, and study the remaining fragments of Sappho's verse, heralded since ancient times as the epitome of love poetry. Although by no means immune from incursions into its realm by the popular image of Sappho, her verse itself rather than her person was the primary focus. The third approach drew on the fragments by Sappho to elaborate or champion a particular poetics in which the link between passion and poetry was thought to give rise to a certain style. In each of these distinct but related interests in Sappho, the figure and her poetry were interpreted through categories of gender to comment on the qualities found or found lacking in the figure, in her fragments, and in their aesthetic style. These three approaches to Sappho provide crucial frameworks for understanding Karsch's use of Sappho's name as poetic alias.

The popular German image of Sappho in the middle of the eighteenth century was most strongly influenced by her seventeenth-century French interpreters, especially Anne Le Fèvre Dacier (*Vie de Sapho* [Life of Sapho], 1681) and Pierre Bayle (*Dictionnaire historique et critique* [Historical and Critical Dictionary], 1697.)[6] In different fashions, they each developed elaborate biographical fictions about Sappho that suppressed the aspect of same-sex erotics and centered instead on her love for the legendary man Phaon. The fictional epistle "Sappho to Phaon" found in Ovid's *Heroides,* long held to be an authentic text by Sappho that shed light on her biography (Rüdiger, *Sappho* 18–20), had popularized the story that Sappho's unrequited love for Phaon had led to her tragic suicidal leap from the Leucadian cliffs. Drawing on Ovid, Dacier wrote against the associations of Sappho with tribadism, or same-sex female love, and attempted to defend her against charges of immorality by recasting her story as one of socially legitimate heterosexual romance. Bayle, in turn, spun an extravagant tale based on Sappho's supposed promiscuous and uncontrollable passion, in which he aimed to include all the reports of Sappho's affairs in one coherent narrative. Bayle's telling identification with the mythic Phaon and his predominant concern with Sappho's sexual reputation suggest both a fantasy of being pursued by such a passionate and demanding lover as Sappho and his pleasure in imagining that a woman so transgressive of gender roles, in literature and in life, would receive her comeuppance.

Bayle's *Dictionnaire historique et critique,* already well-known in Germany among the educated elite who could read it in French, appeared in a German translation under the direction of J.C. Gottsched from 1741 to 1744. Intended for a wide reading public, namely "all types of readers...even simply active minds or women" (Gottsched 1: 3), the translation was reprinted in 1780. Another such influential encyclopedia was Johann Heinrich Zedler's *Universal-Lexikon* (Universal Encyclopedia), published from 1732 to 1750. Like Bayle, Zedler also focused his article "Sappho" on Sappho's biography rather than on her poetry, and he wove together factual information, speculation about Sappho's amorous affairs, and ethical reproaches. Zedler especially took issue with Dacier's attempted rehabilitation of Sappho. With more than a hint of aggression against Dacier as a "learned lady," he rejected her scholarship and underscored for his readers Sappho's alleged ugliness and her poetic hubris (24: 37–39).

The popular image of Sappho transmitted through such reference works influenced the view of Karsch's persona, for example through reviews that included similar charges of hubris and ugliness and assumptions about the link between Karsch's poetry and her experience of passion. A second, contrasting trend to this popular interest in fictions of Sappho is the new philological consideration of her poetic fragments. Many German scholars of the eighteenth century devoted their attention to Sappho's texts, rather than to her biography. The efforts of these scholars to edit, translate, and interpret the ancient fragments inaugurated a new phase in the serious philological study of Sappho's poetry. As DeJean asserts, "At the dawn of the Enlightenment, only German scholars try to advance Sappho's literary stature" (124). An important Greek-Latin edition of Sappho's verse was published by Johann Christian Wolf in 1733 and a first German translation of 29 fragments, by Jacob Stählin, appeared in 1734, followed by Benjamin Neukirch's translated collection in 1744 (Rüdiger, *Geschichte* 10–12). Nikolaus Götz, with assistance from Johann Peter Uz, translated and published Sappho's fragments in 1746 in *Die Gedichte Anacreons und der Sappho Oden* (The poems of Anacreon and Sappho's Odes). The second edition of this translation, published in 1760, was the one used by Karsch in her study of Sappho (Nörtemann 549n25). This renewed engagement with Sappho's texts was one expression of the nascent German Neoclassicism of the mid-eighteenth century, most influentially codified in Johann Joachim Winckelmann's *Gedanken über die Nachahmung der griechischen Werke in der Malerei und Bildhauerkunst* (Thoughts on the Imitation of the Painting and Sculpture of the Greeks; 1755). The interest in classical antiquity and in Sappho in particular was furthered by the excitement of the archaeological discoveries and ongoing excavations at Pompeii. When supposed portraits and busts of Sappho were unearthed at Pompeii in the 1750s, literary scholars hoped (but in vain) that more of her poems would also be found there (Reynolds 165–71).

The pursuit of improved philological tools through which to study Sappho was coincident with debates over how to interpret her aesthetic style. Around 1750, three contesting views of Sappho's aesthetics can be distinguished, each of which surfaces in the reception of Karsch and her poetry. In the first, Sappho's verse is related to that of Anacreon and her presentation of love is seen through the framework of Anacreontic literary conventions. A second interpretation of Sappho arises with the theoreticians of the Storm and Stress and their interest in folk songs and natural genius. Here Sappho is perceived as the best representative of the original genius of her culture. Her song is close to nature, it is not bound by artificial conventions, and it expresses the character of her people and her own authentic emotionality of love. In a third aesthetic program, Sappho is interpreted as the supreme poet of desire. Her ability to express the intensity of love's passions within a rigorous strophic form is the mark of her talent, and her verse exemplifies the aesthetics of the sublime. Three influential interpreters of Karsch and her poetry are closely aligned with these varying aesthetic assessments of Sappho: Gleim advances the image of an Anacreontic Sappho, Johann Gottfried Herder champions the image of Sappho as natural genius in keeping with the aesthetics of the Storm and Stress, and Moses Mendelssohn reveres Sappho as a masterful poet of the sublime.

The painting "Anacreon and Sappho" (1754) by Johann Heinrich Tischbein the Elder portrays the first of these aesthetic interpretations (fig. 1). Tischbein's canvas presents a conventional Rococo scene that includes images of the pleasures of which Anacreontic poets sing: wine, food, and love. Fruit and wine are abundant, and Sappho and Anacreon are shown as a flirtatious couple.[7] On either side of the poets are figures that represent the transformation of this encounter into verse. Sappho's lyre is being played by a female musician behind her, while the putto in the foreground of the image wields Anacreon's phallic quill—or perhaps he too refers to Sappho's poetry and indicates that Sappho should attend to her writing, as Tiegel-Hertfelder suggests (91). In either case, the two symbolic figures observe the scene that is the source of their art. The idyllic natural setting of the tryst is artistically cultivated and adorned with a sculptural stage set of a Bacchic scene mirroring the erotic pursuit pictured in the center of the painting. The pictorial tradition presenting Anacreon in this light—following his self-description as a drinking, joking, flirtatious old man in his odes—is furthered in the second half of the eighteenth century in France, but Tischbein appears to be the first visual artist to bring Sappho and Anacreon together in this fashion, and his image reflects the association drawn between the two poets in the German cultural imagination at this time (Tiegel-Hertfelder 92-93).

Figure 1: Johann Heinrich Tischbein the Elder, "Anacreon and Sappho" (Staatliche Museen Kassel, Neue Galerie)

The Anacreontic interpretation of Sappho's aesthetic style likewise built on the myth of the two poets as lovers, and it was furthered by the publishing history of Sappho's texts. Sappho's verse fragments were often published in one volume together with the verse of Anacreon, following the example of the first modern edition of Sappho issued in 1554 by Henri Estienne. This practice encouraged readers to associate the two poets and therefore to interpret Sappho's love poetry as similar in style to the playful erotic conventions of Anacreontic poetry. Despite the intensity of passion expressed in Sappho's verses, she was thus often interpreted through an Anacreontic lens as a cheerful poet of pleasure and love (Zeman 88). In the translations and edition of the poems of Anacreon and Sappho by Götz of 1746 and 1760, Götz also emphasizes a stylistic connection between the poets by publishing their work together and by incorporating the fictional tale of their mutual love into his own poem, "Lob des Anakreons und der Sappho" (In Praise of Anacreon and Sappho), with which he introduces his volume.

The associations made between Anacreon and Sappho around 1760 inform the role-play between the "German Anacreon" Gleim and Karsch as the "German Sappho" and are one nexus of the popular, philological, and aesthetic interests in Sappho. Through these associations, eighteenth-century philology also contributed to domesticating the figure of Sappho to fit contemporary gender norms. Sappho's originality was obscured by the interpretation of her poetry as stylistically related to that of Anacreon, and her odes in translation were given "a milder and softer, often weak tone that is not found in the original" (Rüdiger, *Geschichte* 13). Even within the framework of Anacreontic conventions, eighteenth-century conceptions of gender differences further influenced how Sappho's poetry was perceived. Rüdiger summarizes this tendency of the time, in which Horace, Sappho, and Anacreon were all seen "as poets of eudemonism and pleasure in life, only that Sappho was given a sentimental quality" (*Sappho* 57). Sappho and her songs were described through adjectives like "sweet" and "dear" (Derks 154) or "graceful" (Rüdiger, *Geschichte* 11) and "tender" (Rüdiger, *Sappho* 50; Zeman 88) that emphasized Sappho's femininity. Sappho's style was thereby distinguished from the common Anacreontic one of jovial masculine conviviality, and the distinction furthered the widespread contemporary notion that women writers were more likely than their male colleagues to express sentiment in a natural style free of stilted conventions.[8] Thus an emphasis on Sappho's quality of feeling over the technical artistry and mastery of Anacreontic convention was a way to mark her literary style as feminine, according to mid-eighteenth-century categories of gender and aesthetics. Such historically particular associations of aesthetic style and gendered attributes help explain how the image of Sappho as a shepherdess in an Anacreontic landscape came to overlap in mid-eighteenth century Germany with the image of Sappho as a poet of sentiment and nature.[9] This view, in which her verse was related to the poetic expression of folk songs (Derks 92), further diminished the aspect of an artistic stylization of emotion in connection with Sappho, an idea that corresponded to notions about Karsch's natural poetic expression.

The Anacreontic interpretation of Sappho was transformed by the theorists of the Storm and Stress, who articulated new conceptions of the links between nature, emotion, and poetic expression. They rejected formal literary conventions as confining and embraced the inspiration of nature and genius. The value placed on expressive, poetic enthusiasm motivated an interest in historically earlier cultures and their songs, which were accorded a new theoretical significance as original poetry. Within this aesthetic program, most importantly for Herder, Sappho was still associated with folk song, but now the association implied a primal poetic power (Scholz 142–45). In this view, Sappho was an example of a poet of genius whose unstudied song gave voice to her native culture and her personal emotions. Eighteenth-century conceptions of the link between gender and literary creativity also inform this image of Sappho, for the natural, authentic emotion attributed to a woman and perceived by Herder in Sappho's verse was the quiet tenderness of love. In a preface to his *Alte Volkslieder* (Old Folk Songs) of 1774, Herder delimits clearly his notion of Sappho's aesthetic as one that reflects her feminine emotionality: he presents her as "Frau Sappho" and "the dear Sappho" repeatedly and describes her verse as "sweet love songs" (25: 85–86) into which she "pours her whole heart" (25: 87).

Throughout his writing, Herder maintains a clearly defined view of Sappho as an ancient poet of natural genius with an exemplary feminine poetic sensibility, and he invests Sappho with an iconic status that influences his reception of Karsch, as will be discussed below. Herder's later text of 1795 on the original forms of the Greek ode, *Alcäus und Sappho* (Alcaeus and Sappho), divides its thematic and aesthetic reach into two realms that are defined, in accordance with the gender norms solidifying in the second half of the eighteenth century, as masculine and feminine subgenres. For Herder, Alcaeus represents the forceful, sublime ode that he calls the daring genre, while Sappho represents the calm, tender ode of love (27: 183). The first of these two original forms of the ode lifts and excites the spirit, while the second calms it. The tender ode does not admit the same extreme expression of passion as the daring form: "The voice of compassion demands a softer tone. The breath of love cannot bear storms" (27: 192). Herder's employment of gendered, polarized attributes to describe aesthetic terms is even more explicit in this piece in his discussion of the hexameter and the pentameter as the "heroic man" and the "heroic virgin" that are brought together "in a kind of marriage, as it were, in which sovereignty and mildness, glory and pleasure, in emotions joy and sorrow mate" (27: 185).[10] For Herder, the masculine and the feminine aesthetic are complementary, and he presents Sappho as the supreme poet of the genre that is "feminine" in both content and tone.

Other eighteenth-century aesthetic theorists, however, perceived Sappho as a poet who did indeed exemplify the power and emotional intensity of the sublime that Herder reserves for the masculine ode. The interpretation of Sappho's centrality for the aesthetic of the sublime had its origins in the first-century treatise "On the Sublime" by (Pseudo-) Longinus, popularized in the modern era through the influential French translation by Boileau of 1674. Longinus was an authoritative source not only for aesthetic theorists, but also for scholars of Sappho, because he quoted and thus preserved the fragment of her second ode on the symptoms of love. Two German translations of Longinus attest to the renewed eighteenth-century interest in the aesthetics of the sublime. The first, by Carl Heinrich Heineke, appeared in 1737, and another, by Johann Georg Schlosser, in 1781 (Rüdiger, *Geschichte* 11; 23). Longinus cited Sappho as an example of a poet of great literary talent who communicated and inspired the feelings of the true sublime. Sappho's genius in presenting the symptoms of love unites in one poem "a whole congress of emotions" into a harmonious whole that elevates the soul of her audience (157).

The image of Sappho found in Longinus's treatise was taken up by Moses Mendelssohn in his theoretical essay "Betrachtungen über das Erhabene und das Naive in den schönen Wissenschaften" (Considerations on the Sublime and the Naive in the Beaux Arts; 1755). For Mendelssohn, Sappho's ode represents the sublime both because of its topic, the extremity of love's passions, and its magnificent composition. The perfection of her poem fragment itself and of the artistic skill it demonstrates elicits the admiration of the audience (1: 208). Mendelssohn underscores Sappho's importance by reminding his readers of Addison's commentary of 22 November 1711 in the *Spectator* that Sappho's fragment is for poets and critics what the Belvedere Torso is for sculptors and painters (1: 208). In Rome, writes Addison in this comparison, "there is the Trunk of a Statue which has lost the Arms, Legs, and Head; but discovers such an exquisite Workmanship in what remains of it, that *Michael Angelo* declared he had learned his whole Art from it" (*Spectator* 2: 84–85). The Belvedere Torso became for Neoclassical theorists and artists a central symbol of the lost grandeur of antiquity that modern artists could only glimpse through its remaining ruins. Mendelssohn praises Sappho's fragment, following Longinus and Addison, as just such an artistic example of skill and originality to respect and to study. Mendelssohn thus represents both a Neoclassical sensibility that values the elegance and precision of Sappho's composition and the incipient aesthetics of the sublime that values the emotional intensity and power of Sappho's depiction of love. While the aesthetics of the sublime will develop in the course of the eighteenth century in the direction of Romanticism and define itself in opposition to Neoclassicism, here the aesthetic virtues of formal clarity and vehement emotion are still regarded together as two aspects of the poetic expression of natural beauty. For Mendelssohn, as for Herder, Sappho's iconic position in defining the aesthetics he promotes strongly influences his reception of Karsch's poetry and her alias as a modern Sappho, as will be shown.

The interpreters of Sappho who viewed her as a representative poet of the sublime were the least inclined to judge her verse through categories of femininity, yet they too employed gendered terms to evaluate her style. There was a tradition of describing her poetic command of the aesthetic of the sublime as a masculine quality. The attribute "mascula" remarked by Horace in his epistles and transmitted over centuries through commentaries was puzzled over by Sappho's critics. It was interpreted either as a sign of her erotic interest in women, as a description of the courage she showed in leaping from the cliffs to her death, or as a recognition of her literary strength, a reference to her "virile genius" (Rüdiger, *Sappho* 5, 23–24, 27). The critics who, following this last view, read Sappho as a masterful poet of the sublime were also unlikely to equate Sappho's poetry with a naive expression of emotion. Friedrich Grillo, for example, whose translation of Sappho appeared in 1767, praised Sappho's sentiment and fiery imagination, but insisted that the poetry that so successfully mediates these emotions was produced in "cold blood" (Rüdiger, *Geschichte* 16). This view of "the sublime Sappho" rejects the idea of an unreflected feminine outpouring of sentiment and instead underscores and lauds her artistic sensibility, her skill, and her discipline.

A "Heart" Like Sappho's: Gleim's Reading of Karsch

The horizon of expectations established by these conflicting mid-eighteenth-century German fictions of Sappho's life, character, and poetry circumscribed Karsch's authorial performance as Sappho. It also permitted Karsch to develop an act that privileged certain aspects of the cultural material surrounding Sappho and thereby to advance her own poetic reputation. Karsch's identification with the Greek poet that secured the sobriquet "Sappho" for Karsch from the 1760s onward was furthered especially by Gleim. Gleim was in a good position to comment upon the figure of Sappho with regard to all three predominant approaches: the popular, the philological, and the aesthetic. He was familiar with the myths and facts about Sappho's life, those in his circle participated directly in the philological revival of interest in Sappho's verse, and he and many of his friends sought to prove their aesthetic appreciation of Sappho by imitating her poetic style. Gleim's influence on Karsch makes the particular manner in which he encouraged her to identify with the figure of Sappho important for an analysis of her performance of that role for her wider reading public. In a letter to Karsch written on 29 November 1761, Gleim elaborates on the affinities with Sappho that he perceives in his new friend:

> Yesterday I read the Greek Sappho. Everywhere a remarkable similarity with the German one! I would acquit her of certain reproaches that the all-too-serious critics make. I could also prove that she did not jump from the cliff: the ancients gave all great poets an unnatural death. Anacreon had to choke on a raisin, Sappho had to jump from the cliff, both went to sleep in the arms of their friends, but people of genius are not allowed to die like other honest people. Just one free week and I would tell my friend many nice things about the Greek Sappho: the critics, who have collected all her words, have understood little of them, they all had much learnedness and as little heart as taste; and who can understand a Sappho without a heart? (Karsch and Gleim 1: 50).

This passage offers a condensed version of the mid-century approaches to Sappho. It demonstrates Gleim's knowledge and attitudes about the figure and his sense of his unique insight into both Sappho's and Karsch's poetry. Gleim identifies and rejects important aspects of the popular, the philological, and the aesthetic interpretations of Sappho that are predominant in the German cultural imagination of the time and specifies the kind of identification with Sappho that he envisions for Karsch.

The most widespread story about Sappho, that of her suicidal leap because of her unrequited love for Phaon, is evoked by Gleim only to be rejected. He shows his familiarity with this image of Sappho popularized by encyclopedias like those of Zedler and Bayle, yet he dismisses the image as legendary.[11] In doing so, in emphasizing Sappho's genius, and in stating that he would defend Sappho against those critics who reproach her, Gleim distances himself from a moralizing stance toward

Sappho and her literary descendent. Instead, Gleim explains the persistence of sensationalist stories about Sappho as an effect of her audience's preoccupation with "people of genius." Gleim's shrewd understanding of the interplay between fame, a dramatic personal story, and public fascination parallels and encourages the consciousness about her public performance as poet that Karsch demonstrates in her poetry and her letters.

Not only are the popular views on Sappho false, Gleim states, but the philological interpretations of Sappho's work are likewise lacking in true understanding. Götz and Uz were friends of Gleim's from his time as a student in Halle, when the plan for their joint translation of Anacreon and Sappho was conceived (Zeman 97–108). As noted above, both the convention of publishing Sappho's odes with Anacreon's verse and Götz's introductory poem in praise of the two poets contributed to the interpretation of Sappho as a lighthearted poet of love. Yet despite Gleim's close association with these important philologists, he dismisses their approach to Sappho in his chosen role as poetic mentor to Karsch. The scholars are diligent and knowledgeable, but have no true understanding of Sappho's poetry, he claims. Just as Gleim begins to move away from a frivolous Rococo vision of Anacreon as a model for his own verse to adapt to mid-century aesthetic currents and moral norms (Zeman 86), he also advances a more contemporary image of Sappho as a poet of heartfelt sentiment.[12]

If Gleim rejects the popular myths about Sappho from the position of the learned and objective modern scholar, he reproaches the philologists and critics from the position of the sensitive reader when he asks, "and who can understand a Sappho without a heart?" He thus identifies the third approach to Sappho noted above, that based on aesthetic taste, as the one that is decisive. An adequate appreciation of Sappho requires both poetic skill and emotional understanding, he claims. By imitating and translating her verse, eighteenth-century poets vied to prove their own literary and aesthetic sensibility. Gleim himself attempted a translation of one of Sappho's odes and wrote poems imitating her style. Gleim's close friend Ewald von Kleist translated an ode of Sappho's. So did Gleim's later protegé Wilhelm Heinse, and others, such as his literary friends Christian Felix Weisse and Karl Wilhelm Ramler (Rüdiger, *Geschichte* 12–33). Gleim requested that Karsch, too, attempt her translation of Sappho's remaining odes so he could compare the German and the Greek Sapphic sensibility, and his assessment of Karsch's efforts in this regard is the occasion for the passage from his letter cited here. In responding to his demand, Karsch thus enters into an ongoing tradition of masculine intellectual companionship and competition in ventriloquizing (and thereby mastering) Sappho, and she bears the burden of having to live up to—or prove her distance from—conflicting expectations that are raised in her audience through her identification with this famous precursor.[13]

The similarity that Gleim perceives between the literary styles of Sappho and Karsch rests, he makes clear, on a commonality of sentiment and taste. The name of Sappho for Karsch also signifies her inclusion in Gleim's circle of friends, literary men with whom he corresponded and socialized, and it marks a particular bond with Gleim himself as "the German Anacreon." Gleim alludes to this role in the passage cited when he discusses the reception history of Sappho and Anacreon and identifies both figures as potentially misunderstood poetic geniuses. But even in Gleim's modified interpretation of the link between the figures, the parallels drawn between Sappho and Anacreon in fictions of the time implied both a poetic and an eroticized relationship. Gleim's inclusion of Karsch as Sappho in his own poetic circle is thus a recognition of her poetic talents that is also fraught with the suggestion of poetic and personal expectations and gendered power relations. The context of the fictions of Sappho is one cultural factor informing the exchanges between Gleim and Karsch as Anacreon and Sappho, as poetic colleagues, as friends, and as mentor and student; it also enters into the relationships between Gleim, Karsch, and the male critics whom Gleim chastises for lacking the emotional insight to understand a Sappho.

The above passage from Gleim's letter not only distinguishes between the popular, the philological, and the aesthetic reception of Sappho, three approaches to the figure in which he asserts his expertise. It also conflates these modes of reception and thereby illuminates some of the complexities of the position Karsch occupied as the German Sappho. In Gleim's comments on the similarity of Sappho's and Karsch's literary styles he reveals his expectations of a sentimental Sappho. Gleim proffers the word "heart" as the key with which to unlock the true Sapphic sensibility that is founded on sentiment in opposition to learnedness, on emotion that speaks to good taste but is inaccessible through philological pedantry. Even as Gleim dismisses as legendary the stories invented around Sappho's tragic passions, he reinforces the image of Sappho as a woman whose poetry emanates from her emotions and thus confirms that image as the paradigmatic female poet of love. Karsch, Gleim effuses, is able to capture Sapphic sentiment in her verse because of her emotional affinity with the ancient poet, whereas he and his male literary friends, despite their education, their knowledge of literary tradition, and their ability to read Sappho in the original Greek, can only approximate her qualities. The contention that women's writing stands beyond the reach of the critics, as an expression of the heart whose essence can in turn only be understood through the heart, is a familiar eighteenth-century topos of female poetic creativity.[14] It is used to define and contain women's texts as something fully other than those of artistic men, or to disparage and dismiss them (expressly or subtly) as unreflected and instinctive, for if masculine learnedness is not adequate to understand the mysteries of female and feminine creativity, then neither is feminine creativity adequate to the rigors of art founded on knowledge. Here Gleim employs this topos to praise Karsch's sensibility and to claim for himself a singular understanding of both modern and ancient Sapphic writing based not only on his ability to criticize the philologists from the position of a learned insider, but also on his aesthetic taste and his emotional wisdom. "Just one free week and I would tell my friend many nice things about the Greek Sappho...." Gleim's promise of insights into the true qualities of Sappho's verse tantalizes his reader Karsch by offering, but as yet withholding, his privileged interpretation of Sappho. He suggests an emotional closeness to both the German and the Greek Sappho, a common understanding of the heart. And he claims a poetic and philological mastery of the Sappho figure and her fragments that Karsch—given her class status, her gender, and her resulting lack of education—cannot approach. Gleim thus emphasizes that Karsch is dependent on him if she is to understand the ramifications of identifying with the fabled figure he has held out to her, or indeed, if she is to understand her own poetic production.

Karsch's Public Enactment of Sappho

The cultural fascination with Sappho, the developing philological interest in her verse, and her instrumentalization in the debates on poetics and aesthetic theory of the mid-eighteenth century all contributed to the kinds of expectations and associations raised by the public identification of Karsch with Sappho. Karsch's enactment of Sappho for her public is an ongoing improvisation in which she responds to, but also resists Gleim's direction. Just as Gleim shows his awareness of the importance of role-playing for achieving poetic fame, Karsch, too, articulates her knowledge that her new-found social status is dependent on public fascination with the poetic persona she cultivates: "People want to satisfy their curiosity, they stare at me and clap their hands and call out a bravo as if all my speeches were little magic spells" (Karsch and Gleim 1: 5). Critics debate about Karsch's ability to shape her audience's reception of her poetry and person by manipulating the roles she adopted in her poems. While some scholars, for example Becker-Cantarino, have underscored the creative ways Karsch used these roles to present a particular image of herself as poet ("Belloisens Lebenslauf"), others, like Mödersheim, have suggested that she was, rather, confined and controlled by them ("Igel oder Amor?"). Karsch's public and private role-playing certainly provided her with poetic and social freedoms, but also imposed limitations.[15] This conflict can be illuminated in exemplary fashion through her negotiation of the role of Sappho.

There is an interesting tension between Karsch's acceptance of the classical figure as a poetic persona and her rejection of Sappho, especially as a poet of erotic desire, as a model through which her poems can be interpreted. In this respect, Karsch's public enactment of the role of Sappho differs importantly from her identification with Sappho in her private correspondence with Gleim, where the inspiration of love is indeed central—but the specific complexities of the role of Sappho in Karsch's letters to Gleim would merit an extended analysis of their own. Although a rigid distinction between a "public" and a "private" forum is often problematic when discussing eighteenth-century epistolary exchange, in this case it is justified to consider Karsch's Sappho-identification in the correspondence with Gleim as a topic related to but distinct from her public image as Sappho, not least because of Karsch's vehement insistence that the letters she writes to Gleim belong in the private realm (Mödersheim, "Igel oder Amor" 38) and because of the disagreements over a publication of the "Sapphische Lieder" (Sapphic Songs), love poetry written in the role of Sappho by Karsch to Gleim. While scholars have begun to investigate the way Karsch uses the role of Sappho in her private letters and unpublished poems,[16] her public impersonation of Sappho is often mentioned without further examination. Here, then, the focus is on Karsch's published poetry and her social self-definition, in which she consistently uses Sappho in part as a figure of identification as a creative, expressive poet and in part as a foil against which she insists on her own unique qualities and independent poetic voice.

Many of the poems from the *Auserlesene Gedichte* (Selected Poems) of 1764, instigated and mentored by Gleim and introduced by Sulzer, as well as poems from the period of the early 1760s that were first published later, bear witness to Karsch's interpretation of the image of Sappho in relation to her own verse. In a letter to Uz dated 16 January 1762, Gleim remarks on Karsch's use of Sappho and provides a clue as to her sources: "She reads but little, but whatever she reads, she immediately puts to use; ...I told her a great deal about the Greek Sappho and Wolf's collected reports, everything was applied" (Schüddekopf 320). Wolf's 1733 edition of Sappho's poetry was one of the new scholarly achievements of the time, as noted above. It included a biographical sketch of Sappho that dwelt on the popular legends of her life, while the second edition of 1735, which Gleim also owned, included an appendix by Olearius that presented a more restrained scholarly assessment of the poet and her work (Rüdiger, *Sappho* 71). Karsch's sources on Sappho received from Gleim thus included both the popular stories and the newest critical approaches to the poet. How, then, did she "apply" this information in her poetry, and to what end? In a simple fashion, Karsch used the figure first of all as a kind of stage prop, to solidify the association between herself and Sappho. More substantially, Karsch established a connection between her aesthetic style and attributes ascribed to Sappho in the mid-eighteenth century. And finally, Karsch defined her own poetic voice in contrast and in comparison to the ancient figure.

Karsch integrates images of Sappho into her poems from the 1760s in order to play with and strengthen the personal association between herself and Sappho that had become popular in her social circles and was well-known beyond them. Karsch refers to Sappho either directly by name or indirectly through the attributes and symbols that denote the figure Sappho at this time: her fame, her lyre, her passion (especially for Phaon), and her suicidal leap from the cliffs. Often these allusions are fleeting, as in "Eine kranke Braut an ihren Geliebten" (A sick bride to her beloved): a passing mention of Sappho is used to augment the image of the love-sick bride, who will imagine even sweeter names for her beloved than Sappho ever could (*Auserlesene Gedichte* 238). Karsch also uses the name of Sappho to represent the poetic voice that is identified overtly with Karsch herself. This sometimes occurs with no particular connection to the theme of the poem, simply to remind the readers that Karsch is identified as the German Sappho, for example when she writes in "An die Prinzessin Heinrich" (To the Princess Heinrich) that even the Greek Sappho could not have been happier than the German one is to sing the praises of the royal princess (*Gedichte* 148).

Karsch clarifies her identification with Sappho in a note at the end of the poem "Die Sehnsucht der Freundschaft" (The longing of friendship): "Mr. Gleim named the poet the German Sappho" (*Auserlesene Gedichte* 166). By reminding her public that it was Gleim who had given her this famous name, Karsch emphasizes both her poetic affinity with Sappho and the legitimacy of her alias. She builds her identification with Sappho on Gleim's literary and social authority and, by giving him the responsibility for the name Sappho, she attempts to deflect the reproach of arrogance that she often encountered (a reproach also made against Sappho herself in many commentaries over the centuries).

Moreover, the public explanation for Karsch's adoption of Sappho's name signifies her inclusion in a circle of poetic friends. The association with her well-known contemporaries that had brought about and furthered Karsch's change of fortunes in life was at least as important to her as her association with the figure of Sappho. But the identification with Sappho served to link her poetic image more strongly to that of Gleim, Ramler, and others who adopted classical poetic aliases. Both the comparison with Sappho and its value as a sign of acceptance and praise on the part of these literary men were significant for Karsch in establishing her authority as a poet. Her many passing allusions to Sappho remind her audience of this recognition and set the stage for her role as the German Sappho.

Karsch uses Sappho as a figure of identification in a more complex fashion in poems that describe her literary style and establish her aesthetic values. One common eighteenth-century view of Karsch and her remarkable poetic facility was the interpretation of her as a natural talent and of her verse as the pure voice of nature. Scholars have clearly shown that Karsch cultivated this image as a mode of self-definition in her poems through the stylization of her biography and her poetic style (Schaffers; Becker-Cantarino, "Belloisens Lebenslauf"), and they have elaborated on how it relates to poetic theories and notions of gender of the time (Barndt, "Mit natürlichem Genie"; Bovenschen; Mödersheim, "'Auch die fruchtbarsten Bäume'"; Scholz). Yet the relationship between this context of reception and the association of Karsch with Sappho has not been recognized. Karsch often employs the image of Sappho to develop her own self-presentation as a natural poetic talent; indeed, as shown above, the iconic female poet Sappho had already come to represent proximity to nature and the literary expression of emotion in the eighteenth-century cultural imagination.

Using the same key word "heart" that Gleim identified as the source of similarity between the Greek and the German Sappho, Karsch evokes Sappho in the poem "An Palemon" (To Palemon) and identifies with her to describe her poetic voice as "the language of the heart" (*Auserlesene Gedichte* 184). The poem elaborates on the notion that Sappho's soul finds direct expression in her song. Karsch compares the reflection of Sappho's soul in her poetry with the moon's reflection in water, thereby linking the poetic expression of emotion and an identification of both soul and song with natural beauty. As figures of identification for herself, Karsch's metaphors of Sappho's poetry provide yet another reflecting surface for her own soul's articulation in verse. The association of this type of peaceful aesthetic of nature and emotion with the feminine qualities of the poet and her poetry is underscored through the figure of Sappho herself as the original female poet, but also through the image of the moon, a traditional symbol of the feminine. The aesthetic for which Sappho stands here is related to the aesthetic of the Storm and Stress that privileges a unity of poetry, emotion, and nature, and the quality of that unity is presented in this poem as one that is feminine.

Yet the figure of Sappho is claimed by more than one aesthetic program, as outlined above, and eludes a definitive categorization. Sappho can thus serve Karsch as a name for multiple roles that are related through their emphasis on the poet's proximity to nature. Karsch employs another image of the ancient poet in "An den May" (To May), where Sappho again represents an aesthetic of nature and sentiment, this time in her Anacreontic guise. "An den May" presents itself as a lighthearted song of nature and love. In the fourth strophe Sappho appears as a model for, and a kindred spirit of, the birds who sing of love: "Von der Liebe treulich unterrichtet / Singt ein Vogel, der wie Sapho dichtet, / Ganze Nächte in der Ode Thon" (Faithfully informed about love, a bird who rhymes like Sappho sings for entire nights in the key of odes; *Auserlesene Gedichte* 40). The images of Sappho mediated in these two poems as poetic mirrors for Karsch each emphasize her aesthetic style as one of simple beauty. Her verse—always presented as her song—is compared to the direct, unreflected voice of nature that expresses the soul's emotions. Karsch's stylization of her poetic voice as a naive, natural expression draws on familiar traditions and literary conventions (Becker-Cantarino, "Belloisens Lebenslauf" 15–17), while her use of Sappho as a figure of identification in this context underscores the poet's privileged emotional access to nature and a poetic immediacy that is associated with femininity in the mid-eighteenth century. The image of the archetypal female poet of love and the concept of a proximity to nature that permits the poetic mediation of authentic emotion reinforce each other: Karsch stakes her claim to the name of the German Sappho by emphasizing her natural poetic talent and her claim to her status as poet of nature by emphasizing her identification with Sappho.

Karsch's identification with Sappho helps her to assert her literary authority and to describe her aesthetic style, but her very success in associating her name publicly with Sappho's also presents Karsch with challenges. Sappho's poetic fame and the cultural interest in Sappho's reputation threaten to overwhelm Karsch's own poetic voice. Even as Karsch employs contemporary fictions of Sappho in her poetic role-play to further her own aims, the mid-eighteenth-century German images of Sappho elicit audience expectations about Karsch's verse and influence the ways in which her poetry and she herself are perceived. Karsch's poetry is marked by these tensions. While she attempts to satisfy her audience when playing the role of her famous alias, she also strives to distinguish herself from her Greek model. In her poems, Karsch maintains a modern poetic voice and resists an interpretation of her poetry and her person that would subsume her individuality under the name of Sappho. Karsch asserts her poetic autonomy when her public role-play as Sappho steers her too far toward a confining idea of female authorship or toward expressions of erotic passion or desperate love.

The association of Sappho with a natural, unreflected poetic style overlapped with common eighteenth-century notions of female authorship, as shown above. While Karsch often drew on this convergence to present a stylized poetic self-image, her use of topoi of female poetic creativity was rarely as conventional and heavy-handed as in her poem "Der unnachahmliche Pindar" (The Inimitable Pindar) of 1763. Her overt role-play allows her to experiment with such an aesthetic stance, yet Karsch's struggle to negotiate between the demands of this role of "the poetess" and her own poetic pride becomes tangible in this poem.

> Ich gleich der summenden Biene,
>   Die saugt an blühendem Klee,
>   Ich sinn' am Ufer der Elbe,
>   Auf mein zu niedriges Lied.
>
> Ich rühre Saphische Sayten
>   Mit ungeregeltem Griff;
>   Mir fehlt zum Heldengesange
>   Gluth und ein männlicher Schwung (*Auserlesene Gedichte* 169).
>
> [I am like the buzzing bee
>   that sucks on blooming clover,
>   On the banks of the Elbe I consider
>   my too lowly song.
>
> I touch sapphic strings
>   with an unregulated grasp,
>   For heroic choruses I lack
>   fire and a masculine energy.]

Karsch constructs an explicitly gendered distinction here between the feminine, inferior song of nature—the sapphic strings that sound a lowly song—and the heroic choruses infused with masculine energy that the poet herself claims she lacks. Significantly, in rejecting the specific attribute of a "fiery glow" identified here as masculine, Karsch is rejecting a characteristic associated over the centuries with Sappho (and especially with Sappho as "masculine"), and thereby is rejecting for herself the image of Sappho as the passionate and skillful poet of the sublime. The distinction she draws between poems inspired by nature and heroic songs simultaneously supports the image of an Anacreontic Sappho, for the contrast between idylls and poetic depictions of heroism is a long-standing topos of Anacreontic verse.

Here Karsch displays a stylized feminine modesty about her poetic talents and subordinates her verse to that of Ramler ("the Berlin Pindar") and of Gleim, who figure in this poem.[17] She also, however, recuperates for herself a supporting role in the "masculine" poetic project of lauding the king's exploits: leaning on the arm of the "singer of the war songs," she writes, she will add her voice, "my more weakly sounding song," to the voices of her friends and they will sing together, "we will sing as a trio" (171). In this poem, Karsch's use of the figure of Sappho as a feminine singer to describe herself as poet entails evident ambivalence. The comparison elevates Karsch by acknowledging her fame and talents, yet she is at pains to occupy a lower place in the poetic hierarchy than her male friends, and to this end employs Sappho to emphasize her femininity as a sign of inferiority. Interestingly, though, she does not turn to Sappho in this poem to identify herself as a poet of a typically feminine realm of love. Instead, her poem indirectly reminds her audience of the fame Karsch herself has achieved through her poetic celebration of the battle victories of Frederick II. Since she defines this kind of verse as a highly valued field of masculine poetic production, she thus also asserts her own worth as a poet who can compete successfully with her male friends, her poetic feminine modesty notwithstanding.

"Should I tell you who I am?": Karsch's Assertion of Independence

Karsch's assertion of independent agency as a modern poet becomes most apparent in the thematic presentation of erotic passion. Although Karsch declares her emotional resemblance to Sappho, through the tenderness of feeling that characterizes each of them and motivates their verses, she distinguishes clearly between her own emotions and the desperate passion ascribed to Sappho in the popular imagination. When Sappho's love for Phaon is evoked in Karsch's poems, it is almost never as point of comparison between the ancient and the modern Sappho. In "An den Phöbus Apollo" (To Phoebus Apollo), for example, Karsch sketches the familiar image of Sappho pining for Phaon, but instead of relating to Sappho through the experience of love, Karsch lays claim to Sappho's lyre and laurels and thus emphasizes their common attributes of literary creativity and fame (*Gedichte* 34-35). The poem's title remarks this significant distinction as well: it is Apollo, the god of music and the lyre, to whom Karsch sings in this poem, and not Venus, the goddess of love addressed in Sappho's surviving complete ode. By presenting herself repeatedly as the inheritor of Sappho's lyre or laurels, the signs of Sappho's poetic talents and of her renown, Karsch suggests a literary continuity between Sappho and herself, but simultaneously marks the temporal difference between them.

There is just one poem intended for public view by Karsch in which she draws a parallel between her own emotions and Sappho's love for Phaon, and this poem is written in response to the explicit demands made on her as the new Sappho by Uz. In a letter to Gleim, Uz describes his expectations of Karsch: "What I most desire are her sapphic songs. I wrote to her that what I seek in them is love, and particularly burning love" (Schüddekopf 317). When Uz urges her to impersonate Sappho as passionate lover, Karsch fully grasps Uz's voyeuristic interest. She writes as much to Gleim in her letter of 5 January 1762: "...but go ahead and satisfy his lustful curiosity, my dearest, read him the most fiery songs and tell him that the Greek woman did not love her Phaon as much as the German Sappho loves her Thyrsis" (Karsch and Gleim 1: 57–58). Karsch plays to Uz's desires in a poem addressed to him, in which she points to Gleim's role in giving her "the lyre of the cliff-jumper" and describes her sweet tones of love that will reflect her affection for Gleim (*Auserlesene Gedichte* 187). At first glance, her role-play appears to be a straightforward identification with Sappho as lover. Yet the comparison between Sappho and Karsch established here by Gleim, as a figure in Karsch's poem, is one between two poets, not between two lovers. As object of desire and as the one who named Karsch the "German Sappho," Gleim mediates the identification with Sappho, but instead of transforming her into a second "cliff-jumper," he presents her with Sappho's "lyre." This distinction may at first seem negligible, but Karsch maintains this description of herself as a modern player of Sappho's lyre throughout her published oeuvre, and in doing so, she emphasizes a symbolic link between two creative women, while resisting a full merger of her poetic identity with that of the Greek Sappho. Furthermore, although she portrays her tender emotions as "Sapphic," even in this poem for Uz she abjures the role of a hapless, lovelorn Sappho and instead foregrounds her conscious role-play and the power of her song: "I became trusted by the gods of love and I now have control over hearts!" (187). The image of her own literary agency is predominant, rather than an image of despair.

The primacy Karsch gives to her creative voice is reminiscent of the portrait of Sappho (sometimes taken to be an implicit self-portrait) painted by Angelika Kauffmann in 1775 (fig. 2). Alone but for Cupid,

Figure 2: Angelica Kauffman, Swiss, 1741–1807
Sappho, 1775
Oil on canvas, 52 x 57 1/8 inches, SN329
Bequest of John Ringling, Collection of The John and Mable Ringling Museum of Art, the State Art Museum of Florida

who whispers in her ear, she is conventionally depicted with bared breast to connote her passion, yet one hand holds a quill and the other points to the ode to Venus that she is in the act of composing. Although a favored theme in Kauffmann's paintings was the figure of the abandoned woman, and although she composed images of Sappho and the abandoned Ariadne as counterparts (Baumgärtel 244, 407), the actual figure of Phaon plays no part in this image. Sappho's inspiration by Amor and her poetic productivity are the topics of the portrait.

Karsch repudiates an identification with Sappho as passionate lover most emphatically in her poem that bears the explanatory title "An den Dohmherrn von Rochow, als er gesagt hatte, die Liebe müsse sie gelehret haben, so schöne Verse zu machen" (To the Canon von Rochow, when he said that love must have taught her to write such beautiful verse) (*Auserlesene Gedichte* 110-12). She addresses her audience in the first line as "connoisseur of the Sapphic songs," and draws on the name of Sappho to describe the emotional character of her own writing. However, she explicitly counters the assumptions of her audience about her experience of love (and thus the potential reproaches against her behavior in this regard) that stem from the association with Sappho. Karsch distinguishes herself pointedly from Sappho by emphasizing the particularity of her own biography as it affects her poetic production. The idea that she herself has learned to write poetry through the experience of love is one she declares to be "a complete fiction." The following stanzas refer her reader directly to the harsh conditions of her youth and the abuse she suffered in marriage. She accentuates her lack of the experience of love, only then to identify this lack as one that gives rise to a poignant, unfulfilled desire, itself an inspiration for her writing. Karsch simultaneously describes and denies this closest moment of identification with Sappho as the poet of love by presenting her artistically inspiring erotic desire, her experience of "Sappho's soft fire," as imaginary: "Keine Gattin küßte je getreuer, / Als ich in der Sapho sanftem Feuer / Lippen küßte, die ich nie gefühlt!" (No wife ever kissed more faithfully than I, in Sappho's soft fire, kissed lips I never felt). Thus here too, Karsch underscores her creative literary powers that allow her to transform biographical fact and imaginary experience into poetry. Karsch thereby resists a facile conflation of her poetry—including her poetic alias—and her person (Barndt, "Mit natürlichem Genie" 18). Into her poetic identification with the Greek Sappho she weaves insistent reminders of her independence as a modern woman whose lived experience and creative talents are unique and uniquely shape her individual poetic voice.

Karsch values the originality of her aesthetic sensibility and self-assuredly pursues her poetic independence. She finds theoretical support for her convictions about her poetic production in Edward Young's *Conjectures on Original Composition* (1759), as she writes to Gleim on 28 March 1762 (Karsch and Gleim 1: 92). Although she compares herself to Sappho in this letter, she explains that she would never turn to Sappho with the intention of imitating her, but only for inspiration. Karsch trusts in her own genius (Kitsch 43–46); she identifies here with Sappho as an original poet. Her own verse necessarily reflects her natural talents, she writes, and to those she must be true if her poetry is to have value. The contemporary aesthetic precepts of the Storm and Stress in Germany, the theoretical embrace of a poetry of natural genius, were congenial to Karsch's self-understanding as an original poet of nature and sentiment, in turn influenced by mid-eighteenth-century images of Sappho. And even in jest, Karsch insists on her right, as the modern German Sappho, to poetic independence. The following impromptu of 1762, "Eigenschaften der Sapho" (Sappho's Traits), was composed with prescribed final rhyming words for social amusement and to demonstrate Karsch's talents at spontaneous rhyme:

> Nicht immer will ich so, wie andre Leute wollen,
> die nicht Gesetze geben sollen
> Der Sapho, der Empfindungsvollen,
> Die um den schönen Geist nicht trägt ein schönes Kleid,
> Der in den Adern ist ein Dichter-Quell gequollen
> Zu aller Lieder Möglichkeit,
> Der hoch von Zärtlichkeit der Busen aufgeschwollen,
> Die aus den Augen oft läßt Thränen nieder rollen,
> Dem Himmel ihren Dank zu zollen
> Für diesen goldnen Theil in ihrer Lebenszeit (*Gedichte* 316).

> [I don't always want to do what other people want me to;
> they should not make laws
> for Sappho, who is full of sentiment,
> who does not wear a beautiful dress around her beautiful spirit,
> in whose veins a poetic source runs
> that makes her capable of all songs,
> whose breast is filled with tenderness,
> who often allows tears to run down from her eyes
> in order to give thanks to heaven for this golden fate in her lifetime.]

The attributes of natural poetic talent, tender sentiment, and also ugliness that Karsch includes in her self-description as Sappho are all ascribed by her eighteenth-century contemporaries to both the classical Sappho and Karsch herself. Karsch sketches a poetics for Sappho that favors nature over rules and sentiment over artifice; both the ancient and the modern Sappho resist conventional rules and the pressure to conform to others' expectations. Thus independence and poetic originality are for Karsch important points of identification with the ancient Sappho. The subtext of individualism evident even in the identification with the famous Sappho is palpable from the first line of the impromptu and its emphasized "I."

In a poem addressed to her friend Frau v. Reichmann, Karsch asks "O you, to whom my heart recommends me, / Should I tell you who I am?" (*Auserlesene Gedichte* 87–88). Here and in similar poems, Karsch offers her readers poetic self-portraits that describe her self-image and fundamental aspects of her poetic voice. She portrays herself and her verse as pious, modest, loyal, and truthful, as well as emotionally sensitive, natural, and sincere. Karsch's public pose as Sappho stresses those qualities that confirm this more extensive self-portrait, as she uses the name Sappho to signify a female poet of sentiment whose song is a natural expression of her authentic emotions. Yet against the growing pressure of the late-eighteenth-century "international cult" of Sappho as the abandoned woman humiliated through her tragic love for the unresponsive man Phaon (Tomory 124), Karsch underscores the "German Sappho's" authenticity of sentiment through images of her loyal friendship as one of her defining traits.

Karsch explicitly links her poetic sensibility to her qualities as a friend and to her long search for friendship and recognition, now achieved through her poetry. The poem "An Palemon" (To Palemon) presents a literary self-portrait prompted by the portrait painted of her by Adam Friedrich Oeser. She draws on the familiar image of Sappho as an unattractive woman to contrast her physical plainness shown in Oeser's portrait with the inner beauty of her soul. Like Sappho she is "a singing woman, poor in external beauty and rich in sweet feeling," and "with her tender heart, she was once called Sappho." The image of her that she hopes her friends will remember, as they gaze at her portrait, is that she was favored by the muses and was loyal to her friends (*Auserlesene Gedichte* 228–30). Friends inspire her creativity, she insists, and "my pride lies in my friendships" rather than in fame ("Ueber den Unbestand des Ruhmes" [On the Ephemerality of Fame], *Gedichte* 81). Similarly, she constructs a contrast between writing for fame and writing for her friends in a poem in which she again appears as Sappho, "Ob Sappho für den Ruhm schreibt?" (Does Sappho Write for Fame?) (*Gedichte* 268–69). In this poem, Karsch maintains that she writes "for the pleasure of my friends!" and not out of ambition for fame. She recalls the great achievements of the ancient Sappho and the praise garnered by her poetry and then reminds the readers that only fragments of her work remain, in contrast to the works of the men Homer, Virgil, Horace, and Pindar. Karsch identifies Sappho, "who bore my lyre, who was as tender as I am," as her poetic ancestor and imagines that a similar fate of oblivion awaits her songs. But although the world will forget her, she writes, her friends will mourn her death at her grave. For Karsch, her friendships attest to her virtues and to her emotional sensitivity and authenticity that also, in her view, build the foundation for the quality of her poetry.

Karsch is acutely aware of the tenuousness of literary fame and fortune. But when she insists in her poetry that for her, lasting and reciprocal friendships are of higher value than poetic recognition, the contrast she draws is not completely convincing. For Karsch, the recognition of her poetic talents, of the value of her "songs," is the very foundation of the new life instigated for her by her benefactors.[18] Literary recognition is therefore the basis of her important friendships and her integration into an intellectual community, as well as her financial support;[19] emotionally, socially, and financially, the acceptance of her poetry has existential meaning for Karsch. Apostrophizing Karsch as Sappho, the icon of female poetic achievement, demonstrates such literary recognition, and it simultaneously casts Karsch, in complex and contradictory ways, in a social role that assures her a place in a community and supports the friendships through which she defines herself and her poetic expression. There are thus immense motivations for Karsch to adopt the role and to attempt to fulfill expectations that accompany it. She courts her public as Sappho and seeks reassurance that her songs, as images of her affections, of her heart and soul, will not be rejected.

Reception as "the German Sappho"

Does an association with "Sappho" serve more to liberate or to control female literary creativity? In the intimate correspondence with Gleim, the role of Sappho seems indeed to have facilitated her poetic expression. In Karsch's public poetic performance as Sappho, she strives to adapt the role to her own ends to support her stylized image of herself as poet. Karsch profits from Sappho's literary authority, as she claims an affinity with the exquisite sensibility and the natural poetic style sometimes ascribed to Sappho. In many ways, the contemporary images of Sappho as a poet of nature and sentiment that she cites (both as Anacreontic poet and as native genius) correspond to the poetic persona that Karsch constructs of an untutored natural talent and an original poet whose verse is integrally linked to her biography. Yet the image of the Greek Sappho and the aesthetic debates over the proper interpretation of her style ultimately obscure the original qualities of the "German Sappho," at least in the contemporary critical reception of Karsch and her published poetry.

It was Karsch's alias as Sappho and the public curiosity about the life of the unconventional woman who took on this role that were instrumental in transmitting cultural knowledge about her and her verse. The image of Sappho also informed the reception of Karsch in a less obvious fashion, such as in the physical descriptions that emphasize her reputed unattractiveness or her lively eyes that reveal an active mind, traits similarly remarked throughout centuries of commentaries on Sappho. Most scholarly work on Karsch makes some passing mention of the association with Sappho, and the tag "the German Sappho" recurs in the titles about Karsch, adding a legendary dimension to her biography.[20] The stuff of the sentimental stories told about her in the nineteenth century included her unreturned love for Gleim and explained the story through a comparison to Sappho. Certainly Gleim consciously played out the role of Phaon (although as Nörtemann remarks ["Nachwort" 528], this was not a name Karsch used for him), at times writing of Karsch's affections to Uz and sharing her love letters to him with visitors like Wieland.[21] But the reception of Karsch that makes of her love for Gleim a modern romance of the unhappy Sappho overlooks the resistance Karsch herself establishes to this interpretation, such as her insistence on her agency and poetic power as Sappho and her position as the inheritor of a noble literary tradition, signified by Sappho's lyre and her laurels.

For Karsch's contemporaries, her public performance as Sappho seemed to demand a judgment of her poetry that addressed this comparison. Karsch received extensive critical attention from Moses Mendelssohn and Johann Gottfried Herder because, for each of them, the figure of Sappho occupied an important symbolic position in their aesthetic programs. In their reviews of Karsch, Mendelssohn and Herder were not only assessing her poetry. They were also articulating their aesthetic convictions and defending their conceptions of the classical Sappho as an exemplary poet. The reviews of Karsch by these influential critics that focus on her identification with Sappho in order to clarify or dismiss the association are thus also contributions to the reception of the classical Sappho.[22]

Mendelssohn's first review of Karsch, on her "Sieg des Königs bey Torgau" (Victory of the King at Torgau; 1760), appeared in letter 143 of "Briefe, die neueste Litteratur betreffend" (Letters on the Newest Literature), before the associations of Karsch with Sappho had become fully current (5.1: 330-37). He lauds the poet's originality and talent in oft-quoted phrases: some of the verses reveal "a masculine, almost wild imagination...that decisively betrays an unusual genius" (5.1: 335). His later critique of Karsch's collected poems of 1764, however, elaborated in letters 272-76 of "Briefe, die neueste Litteratur betreffend," responds negatively to Karsch's self-identification as Sappho and becomes a statement of aesthetic principle (5.1: 574-601). He is willing to grant Karsch some lines worthy of "Sappho's glowing passion of love" (5.1: 585), yet he emphatically dismisses the characterization of many of her poems as "odes" on generic grounds and criticizes the verses in which Sappho is associated with quiet images of nature and a tender soul (5.1: 593). Mendelssohn maintains that these associations, which run contrary to his interpretation of Sappho as a poet of the sublime, are purely arbitrary. He thus rejects the use of Sappho as a figure that would excuse imperfect artistry and legitimize the notion of a feminine aesthetic of sentiment (found in differing fashions in the concepts of Sappho favored by theoreticians of Anacreontic and of Storm and Stress aesthetics). While he acknowledges Karsch's difficult life and the place of her poetic production in it—"It is a glorious triumph of natural talent over all difficulties of fortune, birth, and education" (5.1: 575)—Mendelssohn attacks the lack of polish in Karsch's poetry. He argues for aesthetic standards of classical form and compositional rigor that should be applied with equal measure to all: "A King, a woman, a Jew, what does that have to do with the issue?" (5.1: 578). Mendelssohn's own pride and biography enter here into this literary feud, in which he champions mastery of form and emotional intensity and rejects the image of Sappho as a sentimental, unreflective poet.

If Mendelssohn reproaches Karsch for arrogating the name of Sappho for herself with no trace of her sublimity, Herder denies the identification of the two for different reasons. The importance of Sappho as natural, feminine genius for Herder's aesthetic theories is, as for Mendelssohn, not coincidental to his influential review of Karsch, in which he takes the comparison between the two female poets as a point of departure and uses Sappho's femininity as a measure against which to judge Karsch. Since Sappho represents a touchstone of Herder's gendered aesthetics, Herder cannot leave unanswered what he sees as Karsch's illegitimate appropriation of Sappho's name. Throughout his comparison of "Sappho and Karsch" of 1767, Herder employs gendered terms to criticize Karsch and her verse. Her inappropriate identification with Sappho is a "woman's notion" and not "masculine truth," Karsch's poems are unreflected "births, simply thrown down," and instead of sharing the "gentle Sapphic fire" of the tenth muse, Karsch proves herself too unrestrained to merit the name of the Greek poet. Herder wishes that she would indeed emulate Sappho, whose verse is emotive, harmonious, and full of "tender fire that melts everything away." But instead, Karsch nearly presents a "counter-image" to Sappho: "the German Sappho, whose fire is more wild than gentle, more stormy than melting, seems rather to be androgynous in her works than to be a tender female friend of Venus, as the Greek woman was" (1: 351). Yet Herder's characterization of some of Sappho's fragments, her "little, charming, untranslatable leftovers," as "impromptus" (25: 86), also seems a reflection of Karsch's fame at spontaneous rhyming.

In the 1760s, the literary game of appropriating historical names to indicate aesthetic affiliations, familiar since ancient Roman times, is soon to lose favor in the wake of the poetics of originality and genius. Karsch's enactment of Sappho occurs on the cusp of shifting aesthetic ideals in the eighteenth century, and her poetry reveals her efforts to simultaneously claim Sappho as a poetic ancestor and, through identification with Sappho as an original poet of genius, to assert her own independent, modern poetic voice. While eighteenth-century critics of Karsch's published poetry addressed her evocation of Sappho to take issue with Karsch's departures from their poetic standards, Karsch herself employed the figure of Sappho in her published poetry and in her social self-definition to insist on her own originality and literary merit. But Sappho's symbolic value for competing aesthetic movements constrains Karsch's performance as Sappho and its public reception. Just as Karsch does not conform to Gleim's idea of an Anacreontic Sappho (Nörtemann, "Nachwort" 531; Kitsch 39), Karsch cannot fulfill the other aesthetic demands, either the rational and Neoclassical or the pre-Romantic and national, for which Mendelssohn and Herder each claim Sappho as an ideal. Karsch is successful in employing the identification with Sappho to attract wide public recognition and attention for her poetry, but her poetic attempts to specify who she is as the "German Sappho" are largely obscured by other, predominant ideas about the ancient figure. The tensions that arise in her poetry through her performance as Sappho, however, illuminate some of the conflicts engendered for the modern female poet by the competing cultural images of Sappho and their accompanying definitions of gendered poetic styles in the mid-eighteenth-century German context.

Notes

All translations from the German are my own.

[1] Greene, Introduction (1). Regina Nörtemann ("Nachwort" 528) points out that, although much is made of Gleim's initiative in naming Karsch "Sappho," there is no written evidence that he was the first to do so.

[2] The *Neue Gedichte* (1772) contains no poems in which Karsch's poetic persona is identified with Sappho.

[3] Among the seventeenth- and eighteenth-century British "Sapphos" were Mary Robinson, Lady Mary Wortley Montagu, and Katherine Philips, as documented by Andreadis (38–39) and Reynolds (123–25). Reynolds also mentions "the Swedish Sappho" Hedwig Charlotte Nordenflycht (8). Derks lists several early modern women known as modern Sapphos in the German context, including Elisabeth Johanna Weston, Eleonore Dorothea von Rosenthal, and Sibylle Schwarz, who appeared as "die pommersche Sappho" (62–63). Goodman writes that Erdmann Neumeister called Anna Maria Pflaum "die Teutsche Sappho" (118); she also discusses Gottsched's concern to promote a national Sappho, and his unsuccessful efforts to interest Luise Kulmus in that role (151, 221–22, 255). Catling mentions Louise Brachmann as the German Sappho, while Gabriele Baumberg was considered the Austrian Sappho.

[4] Alexander Pope, for example, attacked Lady Mary Montagu viciously through her alias as Sappho. See Reynolds on Pope and others in her chapter "Wanton Sapphoics," 123–46.

[5] See Reynolds (69–78); Campell (2–52).

[6] DeJean presents the seventeenth- and eighteenth-century French creations of Sappho in her first two chapters (43–197).

[7] Tischbein's image rendering Sappho and Anacreon as lovers draws on a long-standing popular myth about Sappho and Anacreon as an amorous couple, despite the difference in their biographical dates: Sappho lived around 600 BCE and Anacreon lived from 589 to 495 BCE.

[8] In *Die vernünftigen Tadlerinnen* of 1725, for example, Gottsched defends women's poetic abilities through reference to their natural style (414–18). In the mid-century, Gellert asserts in his influential guide on letter writing (1751) that women often write more naturally than men, because of their greater sensitivity and emotionality, as well as their ignorance of artistic convention (4: 136–37).

[9] Kitsch cites Gleim's poem to Karsch that presents her as both Sappho and an Anacreontic shepherdess (39).

[10] The last two terms, joy and sorrow, had been aligned as masculine and feminine attributes in the context of visual allegory by Winckelmann in

1766: he contrasted the masculine joy in activity with feminine sorrow and suffering (Winckelmann 1: 210).

[11] Both Bayle's and Zedler's encyclopedias were part of Gleim's library, as Schulz's catalogue documents (45; 744). One of Gleim's sources about Sappho was perhaps the Latin lexicon by J. Albert Fabricius, which ventured that she may have simply died of old age (Rüdiger, *Sappho* 44 and DeJean 124–25).

[12] In his presentation of Lessing's *Kleinigkeiten,* Meyer nicely describes the pressure felt by eighteenth-century Anacreontic poets to defend their propriety and to explain the relationship between their morally lax verses and their lifestyles (Lessing 204–28).

[13] Elizabeth D. Harvey's article "Ventriloquizing Sappho, or the Lesbian Muse" theorizes the "politics of gender and the poetics of plagiarism" in this kind of intertextuality through interpretations of John Donne.

[14] It is famously employed a decade later, for example, by Christoph Martin Wieland in his introduction to Sophie von La Roche's novel *Die Geschichte des Fräuleins von Sternheim,* but also in reference to Sappho by Herder and even Ramler.

[15] Nörtemann considers the role-play in Karsch's letters in "Nachwort" 527–32 and "Verehrung, Freundschaft, Liebe"; Pott emphasizes Karsch's ability to juggle multiple roles in her letters to Gleim in *Briefgespräche.* See also Mödersheim, "Igel oder Amor?" and Schaffer's study of the stylization of Karsch's biography in her letters.

[16] Nörtemann discusses Karsch's role as Sappho in her letters with Gleim and the "couples" Sappho/Phaon, Sappho/Anacreon, Sappho/Thyrsis, and Sappho/Tyrtäus ("Nachwort" 527–33). Kitsch investigates Karsch's role-playing of Sappho (61–63 and passim) with a focus on the unpublished "Sapphische Lieder"; Reinlein studies the Sappho-role in the correspondence of Karsch with Gleim.

[17] It is surely not coincidental that this poem is addressed to Ramler, whose poetic dogmatism was a source of frustration to his friends and foes alike, including Karsch. Ramler's expectations of female authorship and of Sappho, who is for him, as for Gleim, a poet to be approached only through the heart, are apparently parlayed into Karsch's self-presentation, and lead to disjunctions in her poem. Ramler's own translations of the verse of Anacreon, together with Sappho's odes, appeared in 1801 (Rüdiger, *Geschichte* 29).

[18] On the complexities of the "politics of patronage" and the importance for "the milkwoman" poet Ann Yearsley, another impoverished female poet, of establishing a relationship of friendship with her benefactors, see Felsenstein, especially 356–65.

[19] As Becker-Cantarino states, the roles ascribed to her were her "Lebensunterhalt und -inhalt" ("Vorwort" 15–16).

[20] See Glaser; Kohut; Beuys.

[21] Böttiger relates Wieland's irritation when, during a visit with Gleim in 1775, Gleim read to him from Karsch's love letters, "die schwärmerischen Herzensergiesungen der Karschin" (257–58).

[22] Even Rüdiger, who despises Karsch, writes of this influence: "Breiteren Kreisen in Deutschland wäre die Gestalt der Sappho ohne Zweifel fremd geblieben, wenn sich nicht für die Anna Luise Karschin der Beiname Sappho eingebürgert hätte" *(Sappho* 59).

Works Cited

Andreadis, Harriette. *Sappho in Early Modern England*. Chicago: U of Chicago P, 2001.

Anna Louisa Karsch (1722–1791): Dichterin für Liebe, Brot und Vaterland. Ausstellung zum 200. Todestag 10. Oktober bis 16. November 1991. Ausstellungskatalog, Staatsbibliothek Preussischer Kulturbesitz 39. Wiesbaden: Reichert, 1991.

Barndt, Kerstin. "'Mit natürlichem Genie wider die Regel.' Anna Louisa Karsch und die Ästhetiktheorie ihrer Zeit." *Anna Louisa Karsch (1722–1791): Dichterin für Liebe, Brot und Vaterland.* 14–22.

———. "'Mein Dasein ward unvermerkt das allgemeine Gespräch.' Anna Louisa Karsch im Spiegel der zeitgenössischen Populärphilosophie." Bennholdt-Thomsen and Runge. 162–76.

Baumgärtel, Bettina, ed. *Angelika Kauffmann, 1741–1807: Eine Dichterin mit dem Pinsel.* Ostfilden-Ruit: Hatje, 1998.

Becker-Cantarino, Barbara. "'Belloisens Lebenslauf': Zu Dichtung und Autobiographie bei Anna Luisa Karsch." *Gesellige Vernunft: zur Kultur der literarischen Aufklärung. Festschrift für Wolfram Mauser zum 65. Geburtstag.* Ed. Ortrud Gutjahr. Würzburg: Königshausen und Neumann, 1993. 13–22.

———. "Die 'deutsche Sappho' und 'des Herzogs Spießgesell.' Anna Louisa Karsch und Goethe." Bennholdt-Thomsen and Runge. 110–31.

———. "Vorwort." Karsch, Anna Louisa. *Gedichte: Nach der Dichterin Tode herausgegeben von ihrer Tochter Caroline Luise von Klencke. Nachdruck der Ausgabe Berlin von 1792.* Karben: Petra Wald, 1996. 1–26.

Bennholdt-Thomsen, Anke, and Anita Runge, ed. *Anna Louisa Karsch (1722–1791), Von schlesischer Kunst und Berliner "Natur." Ergebnisse des Symposions zum 200. Todestag der Dichterin.* Göttingen: Wallstein, 1992.

Beuys, Barbara, ed. *Herzgedanken: Das Leben der "deutschen Sappho" von ihr selbst erzählt*. Frankfurt a.M.: Societäts-Verlag, 1981.

Böttiger, Karl August. *Literarische Zustände und Zeitgenossen: Begegnungen und Gespräche im klassischen Weimar*. Ed. Klaus Gerlach and René Sternke. Berlin: Aufbau, 1998.

Bovenschen, Silvia. *Die imaginierte Weiblichkeit*. Frankfurt a.M.: Suhrkamp, 1979. 150–57.

Campell, David, ed. and trans. *Greek Lyric I: Sappho and Alceaus*. Cambridge, MA: Harvard UP, 1982.

Catling, Jo, ed. *A History of Women's Writing in Germany, Austria and Switzerland*. Cambridge: Cambridge UP, 2000.

DeJean, Joan. *Fictions of Sappho*. Chicago: U of Chicago P, 1989.

Derks, Paul. *Die sapphische Ode in der deutschen Dichtung des 17. Jahrhunderts*. Diss. Westfälische Wilhelms-Universität Münster, 1969.

Felsenstein, Frank. "Ann Yearsley and the Politics of Patronage: The Thorp Arch Archive: Part I." *Tulsa Studies in Women's Literature* 21.2 (2002): 347–92.

Gellert, Christian Fürchtegott. *Gesammelte Schriften*. Ed. Bernd Witte. Vol. 4. Berlin: de Gruyter, 1989.

Glaser, Adolph. "Eine deutsche Sappho." *Aus dem 18. Jahrhundert: Culturgeschichtliche Novellen*. Leipzig: Foltz, 1880. 187–203.

Goodman, Katherine R. *Amazons and Apprentices: Women and the German Parnassus in the Early Enlightenment*. Rochester: Camden House, 1999.

Götz, Johann Nikolaus. *Die Gedichte Anakreons und der Sappho Oden aus dem Griechischen übersezt, und mit Anmerkungen begleitet*. Carlsruhe: Macklot, 1760. Rpt. Stuttgart: Metzler, 1970.

Gottsched, Johann Christoph. *Herrn Peter Baylens, weyland Professors der Philosophie und Historie zu Rotterdam, Historisches und Critisches Wörterbuch, nach der neuesten Auflage von 1740 ins Deutsche übersetzt; auch mit einer Vorrede und verschiedenen Anmerkungen sonderlich bey anstößigen Stellen versehen*. 4 vols. Leipzig: Breitkopf, 1741–1744.

Greene, Ellen. Introduction. *Re-Reading Sappho: Reception and Transmission*. Ed. Greene. 1–9.

———, ed. *Re-Reading Sappho: Reception and Transmission*. Berkeley: U of California P, 1995.

Harvey, Elizabeth D. "Ventriloquizing Sappho, or the Lesbian Muse." *Re-Reading Sappho*. Ed. Greene. 79–104.

Herder, Johann Gottfried. *Sämtliche Werke*. Ed. Bernhard Suphan. Vols. 1–33. Berlin: Weidmannsche Buchhandlung, 1877–1913.

Karsch, Anna Louisa, and J.W.L. Gleim. *"Mein Bruder in Apoll": Briefwechsel zwischen Anna Louisa Karsch und Johann Wilhelm Ludwig*

Gleim. Vol. 1. 1761–1768. Ed. Regina Nörtemann. Vol. 2. 1769–1791. Ed. Ute Pott. Göttingen: Wallstein, 1996.

Karsch, Anna Louisa. *Auserlesene Gedichte.* Berlin: Winter, 1764. Ed. Alfred Anger. Stuttgart: Metzler, 1967.

———. *Gedichte: Nach der Dichterin Tode herausgegeben von ihrer Tochter Caroline Luise von Klencke. Nachdruck der Ausgabe Berlin von 1792.* Ed. Barbara Becker-Cantarino. Karben: Wald, 1996.

———. *Neue Gedichte.* Leipzig: Hinz, 1772. Ed. Barbara Becker-Cantarino. Karben: Wald, 1996.

Kitsch, Anne. *"Offt ergreiff ich um Beßer mein zu sein die feder ..." Ästhetische Positionssuche in der Lyrik Anna Louisa Karschs (1722–1791).* Würzburg: Königshausen & Neumann, 2002.

Kohut, Adolph. *Die deutsche Sappho (Anna Luise Karschin): Ihr Leben und Dichten. Ein Litteratur- und Culturbild aus dem Zeitalter Friedrichs des Großen.* Dresden: E. Pierson's Verlag, 1887.

Lessing, Gotthold Ephraim. *Kleinigkeiten.* Faksimile des Marbacher Manuskripts vorgestellt von Jochen Meyer. Göttingen: Wallstein, 2000.

Longinus. "On the Sublime." Trans. W. Hamilton Fyfe. *Aristotle, The Poetics; Demetrius, On Style, Longinus, On the Sublime.* Cambridge: Harvard UP, 1965. 119–254.

Mendelssohn, Moses. *Gesammelte Schriften Jubiläumsausgabe.* Vol. 1. Ed. Fritz Bamberger. Vol. 5.1. Ed. Eva J. Engel. Stuttgart-Bad Cannstatt: Frommann-Holzboog, 1971; 1991.

Mödersheim, Sabine. "'Auch die fruchtbarsten Bäume wollen beschnitten sein.' Georg Friedrich Meiers Konzept der Einbildungskraft und Dichtungskraft und die Kritik an Anna Louisa Karsch." *Dichtungstheorien der deutschen Frühaufklärung.* Ed. Theodor Verweyen and Hans-Joachim Kertscher. Tübingen: Niemeyer, 1995. 37–54.

———. "Igel Oder Amor? Zum Briefwechsel zwischen Anna Louisa Karsch und Johann Wilhelm Ludwig Gleim." *G.A. Bürger und J.W.L. Gleim.* Ed. Hans-Joachim Kertscher. Tübingen: Niemeyer, 1996. 29–39.

Nörtemann, Regina. "Nachwort." Karsch, Anna Louisa and J.W.L. Gleim. Vol. 2. 523–55.

———. "Verehrung, Freundschaft, Liebe: Zur Erotik im Briefwechsel zwischen Anna-Louisa Karsch und Johann Wilhelm Ludwig Gleim." Bennholdt-Thomsen and Runge. 81–93.

Pott, Ute. *Briefgespräche: Über den Briefwechsel zwischen Anna Louisa Karsch und Johann Wilhelm Ludwig Gleim.* Göttingen: Wallstein, 1998.

Reinlein, Tanja. *Der Brief als Medium der Empfindsamkeit.* Würzburg: Königshausen & Neumann, 2003.

Reynolds, Margaret. *The Sappho Companion*. London: Chatto & Windus, 2000.
Rüdiger, Horst. *Geschichte der deutschen Sappho-Übersetzungen*. Berlin: E. Ebering, 1934. Rpt. Nendeln/Liechtenstein: Kraus, 1967.
———. *Sappho: Ihr Ruf und Ruhm bei der Nachwelt*. Leipzig: Dieter'sche Verlagsbuchhandlung, 1933.
Schaffers, Uta. *Auf überlebtes Elend blick ich nieder: Anna Louisa Karsch in Selbst- und Fremdzeugnissen*. Göttingen: Wallstein, 1997.
Scholz, Hannelore. "'Doch mein Herz,...dieses ist ganz Gefühl, ganz Freundschaft, wie es den Dichtern geziemt': Die Karschin im Kontext der Volkspoesie in Deutschland." Bennholdt-Thomsen and Runge. 132–48.
Schüddekopf, Carl, ed. *Briefwechsel Gleim–Uz*. Tübingen: Litterarischer Verein Stuttgart, 1899.
Schulz, Karl-Otto. *Bestandverzeichnis der Gleimbibliothek*. Vol. 1–7. Halberstadt: Gleimhaus, 1985–1993.
The Spectator: A New Edition. Ed. Henry Morley. 3 vols. London: Routledge, 1883.
Tiegel-Hertfelder, Petra. *"Historie war sein Fach": Mythologie und Geschichte im Werk Johann Heinrich Tischbeins d.Ä (1722–1789)*. Worms: Wernersche Verlagsgesellschaft, 1996.
Tomory, Peter. "The fortunes of Sappho: 1770–1850." *Rediscovering Hellenism: The Hellenic Inheritance and the English Imagination*. Ed. G.W. Clarke. Cambridge: Cambridge UP, 1989. 121–35.
Die vernünftigen Tadlerinnen. Ed. J.C. Gottsched. Leipzig: Brauns Erben, 1725.
Winckelmann, Johann Joachim. *Kleine Schriften und Briefe*. Ed. Hermann Uhde-Bernays. 2 vols. Leipzig: Insel, 1925.
Zedlers Universal-Lexikon. Ed. Carl Günther Ludovici and Johann Heinrich Zedler. "Sappho." *Grosses vollständiges Universal-Lexikon aller Wissenschaften und Künste*. Vols. 1–64. Leipzig: Zedler, 1732–1750. Vol. 34 (1742). 37–39.
Zeman, Herbert. *Die deutsche anakreontische Dichtung*. Stuttgart: Metzler, 1972.

Scandal Writ Large in the Wake of the French Revolution: The Case of Amalia Holst

Carol Strauss Sotiropoulos

If feminist hopes during the French Revolution were betrayed by the wide gap between egalitarian rhetoric and actual gains for women, they were all but quashed following the Terror, when a pan-European conservative backlash snuffed out public debate over improving woman's status and social conditions. Amalia Holst was one of few women willing to put her reputation at stake to rekindle this debate. In her book-length treatise on advancing women's education, Holst traverses a precarious tightrope between feisty rhetoric and cultural accommodation. To walk with her is to witness a dazzling display of innovative strategies that would, she hoped, both inspire contemporaries to take action and deflect those quick to censure her as scandalous. (CSS)

The decades following the French Revolution were a particularly fertile and yet puzzlingly frustrating moment for champions of women's education. On the one hand, eighteenth-century economic, philosophic, socio-cultural, and political currents had given rise to expectations of formal education for women. The Revolution can itself be contextualized as a moment of recognition crystallizing universal demands for access to political and civic rights. On the other hand, these jumps forward in consciousness failed to result in major advances in women's social conditions: included in the Revolution's legacy of stinging ironies is its failure to advance either woman's political status or her education.

In the years following the Terror, the fears of social upheaval that extended across Europe narrowed the space in which feminist educational reformists could propose changes and at the same time avoid being judged as scandalous. Few tried. In France, apart from occasional outbursts by partisans of women's rights such as Charles Theremin and Germaine de Staël, Olympe de Gouges' executioners succeeded in silencing feminist reformists for four decades. In England, Mary Hays and Mary Robinson were vilified in reviews of their treatises. And in Germany, between 1794, the year Marianne Ehrmann's second women's periodical folded, and 1802, the year Amalia Holst published her treatise *Über die Bestimmung des Weibes zur höheren Geistesbildung* (On the Purpose of Woman's Advanced Intellectual Development), not a single voice dared publicly argue for the improvement of women's education.[1] Clearly cognizant of the narrow space within which she worked, Holst deployed novel rhetorical tactics to negotiate the tension between respectable reformist and scandalous revolutionary. By taking a close look at her creative and resourceful strategies, we can better understand the operative challenges facing feminist reformist writers of the day.

While the reprinting of Amalia Holst's treatise in 1984 has elicited discussion among scholars of early feminism, it has received less attention among researchers of education history, a field that has traditionally concentrated almost exclusively on the narrative of male learning.[2] Holst's text invites us to interrogate how early feminist educationists deployed the rhetoric and forms of pedagogical writing to contest the conduct-book literature that substituted for a girl's education, as well as to tell the story of a woman's life beyond marriage.

In the reactionary climate following the French Terror, German humanitarians who had enthusiastically embraced revolutionary ideals downplayed man's social role as citizen and emphasized the cultivation of individual potential. In his influential *Über die ästhetische Erziehung des Menschen, in einer Reihe von Briefen* (On the Aesthetic Education of Man, in a Series of Letters, 1795), Schiller argued that sudden political changes for which immature humanity is unprepared lead only to the violent chaos and repression that undermine the goal of democratic participation in governance. Similarly, in pedagogical circles neohumanist theoreticians contested the philanthropinist ideology of education as training for citizenship, and articulated the imperative of *Bildung* to mold the well-rounded individual.[3] Advanced education for women was excluded from this debate; indeed, neohumanists elided discussion of women's education entirely, while the most influential philanthropinists relegated a young girl's education to training for domestic life and rudimentary literacy.

The theme of revolution as female transgression permeates both literary writings and educational texts of this period.[4] Schiller's lengthy poem *Das Lied von der Glocke* (The Song of the Bell, 1799), for example, operates dually to instantiate the danger of female destabilizing impulses and to intimate how best to curb them: the core metaphors of revolution as female perfidy dominate one verse, while the figure of the good woman quietly celebrating her place in the domestic sphere frames another.[5] Lines of the latter, routinely memorized by girls as a staple of their education diet (Dauzenroth 98), offer a glimpse into girls' indoctrination into patriarchal norms. Letters of Caroline Michaelis Schlegel-Schelling (1763-1809) suggest the pressure brought to bear on female "transgressors." Politically and intellectually active in republican Mainz in the revolutionary years, she subsequently took care to mitigate any potentially damaging effects of her participation, writing that she had never been "an unnatural heroine, rather just a woman" (Schmidt I, 296, qtd. in Tewarson 114). The post-Revolution feminists, determined not to be reviled or dismissed as "scandalous," walked an exceedingly narrow tightrope between affirmation of rights and accommodation to norms.

Holst (1758-1829), too, had little wiggle room. That she was a known figure in northern Germany can be discerned in the contemporary reviews of her treatise, as well as in lengthy obituaries that commend her dedication to the praxis and theory of women's education. The daughter of Heinrich von Justi, a controversial and prolific cameralist, she was reputedly one of a handful of eighteenth-century German women to be awarded a university degree.[6] Although von Justi died when she was thirteen, Holst was undoubtedly aware of his mid-century radical proposals for women's academies and for civil courts administered by elected women officials.[7] Despite extensive efforts on the part of Holst researchers, little is known of her family upbringing and education.[8]

Holst's development as educationist, feminist, and feminist educationist can be discerned in her responses to pedagogical and literary writings of her day. In 1791, when she was 33, her name emerged in Hamburg as the author of *Bemerkungen über die Fehler unserer modernen Erziehung von einer praktischen Erzieherinn* (Obervations on the Errors of Our Modern Education by a Practical Teacher). Here she severely critiqued the contemporary pedagogical literature, particularly that of the philanthropinists Campe and Basedow. Her focus was not on their regressive view of girls' education, however, but on fallacies in their theoretical assumptions about how young children learn. Her critical competence from the stance of a practitioner allowed readers to assume that she had been supporting herself as a teacher or governess. Also in 1791 she married Ludolf Holst, a lawyer with whom she had three children; in subsequent years she opened and closed three or four small schools (*Erziehungsinstitute*), in Hamburg, Wittenberg, and Boitzenberg. The reasons for the schools' closings are unknown.[9]

From her discussion of early childhood education in *Bemerkungen,* Holst moved into literary and feminist debates in 1799-1800, when *A.*

Lindemann's Musarion published her "Briefe über *Elisa, oder das Weib wie es seyn sollte*" (Letters on *Elisa, or Woman as She Ought to Be*), a critique of the immensely popular domestic novel attributed to Karoline von Wobeser (1795, in its fifth edition in 1799).[10] Here Holst decried popular glorification of the character Elisa's self-renunciation and abnegation in an unhappy marriage and called for female autonomy.[11] In *Über die Bestimmung des Weibes zur höheren Geistesbildung* (On the Purpose of Woman's Advanced Intellectual Development), her third and presumed final publication, Holst's rejection of patriarchal ideology and her insights as a practicing educator converge in the recognition that advanced and ungendered education of women is key to women's—and to society's—transformation.[12]

Holst's line of argument is refreshingly unfettered by the conflicts and contradictions confounding slightly earlier German women educationist writers such as Sophie von La Roche (1731–1807), who promoted improved education for women, yet tacitly accepted the notion of distinctly gendered spheres of learning endorsed by figures such as Herder, Kant, Wilhelm von Humboldt, Goethe, and Schiller.[13] Holst instead disentangled current prejudices against female learnedness from accepted beliefs about woman's role and destiny to construct an argument that accommodates both the highest degree of formal study and woman's role in the home. The title of her treatise, an arresting extension of the cliché "Bestimmung des Weibes" (woman's destiny, purpose), set the stage for her to advocate a gendered role enriched and expanded by an ungendered education. Also, she extended the word "Bestimmung" to include alternative destinies for exceptional and unmarried women.

Holst appeared fearless of stepping out on a limb, as she boldly exposed herself to critical censure of both her reputation and her cause. She did not write anonymously. She deployed the term "learned" (*gelehrt*) forthrightly at a time when other post-Enlightenment feminist educationists adopted less inflammatory terms such as "educated," "accomplished," or "cultivated" (*gebildet*).[14] She appropriated neo-humanistic pedagogy for women and considered woman's access to deep "male" learning an imperative. She attacked by name popular writers such as Karl Pockels and Ernst Brandes, who denied women the right to advanced education. And yet this educationist, who founded and directed at least three small schools, insisted on home education under maternal tutelage and resisted discussion of institutional education. On the one hand, this silence problematizes her educational agenda. On the other, it invites us to interrogate context and, as Anton Kaes suggests in his discussion of new historicism, to "reconnect the text to the multitude of discourses inscribed in it" (216).

Against the tide of late-eighteenth-century sentimentalist and Romantic writers who challenged women's intellectual equality, Holst drew upon earlier Enlightenment strategies to redefine higher learning and thereby make it available to women. Invoking the voices of Enlightenment feminists such as her father, the Gottscheds, and Dorothea Leporin, she, like them, turned to the empiricism of Locke, Leibniz, and Wolff to promote female learnedness.[15] Significantly, however, she did not espouse women's active participation in the public sphere, as did Theodor von Hippel, who, at the height of the revolution in France, authored the most radical and extensive treatise on women's education and rights, *Über die bürgerliche Verbesserung des Weibes* (On the Middle-Class Improvement of the Woman, 1792).

Holst's text incorporates dialogical argumentation, mini-narratives, and vignettes of great women to overturn contemporary anthropological and pedagogical misogynist discourse against the learned woman, as well as to pitch an intensive home education program. On the pedagogical front, her participation in the debates between the philanthropinist and neohumanist movements is richly textured by her dual focus on pedagogical and gender issues. In mapping out the terrain for an expanded maternal educative role, Holst argued that only a woman who had herself received thorough academic training could educate the next generation. Further, she extended woman's educative function beyond the maternal, arguing not only for single women to become teachers, but also for woman's lifelong pursuit of perfectibility through continuous engagement in intellectual pursuits.

Most education tracts of this period offer a pedagogical plan and often outline how such a plan should be implemented. In the late eighteenth century, particularly at the time of the Revolution in France, the school was becoming increasingly accepted as the site for collective improvement; the most egalitarian European feminists—Condorcet, Hippel, and Wollstonecraft—proposed advanced public coeducation. Holst instead insisted on the professional maternal educator who would instruct her children in all the academic disciplines, not only during their early childhood, but through their adolescence. It seems unrealistic to expect that most mothers could create the conditions, much less embrace the necessary commitment, to sustain this kind of lengthy educative engagement. If they could do so, however, as Holst's idealistic prescription suggests, their professional role would collapse the dichotomy of separate spheres. Certainly the professionalizing of the maternal educator provided Holst ample justification for adopting "male" neohumanist pedagogy for women. And yet, one asks, how did she foresee generations of women collectively attaining to learnedness? Was home education perhaps a retreat from the argument for national coeducation—a retreat from "scandalous" ideology?

I suggest that in carving out a space for women's education in the era of backlash against the revolution in France, Holst could not align herself with advocates of institutional coeducation. Simply put, the discursive opening occasioned by the events in France and seized a decade earlier by Condorcet, Hippel, and Wollstonecraft had closed.[16] Holst's silence on institutional education may be viewed as a marker of self-censorship and helps us to understand the cultural obstacles faced by any educationist promoting female access to the "male" education required for what Holst termed women's "tiefe Kenntnisse" (deep knowledge, 48).

Just eight years after the publication of Holst's *Über die Bestimmung,* the Bremen teacher and girl's school director Betty Gleim (1781–1827) published her two-volume rationale and model curriculum for girls' schools, *Erziehung und Unterricht des weiblichen Geschlechts* (Education and Instruction of the Female Sex). Gleim did not mention Holst, although she shared Holst's vision of appropriating for women the neohumanistic educational ideology conventionally reserved for men. Unlike Holst, she conceptualized the maternal educative role only in the child's first five years and instead proposed a system of state-supported girls' schools as the educational site for girls aged six to sixteen. While her proposal included training schools that would combine academics and paid work training for older girls of the poorest class, she did not entertain any discussion of coeducation. Here we may ask what events northern German lands experienced between 1802 and 1810 that might well have inflected the two women's writings. Gleim's broad vision of institutionalizing education not only addressed dramatic increases in poverty rates by putting women into the work force—albeit in traditional womanly occupations—but also served as an indictment of the Napoleonic occupation begun in 1806, four years following Holst's publication. Gleim's text, which overtly refers to Fichte's *Reden an die deutsche Nation* (Addresses to the German Nation, 1807–08), can be read as a subversive nationalist manifesto for collective educational and social reform.[17] Yet, as comprehensive as Gleim's curriculum for middle-class girls was—by comparison to that offered in German girls' schools of the day—any hope of realizing state support for girls' advanced education rested on compromises in curricular content that gestured to complementarian doctrine by differentiating female and male education.

I suggest that Holst regarded coeducation as the failsafe means to ensure the educational depth she endorsed. While both Holst and Gleim argued against essentialist differences in the ability to reason and process knowledge, Holst's *"tiefe Kenntnisse"* (deep knowledge) extend further into traditional male spheres of learning than Gleim's *"gediegene Bildung"* (sound education). Among her post-Revolution contemporaries, Holst's pedagogical plan for women was singularly radical. However, to have proposed the praxis of this curricular content in institutionalized settings would have invited precisely the kind of reception she strategically sought to avoid, that of "scandalous revolutionary." Clearly she could have assumed a more sympathetic reception by opening readers' imagination to scenes of siblings as they together, in mixed-sex groups, studied speculative philosophy, higher mathematics, and other "male" disciplines.

The coeducation that grounds Holst's program was at the heart of Hippel's revolutionary proposal for state schools, and Holst was the sole feminist writer of the era to emphatically recommend his work. She encouraged her internal audience of *"Freundinnen"* (female friends) to read Hippel's *Verbesserung* "with fervent aspiration for ever greater self development" (16).[18] She praised Hippel for defending women's rights and thus implied her support of his call for coeducational schools. Holst was careful, however, to distance herself from Hippel's advocacy of woman's active engagement in state operations: "As much as we gratefully acknowledge his laudable enthusiasm...I cannot agree with him in this regard...I believe that such a total revolution in civic affairs would produce much confusion" (19). In situating women squarely in all professions and state operations, Hippel failed to include any substantive discussion of the maternal role; this omission may well have contributed to his dismissal by readers and reviewers.[19] In distinct contrast, Holst's appropriation of the word "profession" (*Beruf*) in the title of the first chapter, "Steht die höhere Ausbildung des Geistes mit dem nähern Beruf des Weibes als Gattin, Mutter und Hausfrau im Widerspruch?" (Does higher intellectual development contradict woman's more immediate profession as spouse, mother, and housewife?), indicates her unequivocal elevation of woman's domestic role to that of a profession.

Although she promoted Hippel's work, Holst was quick to announce that she did not want to be perceived as a "preacher of revolution" (*Revolutionspredigerin*). As Susanne Zantop points out in her discussion of "transgressive femininity," the revolution in France generated an obsession among German male literati of all political stripes "with women who cross the boundaries between the private and the public sphere and become advocates of change" (219). Holst clearly recognized these boundaries. She remained silent on Wollstonecraft, whose *Vindication of the Rights of Woman* (1792, German translation 1793) was widely read and had been praised by writers such as Wieland and

Forster, who had supported the Revolution.[20] The labeling of Wollstonecraft as "a raging enemy of princes and nobles" by the Göttingen professor Christoph Meiners in 1788 (243) would certainly have deterred Holst from encouraging readers' association with her. However, at the same time that Holst worked to accommodate boundaries between the private and the public spheres, she transformed normative definitions of the woman within them. This did not go unnoticed.

While Holst's strategic embrace of home education enabled her to confine the contentious segments of her treatise to an indictment of contemporary attitudes about the content and depth of woman's learning, it is in this indictment and in the implications of her home education program that her reception as scandalous could not be avoided. For example, a reviewer for the *Hamburg und Altona Zeitschrift zur Geschichte der Zeit, der Sitten und des Geschmacks* (Hamburg and Altona Magazine of Modern History, Customs, and Taste) commented,

> A learned woman, in the true sense of the word, is neither human, nor wise nor charming.... All learned women...are and remain anomalies....Learnedness, in its true sense, is a calling that nature appears to have decreed for man; the duties that nature and FEMININITY have imposed on woman allow her no time for it. If a woman wants to be a scholar by profession, she must renounce the titles of spouse and mother, and even more of HOUSEWIFE.... Such a woman wants, like men, to break through the dangerous limits of glory and knowledge. You graces, her faithful companions, I pray you prevent this sad catastrophe! (1802: 95 and 98; capitals in original).[21]

Merely by echoing the words of the patriarchal voices that Holst challenged throughout her treatise, the reviewer evaded any discussion of her substantive points. More importantly, however, charged terms such as "nature and femininity" (*die Natur und die Weiblichkeit*), "a scholar by profession" (*eine Gelehrte von Profession*), "like men" (*männerähnlich*), and "catastrophe" (*Katastrophe*) served not only to pan the book, but to put into question the author's reputation as a respectable member of her sex, that is, to raise the specter of scandal.

Holst's cogently articulated platform, more easily dismissed than addressed by contemporary critics, draws on an array of discourses. On the one hand, Holst appropriated early Enlightenment feminist rhetoric for philosophical support of the ungendered mind and to decry complementarians' conflation of woman's biology and her mind: "There exists no proof that woman's mind cannot comprehend the higher sciences" (53). On the other, her emphases on maternity and individual perfectibility situate her in the wake of Rousseau and in the Romantic ideology appropriated by neohumanists. While Holst derided the mysticism associated with Romanticism, Romantic thought had opened a new space for intellectual engagement, both for men and for those women who refused to define themselves as intellectually gendered. German women organized salons that served as forums for intellectual exchange, women published in unprecedented numbers, and a very few took to attending university lectures.[22] Holst drew peripherally on this informal climate of expanding intellectual participation. Advocating depth of knowledge in history, the sciences, philosophy, geography, and the arts, she identified the internalized possession of knowledge (*Kenntnis inne haben,* 98 and *passim*) and the facility to draw meaningful connections among all disciplines as foremost qualities of the effective maternal educator.

Holst tacitly adopted a neohumanist-Romantic semantic universe to argue that women, too, required scholastic depth to work toward individual perfectibility and that they, like men, wanted and deserved the freedom to develop all their strengths "in the most beautiful harmony toward highest perfection" (41). Thus she openly supported self-development for its own sake, not masked by social function, and she promoted women's participation in Romantic individualism. Indeed, Holst attacked women's partial knowledge as dangerous: "Possessing half knowledge of something is worse than having no knowledge of it at all" (98). To include woman in the neohumanist concept of "human," Holst argued, woman must be defined as human being (*Mensch*) first, and woman/wife (*Weib/Gattin*) second.

In a simple but startling observation, Holst derailed the arguments of male educationists—both neohumanist and philanthropinist—who insisted on a female education geared to training in household management. Men are not criticized, she wrote, for seeking culture and knowledge beyond what they need to know in order to execute professional obligations and fulfill civic duty; on the contrary, she maintained, they are held in higher esteem (64). And she asked, "Why do people not accord women the same right? Why are people so ardently opposed to women's learning? Is erudition a male monopoly?" (64). Holst's questions envision woman's education and future in a lifelong process of self perfection; further, her emphasis on the education of young adult and older women—to which she paid greater attention than to the curriculum for young children—emplots a life outside of and beyond motherhood.

The self-development that underwrites Holst's reform of women's education could serve both maternal and alternate destinies. Her broad demands include complete freedom to study every subject, including all branches of philosophy, and access to original sources instead of the books written expressly for women, which offered only "superficial knowledge" and which "treat us like overgrown children" (43). She advocated formal university education for women of exceptional intellect and she repudiated those who deny woman's capacity to achieve in the highest spheres of abstract thought—that is, in speculative philosophy and higher mathematics. Asserting that the dearth of female models demonstrated no more than women's lack of access to the continuous, uninterrupted formal study that these disciplines demand, she fantasized about the many female "philosophical minds" (*philosophische Köpfe*) that would have rivaled the likes of Kant and Leibniz, had women been granted the opportunity to study.

It is surely no coincidence that Holst selected the celibate figures of Kant and Leibniz to gain reader sympathy for her proposal of parallel scholarly lives for exceptional women. Claiming that exceptional women, too, should be exempt from the pressure to reproduce, she skillfully inserted rhetoric redolent of procreation as a metaphorical hinge to the scholarly contributions and discoveries that expand national progress. The loss to the population of childless exceptional women, she wrote, would be no greater than what the population had lost by the celibacy of Kant and Leibniz, "whose immortal works, the offspring of their minds, have enriched the world" (55).

While Holst emplotted equivalent roles for men and women of genius in suggesting that neither should marry, her line of argument for expanding educational opportunities remains fixed on the learned mother and her need for a thorough education to play the dual roles of teacher and model of learnedness. Not only did she condemn the philanthropinists for their narrow view of woman's educational needs, she assailed them for their fear that higher learning and development of artistic skills would inspire distaste for maternal tasks (108). Holst argued that precisely this mentality about home and children—this devaluing and trivializing of motherhood from its rightful position of profession to one of mindless attention to trivial tasks—had fostered "empty souls" (*leere Seelen*): the vanity, pretentiousness, lack of reasoned judgment, laziness, and foolishness of miseducated women (109).

To blow an alarmist trumpet about miseducated women, Holst, like Wollstonecraft, embedded mini-narratives into her polemical presentation. Empty women become substandard mothers who put their children in double jeopardy. Seeking external self-gratification, they provide neither adequate models nor even safe caretaking: "If graves could speak, what horrid stories about neglected children would we not hear? Neglected not by learnedness, no, rather by ignorance" (109). Echoing

Wollstonecraft's assertions that only miseducated women allow passions and foolishness to rule over reason, she exposed the fallacious belief that childrearing skills are as innate as the mother-child bond; instead, she wrote, miseducation was to blame for maternal deficiencies.

Holst's monitory narratives follow the expected trajectory of miseducated mothers and innocent child victims. One mother who could not spend an evening at home not only went out to play cards as her daughter lay deathly ill, but continued to play upon receiving news of the child's death. Another followed the trend of nursing her own child, yet refused to give up outside entertainment; when a nanny tried to satisfy the baby's hunger with food it could not digest, the baby died, "yet another sacrifice to a mother's addiction to pleasure and comfort, and to her ignorance" (111). In contrast, Holst wrote, the children of learned mothers rarely fall prey to such victimization, and she wondered at the specious arguments of writers who castigated learned women while refusing to recognize the most prevalent and pernicious causes of child neglect.[23]

In deconstructing the arguments of male writers who unleashed their wrath on learned rather than on frivolous women, she suggested deeper causes than the male fear that learned women lack femininity (*Weiblichkeit*). Instead, men feared that, "if women acquired higher education, they would recognize the innumerable injustices they have tolerated and would call men to account" (78). Although to this point Holst had deployed "justice" and "rights" to refer solely to education, the term "injustices" here implies other inequities. That she initiated this discussion and swiftly shifted to another topic is significant in and of itself.

Holst's writerly resistance to elaborating specific political and civic injustices refers us to her fear of being regarded as a revolutionary, particularly by male reviewers. At the same time, silence can work subversively to impart meaning. In her discussion of women novelists' deliberate silence, Susan Lanser notes that "some of the most oppositional voices women novelists created in the second half of the eighteenth century are strategized not simply as speech but as staged self-silencing: ...a rejection of gendered conventions through a willful refusal to narrate" (41). Once Holst posited the notion of an expanding collectivity of thoroughly educated women, "staged self-silencing" could either mask or invite the potential for rebellion that her thesis suggests.

Cautious as she was, however, certain topics incited reviewer alarm. For example, Holst, like Hippel, recognized the power of Biblical misinterpretation to undermine woman, and she presented countering interpretations of Adam and Eve, and of the words of Moses, Jesus, and Paul. That this two-page discussion attracted more hostile reviewer remarks than any of her other arguments points not only to the expected adherence to the doctrine of separate spheres, but to the narrow boundaries set for female argumentation.

> One is astonished to hear the author's claim that "the story of the Creation is a childish fable".... This freethinking is likely here, as in the case of many who brazenly deny the Revelation and Christianity, the result of deficient knowledge of religion (*Kaiserlich-Privilegirte*: 12).

Hippel took far greater liberties than Holst in Biblical interpretation, yet the most hostile reviewers did not wave the scandal scepter at Hippel's radical departure from accepted doctrine.

Although Holst maneuvered cautiously in assuming a heterogeneous audience, her introduction to friendly women readers as internal narratees enabled her to put forth her most subversive claims. From the first page she established this relationship of collective defensiveness: "Men have dared draw the lines and domains of knowledge beyond which our minds may not cross" (17). At chapter openings and endings she invoked the collective "we" to take up "our" cause and she warned her female reader "friends" that those who denigrated women should not be taken lightly. While she encouraged her women readers in a comradely register to seek serious education, she also invited them to share her vexation.

The targets of her anger constitute strategic choices. Aside from the philanthropinists, she named only Rousseau, Jakob Mauvillon, Ernst Brandes, and Karl Pockels. Left unnamed are the contemporary German "greats": Herder, Kant, Wilhelm von Humboldt, Goethe, and Schiller, all of whom adhered to the doctrine that women are intellectually incapable of, or disinclined to engage in, abstract speculation, reasoning, or investigation of truth. The opening line of her text—"So much has recently been written about female destiny"—could as easily have been addressed to them as it was to Pockels and Brandes. One can speculate that Holst strategically refrained from identifying these thinkers in order not to alienate male reviewers, and perhaps even female readers. Or her silence could indicate genuine homage, an according of greater weight to genius than to ideology on women. Perhaps she hoped that her incorporation of women into the neohumanistic theory of education that these figures supported would prove flatteringly persuasive. Pointed rhetorical questions, however, appear designed to shame the distinguished as well as the pedestrian: "Do our minds function according to other laws of logic, do they grasp things in the outside world differently than those of men? Just who would desire and dare to make such claims?" (19).

Holst elected the more plebeian figure of Pockels as a convenient target and inserted his lengthy narrative invective on a learned woman's failure to fulfill spousal, maternal, and housewifely responsibilities as a vehicle for colorful intertextual reading. Pockels's bombastic narrative epitomizes popular misogynist writers:

> A so-called learned woman is and remains either a laughable or an adverse creature. Something is either not right about her learning, or...there's something not right about her as a woman. And so as a woman she's a Nonwoman, something monstrous, and if this is what nature has made her, she deserves only to be gaped at, and certainly never admired (70).

By punctuating Pockels's narrative with critical commentary, Holst formulated a dialogical debate and set her readers up to be awakened to injustice, as well as amusedly offended.[24]

Although Holst specifically exhorted women to pursue their education and to be alert to misogynistic obstruction, it would be shortsighted to imagine a strictly female audience. Holst's "quiet revolution" could not easily be effected without male support, and she takes care to present the ways husbands and fathers (in addition to son-pupils) stood to gain. Particular narratives that speak to negligent paternal care are indirectly addressed to an implied male audience.

Ironically, the philanthropinists' investment in the paternal educator conjoined with particular societal changes that empowered Holst to professionalize the maternal educator. As Karin Hausen notes, gendered characteristics (*Geschlechtscharaktere*) defined parent-children relationships in this era. While the mother, defined as feeling, was responsible for early childhood socialization and for stabilizing the child through her love, "[t]he exclusive responsibility of the mother for the child's welfare...ends as soon as training in the desire to succeed and deal with reality make their appearance on the educational agenda. Now the man, defined by nature as rationality, assumes an active paternal function" (74). The philanthropinists drew on the doctrine of sexual differences in character to expand the father's educative role in the home and the neighborhood. Between the 1770s, when the early philanthropinists published, and Holst's 1802 publication, however, German middle-class men had become increasingly committed to commercial enterprises and bureaucratic service outside the home. Most urban families turned to schools. Few educationists had, like Holst, perceived this shift as opening a space for women to become more educated in order to fill the educative role. Holst's expansion of the maternal educator as instructor in all academic disciplines can thus be viewed as a radical assumption of previously male responsibility. Further, her maternal educator could teach coeducational groups (socially acceptable if within the parameters of the home), unlike teachers in institutional settings.

Within this frame of decreasing fatherly presence, Holst did not, however, exonerate fathers from caretaking responsibilities. Invoking Pockels as a convenient foil, she derailed his derogatory account of a learned mother with her own narrative of a learned father. When the man's wife falls ill, he fails to notice and fetch a doctor; bewildered at the news of her death he, as a member "of the class of beautiful minds" (*der Klasse der schönen Geister*), recovers to compose a praiseworthy history of her life. Until he can find a second wife, he must undertake household management and childrearing. An expert on how Persians and Spartans raised their children, he is incapable of imparting culture to his own. When his house goes up in flames, he rushes to save his manuscripts before thinking about his children. Ever invested in his own poetic skill, however, he nabs this opportunity to compose an eloquent elegy and thus display his sublime feelings to the world (71-73).

While Holst's narrative parodies attacks on the learned mother, it also plots male inadequacy and dramatizes the need for paternal engagement in childrearing. By embracing a hybridity of forms and genres, including rhetorical exposition, dialogical point-counterpoint debate, counter plots, and alternative narratives, Holst subtly shifted address to convince both friendly and resistant audiences, and she cast her thesis accordingly.

Holst further strategically addressed a heterogeneous audience by placing the theoretical question of woman's mental capacity into a comparative historical framework. She descriptively embellished the catalog argument, standard in earlier Enlightenment works on women's education, to demonstrate that women's ability to achieve on an intellectual plane was clear from the annals of history, as was the evidence of women's ability to govern.[25] In this era when the men of science—anatomists, anthropologists, and doctors—increasingly affirmed complementarian claims, Holst underscored the point that despite obstacles to their education, women's outstanding intellectual achievements controverted complementarian theory that ascribed mental ability and talent to gender.[26]

In clearly demonstrating the speciousness of complementarian arguments, Holst likely hoped to alter readers' views. Perhaps she did, in the case of readers who read her work in spite of reviewers' remarks. And perhaps her work was a validating addition to the library of contemporary feminists. But as for reviewers, debating the truth or merits of complementarianism was far too threatening. Most, as seen in previous examples and in the following, impugned her *ad hominem*:

> I find myself in the situation in which one always finds oneself with an intellectually gifted woman; one does not tire of listening, although what one hears does not always appear worthy of approval according to reason. I must break off here, as this makes me so cross (*Hamburg und Altona Zeitschrift*: 101).

> About the author one can guess that she has come so far in the laudable business of developing her mind...that her aim is to charm gallant men by showing off her immature intellect and to hear flattery at the expense of pure truth (*Kaiserlich-Privilegirte*: 12).

By thus evoking the scandalous nature of a woman writer's character, reviewers did not need to engage in argumentation in order to effectively dismiss and de-authorize her text.

Particularly disturbing to male readers may have been Holst's discussion of alternate destinies for single women. Unlike the many writers who ignored the ranks of single women in their articulation of woman's maternal destiny, Holst acknowledged this growing demographic group in her final chapter, "Über die Bildung des Weibes im ehelosen Stande" (On the Education of Unmarried Women). Here, in offering reasons for their high numbers, she alluded not only to the high costs of maintaining a household that legitimately prohibited some men from marrying, but to male "freethinking" (*Freidenkerei*) which, she claimed, had debased the sanctity of marriage. Although these observations are embedded in a discussion of single women, Holst, like Wollstonecraft, called for male reform in her condemnation of male indulgence in luxury, self-interested spending, and fulfillment of sensual pleasure. Excluded from the tripartite role (mother, wife, household manager) without benefit of support for alternate destinies, unmarried women had little recourse but to become dependent on relatives' good will and homes where, she observed, they too easily fell prey to the ills accompanying idleness.

Holst's solution is sweeping and visionary in its implications for women's collective future. Once all women are ensured a thorough education, talented single women could, and should, become teachers—a far cry from the philanthropinists' answer to struggling single women: "It seems to me that this [teaching] is more honorable than to support oneself with handiwork, which is the advice Herr Campe recommends for women in need" (94). By thus inscribing the learned single woman teacher into a wider maternal educative function, Holst also inscribed society as an extension of the family, drawing metaphorically on domestic ideology to justify "world citizenship." Such a woman, she wrote, can become a citizen of the world (*Weltbürgerin*) "only through knowledge. She regards all of mankind as her family; ...the children entrusted to her become her own. To her they owe not their physical, but their moral existence" (135). Meaningful intellectual and societal engagement is critical for all women, both married and single, she wrote, and it is this engagement that could empower women to transform society at large.

In an earlier chapter Holst discussed women teachers and governesses as figures whose "contributions extend across generations to come" (94). From remarks such as this and her closing comments on the importance of intellectual and educative engagement to societal transformation, a reflexive hope can be intuited, one that speaks to the potential for the text itself to educate and have an impact on future generations of women. In the case of Holst's treatise, this was not to be, for to reach a target audience of potentially interested women, the work could not be marketable without passing the scrutiny of male reviewers threatened by claims to gender intellectual equality. To what extent Holst might have more openly addressed woman's role as a subversive agent of reason and republicanism, had she not been writing in the era of conservative reaction, cannot of course be known. It is hoped that this discussion of Holst's text and its reception conveys a story of its own about one woman's valiant effort to creatively adapt the range of rhetorical weapons available to her and win a sympathetic reading for the imperative of *Bildung* for women. Situating her text within its specific historic moment of production, we see that to be a voice for educational emancipation, no matter how strategically constructed, was, simply, scandalous.

Notes

With the exception of the quotation by Karin Hausen, all translations are my own.

[1] Theremin argues weakly for women's education in *De la condition des femmes dans les républiques* (1799); Staël calls for equality in the education of men and women in one line of *De la littérature* (Book II, ch. iv); Hays' and Robinson's treatises are far more strident and detailed, Hays in her *Appeal to the Men of Great Britain,* Robinson in *Thoughts on the Condition of Women.* Arguments over content between Ehrmann and the

publisher of her first periodical, *Amaliens Erholungsstunden* (1790–92), compelled her to move publication for her short-lived second, *Die Einsiedlerin in den Alpen* (1793–94).

[2] Prior to this reprinting, edited by Bertha Rahm, the earliest mention of Holst is in Lange and Bäumer's 1901 publication (15–16). Jacoby's 1911 publication offers the earliest extensive research effort (21–60). Since the 1984 reprinting, Holst has been mentioned by Becker-Cantarino 33–34; Honegger 29–30; Schiebinger; and Schmid 340–41. These contributions, along with Rahm's extensive *Vorwort* and *Nachwort,* attend to Holst, rather than her pedagogy, as feminist. The most recent efforts to incorporate discussion of her pedagogy are Spitzer (163–83) and Felden (152–69). Though Kersting includes a chapter on women's education, she does not discuss texts of women educators. Albisetti does not mention Holst in his excellent scholarship on girls' schooling, most likely because information about her schools is not extant.

[3] The philanthopinists emphasized education in the interest of service and duty to the state, and though they overturned class-based strictures by promoting advancement of male students according to merit, most did not waver in their commitment to separate spheres for men and women. They endorsed a restricted education for girls to age ten on the basis of a girl's "natural" fixed role in the domestic sphere. The most renowned of their theorists, Joachim Campe, authored *Väterlicher Rat an meine Tochter* (1789), "das populärste zeitgenössische Buch über Mädchenbildung" (Schmid 331). Part complementarian exposition, part conduct book, this text links woman's domestic destiny to her utilitarian role in the state. By the time of Holst's writing, the utilitarian thrust of the philanthropinist movement was losing currency to the neohumanist movement.

The aim of neohumanist *Bildung* was to mold the autonomous, wise, and worldly individual. Proponents viewed children's preparation to assume social and civic identities as "citizens" (*Bürger*) as an intrusion on children's "ennoblement" as individual human beings. Neohumanist pedagogical writings gender the ideal human being as male and postulate males as both recipients and purveyors of their educational program. Women are simply omitted. Those who also authored works on gender differences, such as Wilhelm von Humboldt, drew on essentialist notions in line with Idealist and Romantic thought, assigning woman's essence to her maternal spirit (*Muttergeist*) and to a receptive, emotional nature that complements male activity and intellect.

[4] This has been treated more extensively for the French. See Landes and Gutwirth. On Germans, see Zantop.

[5] "Da werden Weiber zu Hyänen / Und treiben mit Entsetzen Scherz;

/ Noch zuckend, mit des Panthers Zähnen / Zerreißen sie des Feindes Herz" (lines 366–69; complete verse lines 362–81). Lines 116–130, given girls to memorize, begin, "Und drinnen waltet / Die züchtige Hausfrau / Die Mutter der Kinder, / Und herrschet weise, / Im häuslichen Kreise" (lines 116–20; complete verse lines 88–132). See Zantop for a full discussion of the theme of revolution as female transgression in Schiller's poem (223–24), as well as in the literary works of other German writers of the period.

[6] The *Damen-Conversations-Lexikon* of 1846 mentions Holst having been awarded the doctor of philosophy ("Ihre ausgezeichneten Verdienste wurden in ihrem hohen Alter durch die Promotion zur Doktorin der Philosophie von der Universität zu Kiel öffentlich anerkannt": cited in Rahm, *Vorwort*); otherwise there is no evidence of the degree. Jacoby reports having inquired at the Universität Kiel in 1911 and been told, "dass es nicht möglich gewesen sei, die Promotionsakten der Jahre 1790–1802 aufzufinden" (7). It remains unclear whether she earned the title of doctor or received it as the wife of Dr. Holst.

[7] On von Justi's *Vorschlag von Errichtung einer Akademie für das Frauenzimmer* and *Vorschlag von Errichtung eines weiblichen Schöpfenstuhls in Ergetzungen der Vernünftigen Seele aus der Sittenlehre und der Gelehrsamkeit überhaupt* (1765–68), see Petschauer 264–67 and Rahm 160–63.

[8] See especially Rahm, Jacoby, Felden, Spitzer. Of Holst's mother nothing is known, other than that she was von Justi's second wife and bore six children, of whom Amalia was the eldest (Rahm, Nachwort 160). Her father's last three years were spent in prison on an ostensibly false accusation of having embezzled state funds. The family dispersed: Amalia's mother to an uncle in Braunschweig, her brothers to a Danish cadet school, her younger sisters to a charity school in Potsdam. Of Amalia's adolescence and young adulthood, no information has been uncovered.

[9] Albisetti details the unstable conditions for initiating and operating private schools for girls (30–36). Käthner and Kleinau discuss the difficulty of obtaining information about eighteenth- and early nineteenth-century girls' schools (394–96).

[10] Schieth presents a convincing argument that *Elisa, oder das Weib wie es seyn sollte* was male-authored.

[11] For an overview of the arguments against the philanthropinists in *Bemerkungen* and in support of female autonomy in "Briefe über *Elisa*" see Spitzer (172–74). Von Felden cogently presents Holst's trajectory from that of educator enamored with the foundations of Rousseau's pedagogy to a radicalized position against Rousseau (160–84).

[12] Little information about Holst's life follows the 1802 publication of *Über die Bestimmung*: it appears that she separated from her husband, as in 1807 she was registered in Wittenberg and later operated a pension in

Parchim, while he remained registered in Hamburg. In 1823, she moved to a son near Boitzenberg, where she died six years later.

[13] See Blackwell; Bovenschen; Cocalis; Sotiropoulos, "*Pomona, für Teutschlands Töchter*"; Weckel.

[14] For example, Sophie von La Roche (especially in her periodical *Pomona* [1781–82]); Marianne Ehrmann (especially in her periodical *Amaliens Erholungsstunden* [1790–92]); Betty Gleim.

[15] Leporin (Erxleben) was the first woman to be awarded a medical degree (1751). Holst reports that she learned of Leporin's feminist treatise *Gründliche Untersuchung der Ursachen, die das weibliche Geschlecht vom Studiren abhalten* (1742) in a biography by Leporin's stepson and laments in *Über die Bestimmung* that Leporin's treatise was no longer available (49–50).

[16] Purver aptly comments: "Far from attempting to dismantle them [cultural barriers to female emancipation] after that event [the Revolution], the leading intellectual authorities of the age—including, besides Schiller and Humboldt, the philosophers Kant and Fichte—sought to entrench them still further by underwriting as permanent the socially conditioned dependence characteristic of late eighteenth-century German women's lives" (70).

[17] Nipperdey addresses dramatic increases in poverty rates in Bremen and other German regions (192), caused in part by the levying of troops and the heavy tax burden (17). Gleim concurs with Fichte in the abstract in openly responding to his proposal to educate the current generation far from their corrupt homes: "Das beste wäre freilich, Fichte'ns Rath zu befolgen, die Kinder von ihren Eltern zu trennen" (2: 151). But tactfully insisting that the state has no right to forcibly impose such separation or to deny children parental love, she recommends a pragmatic plan. Fichte's charged rhetoric claiming German as the sole living and uncorrupted language spills into Gleim's rationale for elevating German over all other languages. While the movement to elevate German as a literary language is traceable to Gottsched's poetics and to Herder's view that language forms collective character, it operated under the Napoleonic occupation as a kind of psychological warfare. A typical rhetorical question Gleim poses, such as "Ist nicht erste Bedingung alles Glücks Freiheit und Unabhängigkeit?" (1: 22), can be understood to mean either intellectual or political emancipation. Other remarks, however, betray an agenda that links the language of oppression to wider political protests: "Der gebildete Mensch allein kann sich in den meisten Lagen seines Lebens unabhängig erhalten, unabhängig wenigstens von der Macht, dem Druck, dem Despotismus anderer Menschen" (1: 21).

[18] Page numbers of quotations from Holst's treatise refer to Rahm's 1984 edition.

[19] For further discussion of the importance of the "maternal argument" to the debate on women's education, see Badinter and Bannet; for specific discussion of Hippel's omission of the maternal argument, see Sotiropoulos, *Frictions, Fictions, and Forms*. Hippel's *Verbesserung* neither engendered any imitations, nor sold sufficient copies to warrant a second printing.

[20] Rahm writes, "Ich bin überzeugt, dass Amalia Holst die Bücher, mindestens den Namen der Engländerin kannte (aus den Büchern von Meiners, Pockels, usw.). Dass sie ihn in ihrem Werk nicht nennt, beruht wohl eher darauf, weil sie die Damen und Herren nicht reizen wollte oder der Verleger ihn strich" (158).

[21] "[E]in gelehrtes Weib, im eigentlichen Sinne des Wortes, ist an sich weder human, noch weise, noch liebenswürdig.... Alle gelehrten Frauen...sind und bleiben Anomalien.... Gelehrsamkeit, im eigentlichen Verstande, ist ein Gewerbe, welches die Natur dem Manne bestimmt zu haben scheint; das Weib hat bei den Pflichten, welche ihm die Natur und die WEIBLICHKEIT aufgelegt haben, nicht Zeit dazu. Will das Weib eine Gelehrte von Profeßion seyn, so muss es auf den Namen der Gattin und Mutter und noch mehr der HAUSFRAU Verzicht leisten.... [E]s will männer-ähnlich die gefahrvollen Schranken des Ruhms und des Wissens durchbrechen. Himmlische Liebe und ihr treuen Begleiterinnen derselben, ihr Grazien, verhütet diese traurige Katastrophe!"

[22] Salons were run, for example, by Sophie Mereau, Caroline Schlegel-Schelling, Dorothea Veit, Henriette Herz, and Rahel Varnhagen. Mereau attended Fichte's university lectures.

[23] "Wie ist es dann möglich, daß Schriftsteller, welche über die weibliche Bestimmung geschrieben haben, weit mehr gegen die seltene Ausnahme eifern, daß ein gelehrtes Weib, ihrer Bestimmung ungetreu, ihre Pflichten als Mutter vernachläßigt, als gegen die tausende, welche dies wegen der oben erwähnten Fälle der Unwissenheiten und der nicht unter dem Zepter einer gebildeten Vernunft stehenden Leidenschaften tun. Woher mag dies wohl kommen?" (112–13).

[24] A brief example of one of her responses suffices: "Mit welchen aftergelehrten Weibern, mag denn ein Unstern die Verfasser zusammengeführt hat, mir ist eine solche nie bekannt worden" (69).

[25] The "catalog argument," a subgenre deployed to prove woman's intellectual and leadership capacities, ranged from lists of great women throughout history to mini-narratives of select women rulers, artists, and scientists. Between 1641 and 1740 both women (e.g., Anna van Schurmann, Dorothea Leporin) and men (e.g., Karl Paullini, Johann Eberti) deployed the catalog argument (and later, La Roche in 1782, Condorcet in 1791, Hippel in 1792). Shortly after Holst's publication, Mary Hays published a

six-volume catalog work (1803) that included the lives and works of more than 288 Greek, Roman, European, and British women.

[26] For a thorough discussion on the role of "men of science" in this debate, see Schiebinger, esp. 214-44.

Works Cited

Albisetti, James C. *Schooling German Girls and Women: Secondary and Higher Education in the Nineteenth Century*. Princeton: Princeton UP, 1988.

Badinter, Elisabeth. *Mother Love: Myth and Reality, Motherhood in Modern History*. New York: Macmillan, 1981. Trans. of *L'Amour en plus*. Paris: Flammarion, 1980.

Bannet, Eve Tavor. *The Domestic Revolution: Enlightenment Feminisms and the Novel*. Baltimore: Johns Hopkins UP, 2000.

Basedow, Johann. *Elementarwerk*. 1774. Hildesheim: Olms, 1972.

Becker-Cantarino, Barbara. *Schriftstellerinnen der Romantik: Epoche-Werke-Wirkung*. München: C.H. Beck, 2000.

Blackwell, Jeannine. "Weibliche Gelehrsamkeit oder die Grenzen der Toleranz: Die Fälle Karsch, Naubert und Gottsched." *Lessing und die Toleranz: Beiträge zur vierten Internationalen Konferenz der Lessing Society 1985*. Detroit: Wayne State UP, 1986. 325-30.

Bovenschen, Silvia. *Die imaginierte Weiblichkeit: Exemplarische Untersuchungen zur kulturgeschichtlichen und literarischen Präsentationen des Weiblichen*. Frankfurt a.M.: Suhrkamp, 1979.

Campe, Joachim. *Väterlicher Rat an meine Tochter*. 1789. Paderborn: Hüttemann, 1988.

Cocalis, Susan L. "Der Vormund will Vormund sein: Zur Problematik der weiblichen Unmündigkeit im 18. Jahrhundert." *Amsterdamer Beiträge zur neueren Germanistik* 10 (1980): 33-55.

Condorcet, Nicholas Caritat, Marquis de. *Sur l'admission des femmes au droit de cité*. 1790. Oeuvres. Ed. A. Condorcet O'Connor and M.F. Arago. Paris: Firmin Didot, 1847. Vol. 10. 121-30.

———. *Sur l'instruction publique. Premier mémoire: Nature et objet de l'instruction publique*. 1791. Oeuvres. Vol. 7. 169-218.

Dauzenroth, Erich. *Kleine Geschichte der Mädchenbildung: Der verbotene Baum oder Die Erziehung des anderen Geschlechts*. Ratingen: A. Henn, 1971.

Ehrmann, Marianne. *Amaliens Erhohlungsstunden*. Stuttgart: Verlag der Expedition des Beobachters, 1790-92. Sankt Augustin: Academie Verlag, 1998.

Fay, Elizabeth A. *A Feminist Introduction to Romanticism.* Malden, MA: Blackwell, 1998.
Felden, Heide von. *Die Frauen und Rousseau: Die Rousseau-Rezeption zeitgenössischer Schriftstellerinnen in Deutschland.* Frankfurt a.M.: Campus, 1997.
Gleim, Betty. *Erziehung und Unterricht des weiblichen Geschlechts.* 1810. Leipzig: J.G. Göschen. Rpt.: Beas, 1997.
Gutwirth, Madelyn. *Twilight of the Goddesses: Women and Representation in the French Revolutionary Era.* New Brunswick: Rutgers UP, 1992.
Hamburg und Altona, Eine Zeitschrift zur Geschichte der Zeit, der Sitten und des Geschmacks. 1802. Ed. Franz H. Nestler. 95–102. Rpt. Jacoby, *Beiträge zur deutschen Literaturgeschichte des achtzehnten Jahrhunderts.* 50–58.
Hausen, Karin. "Family and Role-Division: The Polarisation of Sexual Stereotypes in the Nineteenth Century—an Aspect of the Dissociation of Work and Family Life." Trans. Cathleen Catt. *The German Family: Essays on the Social History of the Family in Nineteenth- and Twentieth-Century Germany.* Ed. Richard J. Evans and W.R. Lee. London: Croom Helm, 1981. 51–75.
Hays, Mary. *Appeal to the Men of Great Britain in Behalf of Women.* 1798. New York: Garland, 1974.
———. *Female Biography; or Memoirs of Illustrious and Celebrated Women of All Ages and Countries, Alphabetically Arranged.* London: Richard and Phillips, 1803.
Herder, Johann Gottfried. *Herders Briefwechsel mit Caroline Flachsland, nach den Handschriften des Goethe- und Schillerarchivs.* Vol. 1. Ed. Hans Schauer. Weimar: Verlag der Goethe-Gesellschaft, 1926–28.
Hippel, Theodor Gottlieb von. *Über die bürgerliche Verbesserung der Weiber.* 1792. Ed. Ralph-Rainer Wuthenow. Frankfurt a.M.: Syndikat Autoren- und Verlags-Gesellschaft, 1977.
Holst, Amalia von Justi. *Bemerkungen über die Fehler unserer modernen Erziehung von einer praktischen Erzieherinn.* Leipzig: Johann Gottwerth Müller, 1791.
———. "Briefe über *Elisa, oder das Weib wie es seyn sollte.*" *A. Lindemann's Musarion.* 1. Brief: Bd. 1 (1799), H. 4, 345–61; 2. Brief: Bd. 1 (1799), H. 5, 30–52; 3. Brief: Bd. 2 (1800), H. 7, 213–27; 4. Brief: Bd. 2 (1800), H. 8, 326–34.
———. *Über die Bestimmung des Weibes zur höheren Geistesbildung.* 1802. Zürich: ALA, 1984.
Honegger, Claudia. *Die Ordnung der Geschlechter: Die Wissenschaften vom Menschen und das Weib 1750–1850.* Frankfurt a.M.: Campus, 1991.

Jacoby, Karl S. *Beiträge zur deutschen Literaturgeschichte des achtzehnten Jahrhunderts.* Hamburg: Lütcke u. Wulff, 1911.

Kaes, Anton. "New Historicism and the Study of German Literature." *German Quarterly* 62.2 (1989): 210-19.

Kaiserlich-Privilegirte Hamburgische Neue Zeitung. 34. Stück (27 Feb. 1802): 12. Rpt. in *Beiträge zur deutschen Literaturgeschichte des achtzehnten Jahrhunderts.* Ed. Karl S. Jacoby. Hamburg: Lütcke u. Wulff, 1911. 22-23.

Käthner, Martina, and Elke Kleinau. "Höhere Töchterschulen um 1800." *Geschichte der Mädchen- und Frauenbildung.* Vol. 1. Ed. Elke Kleinau and Claudia Opitz. Frankfurt a.M.: Campus, 1996. 392-408.

Kersting, Christa. *Die Genese der Pädagogik im 18. Jahrhundert: Campes Allgemeine Revision im Kontext der neuzeitlichen Wissenschaft.* Weinheim: Deutscher Studien Verlag, 1992.

Landes, Joan B. *Women and the Public Sphere in the Age of the French Revolution.* Ithaca: Cornell UP, 1988.

Lange, Helene, and Gertrud Bäumer. *Die Geschichte der Frauenbewegung in den Kulturländern.* Vol I. Berlin: W. Moeser, 1901.

Lanser, Susan Sniader. *Fictions of Authority: Women Writers and Narrative Voice.* Ithaca: Cornell UP, 1992.

La Roche, Sophie von. *Pomona, für Teutschlands Töchter.* 4 vols. Stuttgart: Speyer, 1782-84. München: KG Saur, 1987.

Leporin, Dorothea Christine (Erxleben). *Gründliche Untersuchung der Ursachen, die das weibliche Geschlecht vom Studiren abhalten.* 1742. Hildesheim: Olms, 1987.

Meiners, Christoph. *Geschichte des weiblichen Geschlechts.* Hannover: Helwing, 1788.

Naumann, Ursula. "Das Fräulein und die Blicke: Sophie von La Roche." *Zeitschrift für deutsche Philologie* 107 (1988): 489-516.

Nipperdey, Thomas. *Germany from Napoleon to Bismarck.* Princeton: Princeton UP, 1996.

Petschauer, Peter. *The Education of Women in Eighteenth-Century Germany.* Lewiston, NY: Edwin Mellen, 1989.

Pockels, Karl. *Versuch einer Charakteristik des weiblichen Geschlechts: Ein Sitten-Gemählde des Menschen, des Zeitalters, und des geselligen Lebens.* Hannover: C. Ritscher, 1797-1802.

Purver, Judith. "Revolution, Romanticism, Restoration (1789-1830)." *A History of Women's Writing in Germany, Austria and Switzerland.* Ed. Jo Catling. Cambridge: Cambridge UP, 2000. 63-87.

Rahm, Bertha. Vorwort and Nachwort. *Über die Bestimmung des Weibes zur höheren Geistesbildung.* By Amalia Holst. Zürich: ALA, 1984. 6-10, 157-64.

Robinson, Mary. *Thoughts on the Condition of Women, and on the Injustice of Mental Subordination.* London: G. Woodfall, 1799.
Schiebinger, Londa. *The Mind Has No Sex? Women in the Origins of Science.* Cambridge: Harvard UP, 1989.
Schieth, Lydia. Nachwort. *Elisa, oder das Weib wie es seyn sollte.* By Wilhelmine Karoline Wobeser. Hildesheim: Olms, 1990. 1-39.
Schiller, Friedrich. "Das Lied von der Glocke." *Schillers Werke.* Vol. 1. Ed. Ludwig Bellermann. Leipzig: Bibliographisches Institut, 1895. 245-57.
Schmid, Pia. "Weib oder Mensch, Wesen oder Wissen? Bürgerliche Theorien zur weiblichen Bildung um 1800." *Geschichte der Mädchen- und Frauenbildung.* Vol. 1. Ed. Elke Kleinau and Claudia Opitz. Frankfurt a.M.: Campus, 1996. 327-45.
Schmidt, Erich, ed. *Caroline: Briefe aus der Frühromantik.* Vol I. Leipzig: Insel, 1913.
Sotiropoulos, Carol Strauss. *Frictions, Fictions, and Forms: Woman's Coming of Age in Eighteenth-Century Educational Discourses.* Diss. U of Connecticut, 2001.
———. "*Pomona, für Teutschlands Töchter*: Sophie von La Roche as Editor, Educator, and Narrator." *Colloquia Germanica* 33.3 (2000): 213-38.
Spitzer, Elke. *Emanzipationsansprüche zwischen der Querelle des Femmes und der modernen Frauenbewegung: Der Wandel des Gleichheitsbegriffs am Ausgang des 18. Jahrhunderts.* Kassel: Kassel UP, 2002.
Staël, Germaine de. *De la littérature considérée dans ses rapports avec les institutions sociales.* 1800. Geneva: Droz, 1959.
Tewarson, Heidi Thomann. "Caroline Schlegel and Rahel Varnhagen: The Response of Two German Women to the French Revolution and its Aftermath." *Seminar: A Journal of Germanic Studies* 29.2 (1993): 106-23.
Theremin, Charles. *De la condition des femmes dans les républiques.* Paris: Chez Laran, 1799.
Weckel, Ulrike. *Zwischen Häuslichkeit und Öffentlichkeit: Die ersten deutschen Frauenzeitschriften im späten achtzehnten Jahrhundert und ihr Publikum.* Tübingen: Max Niemeyer, 1998.
Wobeser, Wilhelmine Karoline von. *Elisa, oder das Weib wie es seyn sollte.* 1795. Hildesheim, Olms, 1990.
Wollstonecraft, Mary. *A Vindication of the Rights of Woman.* 1792. Ed. Carol H. Poston. New York: W.W. Norton, 1988.
Zantop, Susanne. "Crossing the Border: The French Revolution in the German Imagination." *Representing the French Revolution.* Ed. James A.W. Heffernan. Hanover, NH: UP of New England, 1992. 213-36.

The Hidden Face of Narcissus: Suicide as Poetic Speech in Margarethe von Trotta's Early Films

Eva Kuttenberg

Internationally acclaimed filmmaker Margarethe von Trotta has inspired astute, psychoanalytically informed scholarship that uniformly shies away from analyzing the taboo act that distinguishes three of her early films. *Sisters, or the Balance of Happiness, Marianne and Juliane,* and *Sheer Madness* are subtle portrayals of female suicides. Von Trotta's nuanced stagings of suicidal depression, fantasies, attempts, and postsuicide trauma; blunt depictions of the female corpse as monstrous feminine; and emphasis on the impact of silenced mothers on their daughters invite critics to question her rigorous use of suicide as an aesthetic strategy. This essay comparing and contrasting the three films draws on Julia Kristeva's seminal work *Black Sun* (1989) to uncover subplots and read suicide as a means to enhance or rupture power constellations written by paternal law. (EK)

Peace bought with such sacrifices was too costly and I could no longer stand the thought of partially destroying myself in order to partially preserve myself. —Karoline von Günderrode (*Der Schatten eines Traumes*)

My passage would always be death and not an island in the South Sea. I would extinguish myself, and not try to find paradise elsewhere. —Margarethe von Trotta (Interview with Heike Mundzeck[1])

Among feminist scholars, Margarethe von Trotta's critically acclaimed films *Sisters, or the Balance of Happiness* (1979), *Marianne and Juliane* (1981), and *Sheer Madness* (1982)[2] have been controversial, seen as undermining a feminist agenda by drawing on the codes of a patriarchal system. However, when it comes to suicidology, the study of suicide, von Trotta's agenda is distinctly feminist, as when the survivor (in *Sheer Madness* coterminous with the victim) fills the void by telling the victim's story and thereby imitates Teresa de Lauretis's action in *Alice Doesn't: Feminism, Semiotics, Cinema,* recuperating women from silence. By linking femininity to suicide, von Trotta steps back into late nineteenth-century thought when suicide was the only form of violence accessible to women; however, she anticipates de Lauretis's question: "What happens...when woman serves as the looking glass held up to women?" (6, 7), and depicts women reinventing themselves to fight suicidal depression.

Unabashedly, von Trotta catches suicidal aggressors in action and maps their intricate narcissistic crises. Creating a psychoanalytic montage, she draws on literature, mythology, music, and politics to show the complexity of melancholic depression as the hidden face of narcissism. Her cinematic trilogy progresses from characters' succumbing to suicide as ultimate regression to overcoming suicidal depression that is marked by dislocation of speech. Moreover, she takes the traditional perception of suicide—as an act that collapses meaning and established systems of order—a step further, and depicts the trauma that it engenders.

Von Trotta subtly portrays the female psyche caught in a patriarchal discourse oscillating between a need for self-expression—vehemently defending her difference—and violent rage when realizing her powerlessness. In her favorite and most personal film,[3] *Sisters,* a compelling emotionally and economically symbiotic relationship between two sisters lasts until suicide parts them, only to reunite them inadvertently through postsuicide trauma. Investigating the alleged suicide of her imprisoned terrorist sister becomes the life goal of the survivor in *Marianne and Juliane.* A suicide attempt triggers an intense friendship between two very different women in *Sheer Madness,* a film that concludes not with a suicide but with an imaginary murder. Except for the self-slaughter of Marianne's husband, von Trotta's cinematographic suicides exemplify female transgressions of and resistance to a patriarchal discourse. These women more or less successfully seek alternatives to the tradition of submission exemplified by their mothers.[4] A seemingly clear-cut power dynamic between protagonists, suggesting, "I perform, therefore I am," and antagonists, claiming, "I control, therefore I am," spins out of control as characters unleash their rage in actual, imaginary, or alleged suicide attempts, traumatizing siblings and partners who then either replace the suicide victim or push the survivors firmly back into the position initially carved out for them. To defend their nonrepressed state as subjects in crisis, the characters must subvert meaning, challenge established systems of authority and order, and become anarchic. And, as Julia Kristeva states, "anarchy is the nonrepressed state of subjectivity and constitutes a permanent state of functioning" (Guberman 37); the narcissist becomes coterminous with the anarchist (Moi 158).

Von Trotta calls the corpse as a finite entity into question, using it to construct pivotal cinematographic moments when it reemerges in the survivor's imagination or is blatantly depicted as a real horror. Either survivor and film viewer stare at the corpse, or the viewer witnesses how the survivor cannot bear to look. Inclusion or exclusion from this most abject experience is given an interesting spin in *Sheer Madness,* where the viewer is privileged to see Ruth's suicide fantasies—a perspective denied to her husband, who triggers them. The distinct real or imaginary presence of the corpse prompts survivors to reexamine parameters of their value system and thus marks a "border" (Oliver 233) between self-reflection and self-destruction. It is surprising that long-overdue monographs, such as Renate Hehr's *Margarethe von Trotta: Filmmaking as Liberation* (2000) and Thilo Wydra's *Filmen, um zu überleben* (*Filmmaking as Survival,* 2000), mention von Trotta's subtle portrayals of suicide only in passing. Similarly, Peter Buchka's inspiring interview film *Never Stop Being Curious* (1995) illustrates her interest in female identity, German romanticism, and psychoanalysis, but not her preoccupation with suicide.

Von Trotta makes visual Kristeva's observations on depression and melancholia as "the hidden side of narcissism" (*Black Sun* 5) and illustrates narcissism as not merely a self-cohesive but also an isolating and subsequently self-destructive endeavor turning the body, engulfed by "cannibalistic solitude," into a "tomb" (*Black Sun* 71). In *Sisters, Marianne and Juliane,* and *Sheer Madness,* relationships are based on needs both participants create to feel needed; characters are caught in what Kristeva calls a "subject-in-process drifting between a position that would deconstruct subjectivity and identity altogether and one that would try to capture these entities in an essentialist mold" (Moi 13). The modern subject, Kristeva argues, ought not to be fixed and stabilized but turned into a work of progress able to express itself (Moi 14). Through suicide, a most violent form of expression, characters resist a too-rigid concept of "self" (Moi 14) that forces them to live up to the expectations of others. Von Trotta's drifters in ill-balanced relationships dramatically respond: dreamy Anna turns into a suicide (*Sisters*), Papa's darling Marianne into a rebel with a cause (*Marianne and Juliane*), and the housewife Ruth, nicknamed *Rehlein* (little deer), into a murderer (*Sheer Madness*).

Female suicide is intimately linked to the body as a stage on which to enact violence, to the psyche mapping narcissism and melancholia, and to a full spectrum of speech acts from silence to screams. Interested in connecting "lived experience and the language in which we articulate that experience" (Oliver xxii), the filmmaker explores linguistic and artistic modes of female self-expression that seek to defy the status of woman as lifeless fetish[5] in a patriarchal society. From a psychoanalytic point of view, suicide constitutes an extremely short-lived moment of authentic speech reconnecting "soma" and "psyche." Margaret Higonnet suggests that suicide may ultimately become for a woman the only available means of speaking or acting that allows her to break out of her muteness and away from patronizing relationships. For Higonnet, "suicide both sets a limit and opens up a gap" ("Frames of Female Suicide" 229) and enables certain questions about how we construct a self as well as a literary or cinematographic narrative. In German literature, it "provokes narrative" (Higonnet 230) and is a common theme, whereas in the visual arts it figures less prominently.[6]

Among the exceptions is the work of Austrian avant-garde filmmaker Valie Export, who explored complex contingencies of female identity in *Menschenfrauen (Humanwomen,* 1979), the story of Franz, involved with a wife and three lovers, one of whom commits suicide by electrocution.[7] The suicide victim, Gertrud Lehner, has been systematically silenced in her public and private life: she lost custody of her daughter, was forced out of her job, and was left by her lover. Immediately before her suicide attempt, Gertrud drinks water from a river; suddenly, an image is blended in that shows her drinking out of a toilet, making visual Kristeva's radical rejection of the self, a transition from object to nonobject to abject (Oliver 232). To the soundtrack of a voice repeating, "Even outside, I lived the life of a prisoner," Gertrud submerges an audiotape and a candle in a river—a gesture that invites several interpretations. She may be getting rid of a tape of phone messages from her former lover, leaving a blank tape ready to be recorded by others, or symbolically silencing her voice to signal her displacement while preserving her body (soon-to-be corpse) as the testament of her muteness. As she climbs up a high-tension pole to grab the power line, she calls for her mother, and conjures up an uncanny suicide vision in which she plays the piano next to dolls and a suicide victim dangling from a rope. Apparently, her mother, who denied her a room of her own as a child and is largely mute throughout the film, is the target of Gertrud's suicide. In addition to her unusual death, which makes headlines in the newspaper and temporarily gives her a voice, suicidal characters speak in a scene in a hospital room where a bank robber, a prostitute, and a mother, all of whom survived their suicide attempts, reveal their motives. In *Menschenfrauen,* intense female bonding is portrayed as equally transgressive behavior. Thus Export avoids conventional cinematic vision, yet plots suicide as a clinical case study, laying out motive and method, whereas von Trotta embeds it in a linear narrative.[8]

Fictional stagings of suicide grant the victim, who has plunged into deliberate absence, a continuous presence through interpretation and reconstruction. In *The Acoustic Mirror: The Female Voice in Psychoanalysis and Cinema,* Kaja Silverman argues that in feminist film practice, the female voice is often shown to coexist with the female body only at the price of its impoverishment and entrapment (141). Von Trotta challenges this expression of female corporeality by juxtaposing suicidal characters draping their bodies in flowing dresses with self-confident women in tight outfits. The female body is subtly rendered in the living corpses of wives condemned to silence in a patriarchal society. She implicitly critiques Maurice Blanchot, for whom suicide is a deceptive mastery of death, and challenges his assertion that the language of suicide is ultimately the language of simulation.[9] While women undeniably rehearse their bodily demise, it is from acute awareness of their role-play imposed by a social order. Their suicide is a dramatic way to stop simulating.

Suicides revert to a language that is partially safeguarded in the subconscious and thus allows them to survive in a world in which they feel at odds. Through her characters' poetic speech, von Trotta visualizes anxieties and maps both an imaginary and imagined side of suicide. Constricted logic and dichotomous thinking characterize a suicidal mindset expressed in a language of binary oppositions between the real and the imaginary, past and present, public and private, immediate and mediated, and pragmatic and enigmatic. These contrasts create symmetry within and among the films. The duplicity of the suicidal act in collapsing victim and murderer is reinforced with visual codes that arbitrarily mark and blur boundaries between self, other, and corpse. Color images suddenly fade into black-and-white suicide fantasies; red signals subliminal aggression; mirrors become revolving doors for swapping conflicting roles, meeting grounds for casual encounters, or immediate threats to self-cohesion and disembodiment by reflecting the victim's face instead of the survivor's. Interestingly, windows mark enclosures and borders, while open windows and windowsills, which traditionally allude to the deadly leap, are largely absent. The ultimate stage for a narcissistic, hysterical performance of, as Kristeva suggests, "an inevitable, irresistible, and self-evident transition" (Moi 157), remains the female body: it either enacts difference or houses a self-imposed, narcissistic indulgence in sadness as life's sole purpose.

Women's fetal positions, as if coiled around an imaginary death, alternate with paradigmatic horizontal death positions.

Death Is Now a Welcome Guest:[10] *Sisters, or the Balance of Happiness*

An intense relationship between sisters gradually goes awry: Maria humbly assists her boss at work while financially and emotionally controlling her sister, Anna, at home and forcing her own ambitions upon her. She uses Anna as a canvas to create a replica of herself—a model of success and accomplishment. Shielding herself from Maria's assertiveness, Anna retreats to a world of dreams and falls back on her precarious mind. Unable to live out her difference and overwhelmed by an existential crisis—questioning the validity of her studies of cell regulation that inevitably erases all individuality—Anna commits suicide. In "Margarethe von Trotta's *Sisters*: Interiority or Engagement?" Anna Kuhn points to Anna's suicide as performance in the style of a *Gesamtkunstwerk* annotated with music and mirror images. In "Images in Balance," Roswitha Müller takes Kuhn's reference to Freud's death wish as her point of departure and reads Anna's suicide as a narcissistic disorder, a classic case of Freudian melancholia (70), without, however, differentiating between ambiguous self-preserving and self-destructive aspects of narcissism. In "Margarethe von Trotta's *Sisters*: Brides Under a Different Law," Janice Mouton explores the relationship between the sisters beyond the Freudian model. What still merits further analysis are Anna's systematic withdrawal from life; her narcissistic and melancholic character traits; the fact that Maria retains her boundaries by quickly averting her gaze from Anna's corpse; and the relationship between the daughters and their mute mother.

Power and control hold Maria and Anna's relationship in balance until two events pose immediate threats: Anna's upcoming final examinations in biology and subsequent financial and, presumably, emotional independence, and Maria's dating Maurice Münzinger, the son of her boss, who begins to claim Anna's place in her sister's emotional life. Instead of openly discussing this reality, the sisters study and work excessively until Anna utters a silent scream: her suicide attempt. Even as a child she would hurt herself to prevent her sister from directing her affection to others. Once again her strategy works, and immediately after Anna's suicide attempt, Maria comforts her sister by coiling her naked, warm body around her sister's pallid, corpselike one. This sisterly embrace prefigures their dance of death. Even before Maria embraces Maurice, the immediate threat to Anna's object attachment, Anna embraces herself, as if to hold the object she is about to lose.

Eager to reclaim her spot as Maria's most significant companion, Anna picks her up from work and buys her gifts. Although she promises not to harm herself, she commits suicide during the only night of intimacy between Maria and Maurice, when she symbolically fails to take the role of the lover and loses control over her loved object. Maria has succeeded in freeing herself from the confinement of Anna's melancholia; Maurice, then, is a welcome pretext for Anna to end her tormented existence. In utter despair, she cuts her veins open and thereby releases the imaginary object and anger held within herself. By turning her body into an empty vessel and inscribing herself on the floor when bleeding to death, she forces Maria to take care of her one last time. Narcissism has run riot: Anna actually watches herself dying, sitting at her desk, a pose she extensively rehearsed when falling asleep over her books.

Anna communicates her intent through an array of intertextual allusions. As if housed in Antigone's death chamber, her body gradually becomes enshrined: cloaked in loose-fitting dark clothes, trapped in her eerie room, and further enveloped by a dark apartment. Although the sisters seal their symbiotic relationship by sharing a bedroom, they lead distinctly separate public lives. Anna leaves the house only to go to classes or to visit their widowed mother in the country. On such a trip and with death on her mind, she points to the birch as the tree of life. Trees, especially the image of the forest, symbolize the bond between the sisters that originates in their childhood when Maria reads a fairy tale to Anna describing a dark forest. She clearly defines her role as active reader and that of her sister as attentive, yet silent, listener. The reappearing image of the forest as a visually coded sign for a suicide attempt alludes to William Blake's (1757–1827) painting, *The Wood of the Self-Murderers,* which poignantly illustrates Dante's *Inferno* (canto 13), where the souls of suicides are trapped in the bodies of trees so that they can do no more mischief to their flesh. Harpies rip off twigs from the branches, which subsequently bleed. Their subsequent eerie moaning is the only way the suicides can express themselves. When Anna sways back and forth, humming the melancholy melody of Dido's *lamento* "When I am laid in Earth" from Henry Purcell's 1689 opera *Dido and Aeneas,* her pose uncannily resembles the suicide trees, with Maria playing the role of the Harpies. Von Trotta juxtaposes Purcell's music, effectively Anna's requiem, to Konstantin Wecker's "Songs of Freedom." On a visit home, Anna overreacts to her mother's choice of literature. In great agony, she reads aloud a verse by the melancholic nineteenth-century poet Nikolaus Lenau—a verse that epitomizes her feeling trapped between her own desires and her sister's expectations, yet also signals her distress and secret longing for death.[11] Quickly

Maria silences Anna's dramatic poetry reading by holding her mouth shut and forcing her to keep her anger within herself. Unsuccessful in communicating her grief, Anna "lack[s] the filter of language, and can't inscribe her violence in 'no' or in any other sign—she can expel it only by means of gestures, spasms or shouts" (*Black Sun* 15).

Anna's diary serves as an immediate projection screen for her fear, mirrors her fractured identity, and casts the shadows of what Kristeva referred to as the black sun. Aphorisms, such as "The dream I have of life robs me of life," and notes of dreams complement her black-and-white illustrations of bodies in pain with frightening, distorted faces, in addition to photos of the sisters and a series of self-portraits, as if she were striving to integrate herself into the history of tormented mankind and store her face in an image before her bodily demise. It also shows her impressive knowledge of burial rites of suicide victims and confirms her secular take on suicide when acknowledging "I am breaking a law of nature." She dedicates her chilling last entry to Maria:

> Place a stone on my face when I am dead. Drive a stake through my chest [breast] to keep me from haunting you. Chop off my hand, when I am dead; bury it at the crossroads [Way of the Cross], so that I won't rise [up] to torment you. I have laid hand on myself, against you [I took my own life in opposition to you]—you [alone] are the target of my death. Beware of me.[12]

Anna's abyss of sorrow is partially self-imposed, as she keeps human contact to a minimum and engages in activities that provide only temporary self-cohesion, such as studying at home or listening to her favorite music. Her narcissistic withdrawal gradually leads to emotional and psychic paralysis, during which, as Kristeva argues, killing herself "is not a choice but a gesture that is imperative on the basis of an elsewhere—a nonact, or rather a sign of completion" (*Black Sun* 73). Whether Anna's suicide is read as an act of liberation or as one of revenge (Hehr 27), the illustrations in her diary, together with her tanks of lizards and her favorite music, point to ancient traditions, such as Ixtab, the Mayan goddess of the noose and the gallows, who took those who committed suicide or died by hanging straight to eternal rest in paradise.[13] This take on suicide runs contrary to contemporary perceptions, and so does Anna's blunt rejection of competitive principles. Not desiring success is a sign of life for her. Her anger and frustration are also directed against a mother who has participated in patriarchal signifying practices as a submissive, now widowed wife and mother, and as such represents a negative figure, an abyss (Creed 60–62) embodied in the dark wood of the fairy tale, the habitat of wild animals threatening to eat the sisters—or, psychoanalytically speaking, female genitalia giving birth to equally horrific offspring (Creed 63). Maria and Anna, in turn, categorically reject motherhood.

As Lacan says, "the most interior part of the psyche has a quality of being Other, of being like a parasitic foreign body" (qtd. in Bronfen 292). While Maria completely represses and denies her inherent otherness, Anna is unwilling to give it up and conveys to Maria that she cannot relate to her fellow students, who eagerly take notes and throw themselves into exams to show off their knowledge. After Maria misinterprets Anna's concern as general fear before exams and explains it away, Anna dramatically responds by doing away with her body, an act that Lacan considers an abortion—a killing off of a part of the self to get rid of an excess, and an act that the suicide victim perceives not as terminal but as a prerequisite for uniting with an idealized part of the self. Since this fusion is denied to Anna in life, she seeks it through death.

Anna's suicide reconfigures the roles of victim and perpetrator by putting "a psychological skeleton in the survivor's closet."[14] In the same systematic manner in which Maria approaches life, she deals with death—through repression and amnesia. After the unexpected loss of their father, she takes over as family caretaker. Anna's suicide suddenly makes this role obsolete. Maria deliberately erases the memory of her sister by packing away her belongings immediately after her death, not keeping a single picture or other memorabilia, except for the diary. Unable to resume her routine, although she feels neither guilt nor remorse, Maria visits Fritz, a friend who lives as a hermit and spends his time recording dreams that signal loss, disorientation, and loneliness. Although Maria cannot grasp Anna's suicide, she does not even try, and neither rationalizes, nor reconstructs it. Anna keeps haunting Maria in surreal, imaginary encounters that traumatize her to the point that she pictures herself lying sprawled across the desk in a puddle of blood, while Anna stands in the doorway and smiles. What Anna failed to accomplish in life, she has succeeded at in suicide—inscribing herself on Maria and thus inverting the power balance. Higonnet calls this a "self-barred signature," suicide tied to destructive narcissism, which is particularly feminine, and aims to inscribe the self on the other ("Suicide as Self-Construction" 70). Without ever attempting to mourn her loss, Maria is her old self again once she dictates Fritz's dreams to her co-worker Miriam and thus mechanically processes someone else's thoughts instead of trying to understand Anna's or her own, both of which are now completely repressed.

Back at her job, Maria, the "irreplaceable" executive secretary, replaces the suicide victim by offering Anna's room to Miriam, who overtly resists her patronizing attitude, decorates their apartment, continues her relationship with her boyfriend Robbie, yet accepts Maria's offer to pay for her English classes—however, not to excel as a bilingual secretary, as Maria hopes, but to sing like Billie Holiday. Despite her efforts to maintain independence, Miriam gradually begins to assume Anna's appearance and position, except when Maria sits at home at night waiting for her. Alarmed by her own increasing apathy and acutely aware of Anna's fate, Miriam splits from Maria by rejecting the lifeless, androgynous female mold—that of a living corpse—in which the latter wanted to cast her. Maria's new attempt at symbiotic life ends with Miriam's suicide threat: "Before I go on a trip with you, I'd rather go into the water."

Now falling back on herself, Maria begins to resemble Anna in dress and hairstyle and to explore an imaginary side of herself by taking time to reflect instead of numbing herself with work. Yet she does so from a safe spot, as executive secretary, a guardian of the status quo and most fervent protector of the established order. The final scene, a close-up of Maria writing in Anna's diary, indicates a dramatic shift from transcribing a dictation to expressing her own thoughts and suggests a fusion of female voice, body, and speech. Virginia Woolf's *A Room of One's Own* turns into von Trotta's *A Voice of One's Own*.[15] The forest blended into the background signals a death sentence for Maria's rigid approach to life and a paradigm for the politics of displacement and replacement.

Marianne and Juliane

Father said: "She won't kill herself. I might, but she wouldn't. Not her. I might, but she wouldn't."—Margarethe von Trotta (*Marianne and Juliane*)

Reconstructing an individual and a national past, an intense competitive relationship between two sisters, and the role of terrorism in postwar Germany are at stake in *Marianne and Juliane*. Flashbacks to their childhood show Juliane as independent, assertive, and nonconformist, whereas Marianne lives up to the expectations of their authoritarian father, whom their mother affectionately nicknames "The Egoist." Kristeva's argument in "The Terror of Power or the Power of Terrorism" (*New Maladies of the Soul* 214–18) explains Marianne's transformation from a bourgeois housewife and mother, whose voice remains powerless in the sociosymbolic order, into a terrorist. She turns to immediate action, investing herself in a system that promises radical change. Undeniably, her terrorist activities gain her instant visibility. Yet for a liberal democratic order, represented by Juliane, she embodies abjection. Her radical, violent actions not only alienate possible supporters in the feminist movement but pose a threat to society at large. Symbolically doubly silenced, first within a bourgeois patriarchal order and then as a prison inmate under special surveillance and barred from any action, all that Marianne has left is her sister's sympathy. After Marianne's alleged suicide in prison, Juliane challenges the official records and meticulously reconstructs the circumstances of her sister's death. Throughout the film their mother quietly submits herself and her daughters to paternal tyranny that goes as far as the father's threat against Juliane, whom he deems more likely to commit suicide than her sister. Suicide thus becomes the ultimate sign of female rebellion and anarchy against the paternal law.

Susan E. Linville, in "Retrieving History: Margarethe von Trotta's *Marianne and Juliane*," explores intersecting personal and collective memory structures and suggests that "Juliane's less spectacular and less simplified feminist commitments and engagements sustain the tenacious resistance to patriarchal repression" (452), a fact Marianne fails to acknowledge: she disdains her sister's grassroots feminist activism, such as her research on the role of women in the Third Reich and her fighting for abortion rights. The complex relationship between the sisters is also the focus of Marc Silberman's "The Subject of Identity: Margarethe von Trotta's *Marianne and Juliane*," which reads their interaction as "a form of role-playing that leads to the recognition of the self in the Other" (202)—also true of the siblings' relationship in *Sisters*. Juliane, the vocal activist, and Marianne, wife and mother, initially replicate their parents' role-play. Then suddenly Marianne resents this and turns violent. Both daughters distance themselves from their submissive mother, who, after all of her children have left the house, turns to music to dispel her fear as if to cover up her inability to speak, especially in the presence of her husband. She confides her lack when she joins Juliane to visit Marianne in prison:

> Once I'd have wept about this or prayed. Do you think I am right not to do either now? I have so many questions to ask both of you. Ought I to write them down? I am used to trusting people, not questioning them. Do you understand?

Maternal feminine speech is strictly limited to an emotional response and the citation of codified scripture, but does not extend to posing questions. When viewing Marianne's corpse, their mother remains remarkably composed, and once again recites a prayer. The language of binary opposites fully materializes in the paternal law that defines suicide as nonconformity and in maternal speech that drifts between their mother's silence, Juliane's critical journalistic voice, and Marianne's violence and aggressive demands. Instead of asking, Marianne commands.

Marianne's ex-husband Werner commits suicide to escape his responsibilities as a single parent after she becomes a terrorist. When Juliane breaks the news to Marianne, she harshly comments, "He has always been suicidal," and "I have no time to mourn the death of a neurotic intellectual." Obviously, suicide is not an option for Marianne. Shortly before her imprisonment, the sisters meet in the art museum. Filled with statues, it is the preeminent site to fix meaning and identity and exhibit the past, whereas in contrast, both of them reject a firm position in the bourgeois family and fight against becoming social icons. Their final encounter prior to Marianne's incarceration is her unexpected intrusion in Juliane's home in the middle of the night, which leaves Juliane helpless and angry at the same time. In Kristeva's terms, it is an attempt to insert herself into her sister's life (Oliver 387). As soon as Marianne is in jail, they see each other regularly and their relationship intensifies. Juliane has more control over their interaction now; she takes days off from work to visit, writes letters, and prepares CARE packages. In spite of her efforts, Marianne quickly loses her strength: she goes on a hunger strike, lives without human contact, and has to sleep in a room with the light on day and night. Via a news broadcast, Juliane learns of Marianne's alleged suicide. Thus suicide is both an event in the media and a mediated event for Juliane.

When viewing Marianne's corpse, particularly her distorted face, Juliane does not avert her gaze. This encounter throws her into a crisis. The boundaries designed to keep the abject at bay actually disintegrate and collapse (Creed 64): while "death images are most likely to cause the spectator to look away to retain his/her boundaries" (Creed 65), as was the case when the sisters watched a documentary about the Holocaust, Juliane keeps looking and subsequently suffers a nervous breakdown. Marianne's imprisonment had already assumed an overwhelming presence in her life; obsessively researching and proving her sister's murder keep her even busier. She studies medical books and builds a dummy to make her point. Finally, she dismantles the political fiction driven by the calculation that if terrorism legitimizes murder for a higher cause, a period of political turmoil legitimizes murder of an imprisoned terrorist to attain political stability and closure. Her narcissistic withdrawal alienates her partner Wolfgang, who vents his anger and need for her attention: "It is self-destruction and you want me to watch. I am no help. I am dying too, or must I also get an autopsy." Once the evidence clearly indicates murder, Juliane intends to go public and is shocked when a journalist responds: "Murder or suicide—snow from yesteryear." Proving the murder and implicitly also the instrumentalization of female suicide for political purposes is more important to Juliane personally than to the rest of the world legally or politically; it allows her to reclaim her position as the stronger partner in the sibling relationship and abets her sustained rebellion against the paternal law. The fact that the media are not interested in the true story of Marianne leaves one pressing question unanswered: if family commitments take precedence over political ones, as Barton Byg argues in "German History and Cinematic Convention Harmonized in Margarethe von Trotta's *Marianne and Juliane*," why doesn't Juliane immediately tell their father that she succeeded in proving the authorities wrong about Marianne's suicide—thus granting her father the triumph of his rightness and conveying to their mother the official end of the siblings' competitive relationship?

With Werner dead and Marianne in hiding, their son Jan lives with foster parents because Juliane resents motherhood and being forced into a life that she never wanted and that her sister no longer wanted to lead. Only after Marianne's imprisonment and death, when Jan is badly hurt in a hate crime provoked by his mother's past, does Juliane take the orphan in. Now that the anger and rivalry between the sisters have finally ceased, Jan displays his narcissistic wounds and tears up his mother's photograph. Eager to fix the rift between mother and son, Juliane offers to tell him everything she knows, and Jan impatiently insists that she begin immediately. The film closes as yet another story about an abject mother begins to unfold.[16] Byg illustrates how Juliane, in spite of her emancipatory efforts, "[carries] on the Oedipal narrative" by becoming a foster parent and "passing on [Marianne's] story to the son, restoring political and moral authority to its rightful place" (263).

Unlike the siblings in *Sisters,* the characters in *Marianne and Juliane* lack suicide fantasies and melancholic traits. Instead they pursue their agendas: Juliane has found her medium in feminist journalism, whereas Marianne initially met mainstream expectations as wife and mother. Kristeva argues that once a woman realizes

> her status as a social being who remains unknown to the discourse and the powers...she can make herself into a "possessed" agent through the counterinvestment of the violence she encounters. She

fights against her frustration, then, with weapons that may appear extreme at first glance, but that are justifiable and understandable once the narcissistic suffering that elicits their use is recognized (*New Maladies of the Soul* 217).

Marianne, seemingly empowered by terrorism, fights the patriarchal order embodied by her father, the passive conformism of her husband, and inadvertently the liberal order, represented by Juliane—a fact Juliane fully realizes when she claims her sister would probably have joined the Hitler Youth had she lived at a different time.[17]

Sheer Madness: "Ruth, where have you left your clothesline?"

Sheer Madness established von Trotta's reputation as a man-hater (Hehr 34), and German critics widely attacked her for reproducing clichés of the women's movement, while women who saw themselves in the film vehemently defended it (Hehr 34). What has gone unnoticed is her astute critique of medical treatment of suicidal female patients who become dysfunctional through sedation, and the women's fate of lifelong confinement. Coincidentally, von Trotta produced part of the script while in the hospital undergoing cancer screenings.[18] Susan Linville and Kent Casper's observation in "The Ambiguity of Margarethe von Trotta's *Sheer Madness*" that "suicidal states of mind may stem not from negative distortions of external reality, but from an accurate assessment of the way things are" (1) is my impetus for further analysis, along with their reading of Olga as a thoroughly negative figure (6), as female abject.

Sheer Madness depicts the friendship between Ruth, an eccentric painter, and Olga, a self-confident university professor, who meet as houseguests in a vineyard in southern France. While hosts and guests enjoy a relaxing evening and listen to Olga and her ex-husband, Dieter, talking about their recent vacation and describing their conscious efforts at "literally producing silence," Ruth's most radical act of speech, her suicide attempt, ruptures the idle conversation. The very first evening after their chance encounter reveals trademarks of their personalities, particularly Olga's eagerness to help and Ruth's suicidal tendencies.

This sequence is preceded by Ruth's session with a psychiatrist that poignantly illustrates her dilemma of expressing herself, and her husband Franz's predicament concerning her need of psychiatric care. The psychiatrist provides verbal cues to elicit responses from Ruth, who cites folklore, nursery rhymes, proverbs, fairy tales, and biblical language. When asked to simply speak for herself, she resents doing so because she feels that the audience already has the transcript of her speech, denying her individuality and originality. Instead, she lies down on the examining table with her hands folded, enacting an imaginary wake. This recurring position of lying in state functions as what Kristeva calls a "poetics of survival," an intense effort to embody an imaginary death (*Black Sun* 73) that paradoxically allows the individual to continue to live. The idea of giving a speech anticipates Ruth's encounter with Renate, Olga's former classmate, hospitalized after a suicide attempt and fixated on the idea of having to deliver a sermon[19] from the top of a mountain she is unable to find. Renate symbolizes a radical dislocation of female speech and a language Ruth can easily relate to and decode.

In Ruth's first suicide attempt, she suggests the fantasy of being rescued, by deliberately leaving traces, such as clothes strewn on the floor, indicating that she took the clothesline to harm herself; indeed, Olga finds Ruth in a cave with a noose around her neck. Three suicide visions, all linked to her husband, her home, and her artwork, as well as a second, nearly fatal, suicide attempt follow, as if to legitimize Franz's fear of a copycat suicide, since Ruth's brother killed himself. Ruth's suicide fictions are the stories of her life, yet also emotional anchors. The stage for her first suicide vision is set as follows: after an enjoyable afternoon with Olga, she gets home and finds her husband furious because she failed to call and let him know her whereabouts. In his anger, he blurts out that without him she would be confined to a psychiatric ward. Shocked at having vented his reproach, he apologetically hugs her, and suddenly Ruth sees herself dangling from a rope in her studio. This suicide vision signals her ego split and poignantly expresses what Kristeva describes as "cadaverization and artifice" (*Black Sun* 73). Picturing herself as a corpse keeps Ruth alive, yet also taints her life with artificiality. In her second suicide vision, Franz finds her hanged in her studio and quickly embraces the corpse. Shortly thereafter, when Franz tells her that the gallery has canceled her exhibit and that he actually arranged what she mistook for Olga's genuine friendship, Ruth makes a second attempt. Thus, Olga, the rescuer in the first attempt, becomes the perpetrator provoking the second. She is manipulated first by Franz, then by Ruth, into the role they need her to play. After Ruth's recovery from this second attempt, Franz immediately reclaims his position as savior and stabilizes their relationship by having her rest on the sofa, pushing her into the paradigmatic horizontal death position. As if lying in state, she is surrounded by flowers.

She fully realizes that in order to survive, she must overcome her insurmountable fear of directly or indirectly communicating with people. An attempt to leave a message on Olga's answering machine conjures up memories of her first suicide attempt. Trying to place a call from a public phone provokes an anxiety attack. Whenever Ruth has to speak, she develops aphasia. She even has to quit teaching because she cannot utter a single word in front of the class, and dedicates herself to her artwork, which gives her identity, and a literal and symbolic place. Her home, furnished by her mother-in-law, constitutes an infinitely controlled space, in which rooms resemble tombs that stifle and chill. The only bright spot in these death chambers is her studio. Her images with halos and circles uncannily recall the scene in southern France when Olga's flashlight cast a halo around Ruth's head as she sat in the cave—both a womb and a death chamber—with the noose around her neck.

Psychoanalysis detects a secret mother behind each work of art. According to Kristeva, the imaginary continuity with the mother is what guarantees identity, while the work of art is the most unsettling imitation of mother-child dependence. The art is a substitute and a displacement, and thus a deceptive form of independence (Moi 14), and indeed, Ruth's mother is omnipresent in her life. Yet, at the same time, as Kristeva argues in *Black Sun,* art fills the psychological need to confront separation, emptiness, and death. Ruth's alternately producing originals and copies shows her dilemma between replicating the female model of quiet submission and trying to break away from it. To escape ordinary speech acts, she turns to her art. But when it is allegedly rejected, she immediately paints over her originals and implicitly erases her individuality and herself.

Ruth's life increasingly becomes one large quotation: pleasing her mother as submissive daughter; copying original paintings in black and white, such as Caspar David Friedrich's (1774–1840) *Die Frau am Fenster* (*Woman at the Window),* an image that points back to the film's beginning; and identifying with literary suicides by emulating Karoline von Günderrode and ambitiously studying her writings as much as her suicide. Paradoxically, the more Ruth talks about literary suicides, the more she becomes alive. Even Olga's lover, a struggling artist, is familiar with Günderrode and argues that her ill-fated love was a mere pretext to end her life; her actual fear was artistic failure. Suicidal thought is literally staged when Olga's former husband, an artistic director at a theater, interprets Georg Büchner's comedy *Leonce and Lena,* which culminates in Leonce's wish to kill himself in order to hold fast to the moment of utmost happiness.[20]

Ruth feels that Franz has created an eccentric image of her that he believes coincides with her secret wishes of narcissistic loneliness and foolish isolation. As in *Sisters,* two people create balance in their relationship by living up to projected fantasies of each other, and any outside intervention becomes an intrusion, as when Olga begins to take Franz's place. Only radical interference will reestablish the couple's power balance—but Franz's attempt backfires. After clarifying Olga's role in Ruth's second suicide attempt, Ruth accepts new challenges from Olga and they even team-teach a seminar on feminist literature in Egypt. By interacting with female students steeped in Islamic tradition, Ruth gains confidence as a teacher and as a woman without letting go of her superstitions; she asks the emancipated Egyptian wife of the German professor about a fortune-teller, whom she eagerly consults. A seemingly random remark by their tour guide in Cairo, that suicide is rare, puts the plot in the Freudian tradition of *Civilization and Its Discontents,* arguing for suicide as the product of mankind and civilization, the repression of instincts and drives for the sake of cultural progress. Ruth's intellectually gifted husband, skilled in peace research and the prevention of nuclear disaster, is unable to help her gain emotional and psychic stability.

Finding positive means of enacting difference is Ruth's challenge. In *Alice Doesn't,* de Lauretis argues that no female self-presentation, as long as it is informed by prevalent cultural expectations of femininity shaped by patriarchal constructions, coincides with the reality of female experience, especially when others narrate the story. But Ruth has reserved that privilege for herself. In the surreal, black-and-white final scene of a trial, Ruth thanks her friend Olga for helping her find the courage to fire a bullet at her husband. This scene invites several conflicting interpretations. Ruth's repeated suicide attempts as a result of a radical transference of self-murder may have led to premeditated murder. The murder may as well have been another of her nightmarish visions; an act of heroic defiance against an oppressive psychiatric establishment for which her marriage is an alternative (at least in the eyes of her husband); a resistance against patriarchal tyranny; or a visualization of the death wish. More important than a conclusive interpretation is its actual function in the narrative. It reestablishes patriarchal order and defies the plea for psychoanalysis at the beginning of the film. The potential self-murderer most likely will be sentenced and possibly confined to a psychiatric ward to establish once again the paternal law.

Conclusion: The Abyss of Female Poetic Speech

If *Sisters, Marianne and Julianne,* and *Sheer Madness* are considered as a trilogy, the suicidal characters progress from hunger artists driven by unfulfilled desires and succumbing to their despair, to individuals who break away from their oppressors. Von Trotta neither stigmatizes nor moralizes suicide but rather strips it of taboo and employs it as an aesthetic strategy to map an aspect of female existence. Peculiarly, the apparently weakest character, Ruth, succeeds in ending and surviving her negative relationship, only to find herself within the confines of psychiatric care. She and successful suicide Anna share a strong nonverbal component: painting is freedom for Ruth, music is freedom for Anna.

Margarethe von Trotta's characters come to suicide in a roundabout way as they seek to fulfill unmet needs or resolve internal conflicts. Through interwoven fantasies, dreams, allusions, quotations, and reflections, they directly convey their presuicidal mindset. This immediacy, however, is frequently undermined by posthumous editorial work, when family members reconstruct events and thereby inevitably blur memory and testimony. Intriguing opening scenes introduce the survivors Maria, Juliane, and Ruth; draw on powerful imagery; underscore the fact that cinematographic suicides are aesthetic, fictional constructs; and poignantly summarize the films' main themes: role-play between uninhibited speaker and reluctant respondent, contrasting interior and exterior spaces along with intimacy and isolation, and collapsing private and public dimensions. *Sisters* opens with the image of a forest, which is intimately linked with an irretrievable past, suicide, and the symbolic, mysterious black hole. *Marianne and Juliane* opens with a shot of a closed window and a sound collage of a person pacing up and down, thus alluding to the trapped individual caught in the archive of the deceased other. In *Sheer Madness,* a woman stretches her arm out of a window to feel the raindrops before resuming her session with a psychiatrist. The woman at the window reappears as Caspar David Friedrich's painting, copied by Ruth, and the scene is inverted when bystanders peek inside a home or when Franz looks at his wife enjoying herself with Olga. In the closing scenes the role reversal has been completed: Maria sits at Anna's desk writing in her diary; Jan's new foster mother Juliane begins to tell the story of his mother; and Ruth thanks her friend Olga, who taught her to articulate her feelings.

Ultimately, von Trotta argues for a capacity of fusion that does not sacrifice autonomy or individuality. She performs a tightrope act between aestheticizing and deromanticizing self-inflicted death. On the one hand, she portrays artists and intellectuals who find their true calling in suicide, links the act to a ritualized performance (*Sisters*), and arbitrarily conjures up seductive scenes and pathos. On the other hand, she bluntly depicts shock, terror, and trauma. She embeds her complex suicide scenaria in "quest narratives" (Silberman 202) that strive for cohesion and maps a wide spectrum of motives ranging from inflicting trauma to seeking revenge, instrumentalizing suicide as an act of political protest, or succumbing to a genetically engineered phenomenon, hereditary and therefore inevitable—an assumption Ruth proves to be wrong.

In the tradition of Kristeva, von Trotta suggests psychoanalysis for treating the maladies of the soul. Furthermore, she attributes her choice of themes to a female cinematographic form of aesthetics and argues that women stand in public for what they think in private (Rentschler 89, 90). Exploring female identity through a Kristevan, speaking female subject, she makes a most intimate trauma of women public, dismantles the violent act as a radical dislocation of feminist speech, and indicates that adequate models of speech may make suicide obsolete. She concludes with the possibility of a way out of suicidal behavior and issues a call for action to break the silence. At the same time, she sends out a chilling reminder to those in power and control that they may find themselves alone at the end. Decidedly, she works against the emotional deep freeze and numbness that characterize later cinematographic productions on suicide such as Michael Haneke's *The Seventh Continent* (1989), which has the film viewer stare at a mysterious black hole after the collective suicide of a family. Instead, von Trotta paints a full panoramic view of female suicide and argues for continuity in spite of all odds. What is somewhat puzzling about von Trotta's cinematographic trilogy is the fact that suicide becomes more and more fictional, surreal, and magical, and a topic of aesthetic imagination. What would technically mean closing in on the nineteenth-century sentiments of the exquisite, aestheticized female corpse is countered by the horrific and traumatic gaze at the corpse of female suicide victims.

Notes

All translations from the German are my own except for the English subtitles of the films. In the case of revised wording, the original is in parentheses.

[1] The original reads: "Meine Fahrkarte wäre immer der Tod und nicht die Südseeinsel. Ich würde mich auslöschen, und nicht versuchen, das Paradies woanders zu suchen."

[2] All dates indicate production dates.

[3] For more, see Fischetti's interview (168). During the last week of shooting, in April 1979, Elizabeth von Trotta died without her daughter at her side—a fact that haunted the latter, although her mother had lost most of her memory and no longer even recognized her. Shortly thereafter,

Margarethe von Trotta learned that she had a sister. For more, see Wydra (esp. 26, 28, 99).

[4] Bronfen argues that parents have endowed their daughters with traditions from submissive mother to submissive daughter, and the constraints and phantasms of the culture in which they were educated (301, 306–07).

[5] Laura Mulvey, qtd. in Byg (260).

[6] For more on suicide and the visual arts, see Cutter. Twentieth-century German painters who depicted suicide include George Grosz, Käthe Kollwitz, and Alfred Kubin.

[7] For more, see Müller.

[8] As Moeller has pointed out, von Trotta's realistic feminist cinema of transgression is reminiscent of Helma Sanders-Brahms's *Deutschland, Bleiche Mutter* (*Germany, Pale Mother,* 1980), particularly Lene, who becomes disfigured and suicidal in the postwar emotional deep freeze (56).

[9] John Gregg in *Maurice Blanchot and the Literature of Transgression* notes, "The error to which suicide victims succumb is, as Blanchot says, like a bizarre play on words; they take one death for another. Their attempt to domesticate death by taking their own life constitutes an act of power. All efforts to have mastery over *le mourir,* to personalize it and render it present, are futile. The perpetrator of suicide sets out with great determination to conquer and possess death, to make it his or her own" (36).

[10] Part of Dido's *lamento* "When I am laid in Earth" in Henry Purcell's opera *Dido and Aeneas.*

[11] Nikolaus Lenau actually wrote a poem entitled "Der Selbstmord."

[12] For more, see Alvarez (esp. 64, 65).

[13] Ixtab is depicted as hanging from a tree with a noose around her neck, her eyes closed in death and her body partly decomposed. In addition to suicides, she also took slain warriors, sacrificial victims, priests, and women who died in childbirth to paradise.

[14] Qtd. from Edwin Shneidman in Jeffrey Berman (114).

[15] Repeatedly *Sisters* has been compared to Woody Allen's 1978 *Interiors* (Wydra 105), in which Eve, a wife and mother of three adult daughters, is unexpectedly heading for a trial separation and divorce at her husband's request. Eve embodies style, power, and control, reflected in her exquisite taste for decorative objects. When suddenly faced with the radical object loss of her soon-to-be-ex-husband, who is another one of her creations, she loses control and turns on the gas. Eve's first suicide attempt brings together the family, haunting them with her imaginary and actual presence and thus exerting control over her daughters, who reflect on their lives and painfully realize their own emotional numbness. Her second, successful, suicide attempt is by drowning the night after her ex-husband

remarries a life-loving, down-to-earth woman, ultimately leaving Eve entrapped in herself.

[16] In *The State I Am In* (2000), director Michael Petzold takes up the issue of motherhood in the underground.

[17] An interesting counterpoint to von Trotta's intertwining terrorism with terror in the domestic sphere is Rainer Werner Fassbinder and Alexander Kluge's landmark film *Germany in Autumn* (1977/78), focusing on institutions, the army, press, and industry in the political climate of that era in Germany. It opens and closes with funerals: that of the industrialist Hans-Martin Schleyer precedes that of three imprisoned Baader-Meinhof terrorists after their alleged suicides. Moreover, the film historicizes suicide and transplants it to Hapsburg Austria and the legendary tragic deaths of Kronprinz Rudolf and Maria Vetsera in 1898, a political gesture to avoid scandal bound to sexual transgression.

[18] For more, see Weber (96).

[19] A sermon about "die Verheißung der Sintflut" recalls Georg Büchner's *Lenz*.

[20] As part of an assignment in high school, Büchner writes in "Kritik an einem Aufsatz über den Selbstmord" that the suicide is only "ein Verirrter," but not a criminal (100).

Works Cited

Alvarez, Alfred. *The Savage God: A Study of Suicide.* New York: Random House, 1970.

Berman, Jeffrey. *Surviving Literary Suicide.* Amherst: U of Massachussetts P, 1999.

Bronfen, Elizabeth. *The Knotted Subject: Hysteria and Its Discontents.* Princeton: Princeton UP, 1998.

Buchka, Peter, dir. *Die Neugier immer weiter treiben: Margarethe von Trotta.* Bonn: Inter Nationes, 1996.

Büchner, Georg. *Sämtliche Werke und Schriften: historisch-kritische Ausgabe mit Quellendokumentation und Kommentar.* Darmstadt: Wissenschaftliche Buchgesellschaft, 2000.

Byg, Barton. "German History and Cinematic Convention Harmonized in Margarethe von Trotta's *Marianne and Juliane.*" *Gender and German Cinema: Feminist Interventions.* Vol. 2. *German Film History/German History on Film.* Ed. Sandra Frieden, Richard W. McCormick, Vibeke R. Petersen, and Laurie Melissa Vogelsang. Providence: Berg, 1993. 259–71.

Creed, Barbara. "Horrors and the Monstrous-Feminine: An Imaginary Abjection." *Screen* 27 (1986): 44-70.
Cutter, Fred. *Art and the Wish to Die*. Chicago: Nelson-Hall, 1983.
de Lauretis, Teresa. *Alice Doesn't: Feminism, Semiotics, Cinema*. Bloomington: Indiana UP, 1984.
Export, Valie, dir. *Menschenfrauen*. Chicago: Facets Video, 1989. Original film: Vienna: Valie Export and Top Film, 1980.
Fischetti, Renate. "Großes Erzählkino mit neuen Inhalten: Margarethe von Trotta." *Das neue Kino: Acht Porträts von deutschen Regisseurinnen*. Frankfurt a.M.: Tende, 1992. 151-74.
Gregg, John. *Maurice Blanchot and the Literature of Transgression*. Princeton: Princeton UP, 1994.
Guberman, Ross Mitchell. *Julia Kristeva Interviews*. New York: Columbia UP, 1996.
Hehr, Renate. *Margarethe von Trotta: Filmmaking as Liberation*. Stuttgart: Edition Axel Menges, 2000.
Higonnet, Margaret R. "Frames of Female Suicide." *Studies in the Novel* (Summer 2000): 229-42.
_____. "Speaking Silences: Women's Suicide." *The Female Body in Western Culture*. Ed. Susan Rubin Suleiman. Cambridge: Harvard UP, 1986. 68-83.
_____. "Suicide as Self-Construction." *Germaine de Staël: Crossing the Borders*. Ed. Madelyn Gutwirth, Avriel Goldberger, and Karyna Szmurlo. New Brunswick: Rutgers UP, 1991. 69-81.
Kristeva, Julia. *Black Sun: Depression and Melancholia*. Trans. Leon S. Roudiez. New York: Columbia UP, 1989.
_____. *New Maladies of the Soul*. New York: Columbia UP, 1995.
Kuhn, Anna. "Margarethe von Trotta's *Sisters*: Interiority or Engagement?" *Women in German Yearbook 1*. Ed. Edith Waldstein and Marianne Burkhard. Lanham: UP of America, 1985. 77-84.
Linville, Susan E. "Retrieving History: Margarethe von Trotta's *Marianne and Juliane*." *PMLA* 106.3 (1991): 446-58.
Linville, Susan E., and Kent Casper. "The Ambiguity of Margarethe von Trotta's *Sheer Madness*." *Film Criticism* 12.1 (1987): 1-10.
Moeller, H.-B. "West German Women's Cinema: The Case of Margarethe von Trotta." *Film Criticism* 9.2 (1984): 51-66.
Moi, Toril, ed. *The Kristeva Reader*. New York: Columbia UP, 1986.
Mouton, Janice. "Margarethe von Trotta's *Sisters*: 'Brides Under a Different Law.'" *Women in German Yearbook 11*. Ed. Sara Friedrichsmeyer and Patricia Herminghouse. Lincoln: U of Nebraska P, 1995. 35-47.

Müller, Roswitha. *Valie Export: Fragments of the Imagination.* Bloomington: Indiana UP, 1994.

———. "Images in Balance (*The Cat Has Nine Lives; Sisters*)." *Gender and German Cinema: Feminist Interventions.* Vol. 1. *Gender and Representation in New German Cinema.* Ed. Sandra Frieden et al. Providence: Berg, 1993. 59–71.

Mundzeck, Heike. "Von Zeit zu Zeit muß ich den Baum schütteln, ob noch alle Früchte dran sind." *"Als Frau ist es wohl leichter, Mensch zu werden": Gespräche mit Dorothee Solle, Margarethe von Trotta, Heidemarie Wieczorek-Zeul.* Reinbek bei Hamburg: Rowohlt, 1984. 53–98.

Oliver, Kelly, ed. *The Portable Kristeva.* New York: Columbia UP, 1997.

Silberman, Marc. "The Subject of Identity: Margarethe von Trotta's *Marianne and Juliane.*" *German Cinema: Texts in Context.* Detroit: Wayne State UP, 1995. 198–213.

Silverman, Kaja. *The Acoustic Mirror: The Female Voice in Psychoanalysis and Cinema.* Bloomington: Indiana UP, 1988.

von Trotta, Margarethe, dir. *Die bleierne Zeit: Marianne and Juliane.* New York: New Yorker Films, 1989. Original film 1981.

———. "Female Film Aesthetics." 1982. *West German Filmmakers on Film: Visions and Voices.* Ed. Eric Rentschler. New York: Holmes & Meier, 1988. 89-90.

———, dir. *Heller Wahn: Sheer Madness.* Water Bearer Films 1997. Original film 1982.

———, dir. *Schwestern, oder Die Balance des Glücks. Sisters, or the Balance of Happiness.* Water Bearer Films, 1997. Original film 1979.

Weber, Hans-Jürgen, ed. *Heller Wahn: ein Film von Margarethe von Trotta.* Frankfurt a.M.: Fischer, 1983.

Wydra, Thilo. *Margarethe von Trotta: Filmen, um zu überleben.* Berlin: Henschel, 2000.

Intertextual Connections: Structures of Feminine Identification in the Works of Karin Struck

Morwenna Symons

The intertextual space is potentially a valuable resource for women authors writing self-consciously within a female literary heritage. For Karin Struck, the intertextual mode is a central feature, reflecting and supporting the thematic concern with making connections that runs through her texts. This article offers a survey of her work, analyzing her intertextual practice and assessing the value of an intertextual mode employed principally to set in place structures of identification with anterior texts. The author argues that the later text *Ingeborg B. Duell mit dem Spiegelbild* is both more ambitious in this respect and less sophisticated than the early texts in its handling of the inherent tensions of intertextual narratives. (MS)

A central aspect of Karin Struck's writing is her use of intertextuality. She makes extensive use of quotation and allusion, drawing her sources from the Bible, from classical and established works from the canon, and from contemporary authors and critics. While her oeuvre is of very mixed quality, it is nevertheless my belief that Struck's intertextual practice is of interest, for two reasons. First, her writing enables us to assess the critical value of an intertextual mode that is employed above all to set in place structures of identification with anterior texts. Second, it contextualizes some issues arising in relation to an intertextual model conceived as a specifically female literary bond and functioning as a symbolic space outside the male preserve. The aims of this article are therefore twofold: to offer a survey of Struck's work, focusing particularly on the contribution made by the intertextual mode to the development of her feminist project; and to reflect more generally on the nature of the tensions inherent in intertextual narratives.

Struck's intertextual methodology can be understood as the structural corollary to a central thematic thread that runs through her works, the constant desire to establish connections. Her texts enact a recurring fear, the fear of the writer's isolation from the rest of the world, and their referentiality bespeaks an attempt to break free from an anxiety associated with pure, unmediated individuality. By setting up narratives that are driven by a technique of speaking across divides, by crossing and transgressing the boundaries between her own work and that of other authors, she wishes to contextualize herself, finding sustenance in the assurance that her words do not act as a barrier to others, as it sometimes seems.

In a reading of *Die Mutter* (The Mother, 1975), Inta Ezergailis suggests that the numerous references to other authors represent an attempt to overcome the sense of total isolation that the protagonist experiences, and to return to a "naïve state where one was in harmony with the natural world and with other people.... [Struck's] particular route...includes researches into childhood and exploration of dreams, but it never becomes solipsistic. A contact with others is essential" (25–26). Manfred Jurgensen, in reference to *Lieben* (Loving, 1977), draws attention to what he calls Struck's "citation mania," describing the work as a "many-layered citation" (89) and assessing it positively as "a living and connecting citation" (93).

As a whole, however, critics have been rather less convinced by Struck's use of intertext. Joanne Leal, discussing *Klassenliebe* (Class Love, 1973), questions Jurgensen's analysis of Struck's citational method as an all-important gesture of contact with others, arguing that the narrator is too fragile to withstand the rigors of social contact and is able only to exist within the closed world of the text. For Leal, the text represents a failure to resolve the dual impulses of "writing for me" and "writing as a cry for help," and so exemplifies the conflict between the private and the political that tends to be a characteristic of feminist thought and literature of this period (521–22). In Peter Handke's review of *Die Mutter* the citational method is dismissed as a "flight into thoughtlessness," and Gabrielle Wohmann's equally scathing account of *Lieben* accuses Struck of bad imitation.[1]

These assessments rightly point toward a certain insecurity that accompanies the intertextual voice and compromises the narrative in these early texts. In that thematic struggle to establish the female self in respect to others, they already strike a precarious balance between highly subjective self-expression and a sometimes rather strained identification of the literary voice with other texts and authors. In a broad sense, the existence of a feminine space self-consciously outside the tradition of male writing is, potentially, of great interest: women writers and theorists have effectively occupied it in various ways to bypass or disrupt the dominant discourses of the literary canon. The particular dynamics of the intertextual mode, moreover, would appear to be especially suited to an exploration of and meditation on a female literary inheritance. Insofar as the intertext challenges notions of singularity and pre-existing authority, it lends itself well to the search for creative alternatives to established literary discourses and might represent a textual complement to that position of non-belonging or non-conformity out of which the female literary tradition has been crafted. However, as a complexly functioning space in a narrative, the intertextual dimension of a text must be managed with dexterity. We are right to question whether the intertextual dimension of Struck's narratives really realizes what the intertextual mode promises in theory, namely a complex and dynamic interplay among writer, text, source, and reader.

Other Models of Intertext: Jelinek and Bachmann

Intertextuality takes many different forms, and its employment and our response to its effects are correspondingly diverse.[2] Most simply, it is direct citation from an anterior work, but it may also be understood as a more broadly based citational framework, a generic discourse, in other words. The reader, too, can be thought of as a generator of intertext, insofar as s/he is in a constant process of following through textual significations for which the author effectively cannot legislate. It is in this sense that we begin to approach Julia Kristeva's formulation of intertextuality, in *Revolution in Poetic Language,* as "a field of transpositions of various signifying systems" whose "place of enunciation and...denoted 'object' are never single, complete and identical to themselves, but always plural, shattered, capable of being tabulated" (60). Kristeva's coining of the term, a direct response to Bakhtin's concept of dialogism in the novel, expresses a notion of an infinitely open and unstable text. This might explain why she later rejected the term "intertextuality" in favor of "transposition," which seemed better to suggest the shifting ground of the signifying practices she sought to describe.

The intertextual voice is a textual exchange functioning at a number of levels within the narrative. First, it depends on a delicate balance of relations between the writer and her/his source. Second, it contributes to the communication between author and reader. Third, it is the site at which textual significations act on the reader in a sphere beyond the author's creative control. Hence, issues of self-legitimation and fragility are always enshrined in the intertextual narrative. In one sense, the intertextual dimension represents an exercise of textual authority over anterior material (which is reintroduced as a controlled repertoire of effects), corroborating the sovereignty of the new text. Yet the return to the past is potentially a passive act, accompanied by the fear of powerlessness and speechlessness, of becoming subjugated by what has gone before.[3] It is the active appropriation of the material that allows it to continue to resonate in its new environment, as Herman Meyer's formulation of the successful citational method makes clear, long before the term intertextuality became current:

> In general it would hold that the appeal of the citation consists in a curious tension between assimilation and dissimilation: [the citation] binds itself closely to its new environment but at the same time stands out from it and in this way allows a different world to shine into the world of the novel (12).

The new text must work hard to sustain the equilibrium of this intertextual tension, that is, it must lend the anterior material a sufficiently robust frame within which to expand and perform its effects.

Each author working self-consciously within an intertextual framework must find her/his own way of containing and exploiting the tension Meyer describes. Struck's model of intertextuality is in theory no more or less valid a practice than that of, say, Elfriede Jelinek or Ingeborg Bachmann, both of whom demonstrate a sophisticated textual control of the intertextual dynamic in their narrative fiction. Before I begin a more systematic analysis of Struck's writing, I would like to bring into focus some of the theoretical issues with which this article engages by way of a brief consideration of the intertextual practices at work in *Die Klavierspielerin* (The Piano Teacher, 1983) and *Malina* (1971).

Jelinek's *Klavierspielerin* finds its narrative force in an essentially negating intertextual fabric. The discursive patterns we find in the text are intertextual in the sense that the narrative recalls a range of pre-established discourses, quoting from a staple repertoire of received ideas and images: about the home and family, about love, about the highs (music) and lows (sex) of the culture industry. Jelinek's writing in this text achieves a particular kind of quotational narrative force, one that is at the same time ironically distancing and compulsively involving. By this means, the study of the miserable existence of a middle-aged piano teacher becomes a powerful critique of the social structures that are shown to produce and control her. One of the main generic intertexts is a pornographic iconography. The text contains a range of staple pornographic images, peep shows, s/m fantasies, role-play, and so on. Yet Jelinek deploys these images, representing the all-consuming turn-on that is pornography, within a radically contextualized environment that is equally forceful in its anti-substantial, anti-obsessional quality. The depiction of sexual frenzy in the peep show scene (46–57), for example, achieves a rhythmic, linguistic energy entirely faithful to the pornographic mode. The sheer excess of detail is fundamentally part of what turns us on, part of pornography's repetitive overkill of image and dialogue. Yet the pornographic element, reinstated into the text, is also hugely discomforting, because it is under constant challenge from cohabiting discourses. The pennies clicking in the slot, the economics of the hard work that is masturbation, the grotesquely exaggerated female performance, the majestically comic invocation of Lacan, all these have a prohibitive effect upon the pornographic fantasy.

Alongside this ironic constellation of quotational narrative modes, the text contains a number of specific musical and literary intertexts. Notable among these is the integration of texts by Wilhelm Müller from Schubert's song cycles "Die Winterreise" (The Winter Journey) and "Schwanengesang" (Swansong). The way in which the lyrical force of these citations is kept intact within their ugly environment is paradigmatic of Jelinek's effective use of the intertextual space. In one respect the radically poetic consciousness comments ironically on the narrative situation. Yet at the same time the modulation between satire and melancholy guides the reader into a differentiated response to the narrative, one that is both cognitively critical of and profoundly involved in the world Jelinek represents.

Ingeborg Bachmann's theory of citation would seem to provide an interesting counterpoint to Jelinek's intertextual methodology. In an interview with Dieter Zilligen, she describes an approach that has primarily to do with a perceived affiliation to the material she uses. Asked about the importance for her of a citation lifted, almost verbatim, from Rimbaud, she replies:

> For me, that is not a citation. For me there are no citations, but rather, the few moments in literature that have always excited me, those are life for me. And I do not cite sentences because I have liked them so much, because they are beautiful or because they are meaningful, but because they have genuinely aroused me. Just like life itself (Koschel and von Weidenbaum 69).

In her writing, though, intertextuality is a multi-functioning strategy that is more complex than the statement cited above would suggest. This is the thesis of Joachim Eberhardt, whose comprehensive analysis illuminates the variety of forms of the intertextual dimension in her lyric poetry and prose. His assessment of *Malina,* for example, discusses the wide range of marked references, thematic intertexts and structural intertexts contributing to the textual fabric. The different functions that these intertexts fulfill, he suggests, overflow the individual theoretical categories that have been developed generally in critical readings of the text. These are, in his summary: "theory of subversion," where intertextuality undermines the surface of the text; "theory of dialogue," where intertextuality places the text in relation to other texts; "theory of appropriation," where the author uses intertextual references to articulate her/his own ideas; "theory of content," where intertextual references are in place to create meaning (419–20).

Eberhardt's thesis is instructive, because it emphasizes the need for text-based criticism that takes account of the narrative dynamics of each intertextual moment within the text as a whole. After all, as the very different approaches of Jelinek and Bachmann show, it is precisely this sense of the intertext as a living linguistic instance within the narrative that ensures their ongoing resonance in the new text.

Struck's Early Texts: The Search for an Authentic Female Voice

The three texts written by Struck in the 1970s, *Klassenliebe, Die Mutter,* and *Lieben,* very much belong to the confessional literature of that period, characterized above all by the desire to identify and articulate an authentic, undivided female self. The self-conscious and troubled subjectivity that becomes, early on, the hallmark of Struck's writing is shown explicitly to be part of the domain of the female subject. In *Klassenliebe,* the intertextual mode is conceived as a predominantly subjective experience, where the narrator can express elements of herself through the selective appropriation of other, often radically different lives. The citational style is described as being the primary means of asserting a link with others as a form of creativity. The narrator justifies this to her lover, Z., in the following terms:

> You said that I assimilate these citations, so then they are hardly citations any more.... My citing so much is an expression of my fear of memory loss, and also an attempt to appropriate something from the monstrous mass of printed texts around me, not for knowledge, but in relation to my subjective experience. Citations also as an expression of my life...(44).

The intertextual mode, as set out here, is in place to provide orientation, insofar as the citations promise a relationship with other authors. The explanation is strikingly reminiscent of Bachmann's theory of intertextuality, cited above, as a fully subjective, affirmative appropriation of texts.

By the time of *Die Mutter,* the intertextual mode is shaped more consistently as a gesture of feminine identification, with the essentialized image of Woman at its root. The figure of the mother as both a literary and a very physical, biological presence plays a critical role in Struck's writing as a whole. The female intertextual bond is invariably underpinned with powerful metaphorical notions of fertility and reproduction, solidarity, and so forth. In *Die Mutter,* these sentiments come to the fore: "But just look what a work of art I have perfected, what works of art you have perfected, mothers" (326), and "I learn to write when I come to acknowledge the mother" (304). The invocation of Sappho (272) places the narrator in a matrilineal tradition of female creativity, sketching out the power of a motherly lifeline from past to present and future. The protagonist Nora is linked historically with other women in a common experience that, self-consciously outside the tradition of male writing, represents the birth and sustenance of a specifically feminine aesthetic.

The "Mother's Letters," which form the first section of the work, lay claim to an organic heritage that rests on the literary transferral from mother to daughter. Nevertheless, the letters also recall Kafka's *Brief an den Vater* (Letter to His Father), and this intertext, along with other more explicit references to Kafka, supplies a counter-voice to the simple embrace of the mother muse: "I say I want to write like Sappho. But all literature throws me back. I read 'The Castle' but I am thrown out from it. I read 'The Castle' for the third time, discover the word home in the first three chapters, but literature is foreign to me, it will not let me penetrate it" (273). Here, ambivalence and anxiety are inscribed in the narrator's desire to reach out to others. The belief that the mother's tongue will ward off the threat of silence is countered by an awareness that it is equally difficult to write self-consciously within the framework of a tradition. The dream of unity with the literal and metaphorical mother cannot be realized, and the closing words of the text, an allusion to Heine's "Morphine," admit to the impossibility of sustaining the utopian pretensions that gave birth to the textual figurations: "Not to be born is the greatest joy" (385). The intertext recalls the mythologized personification of drug-induced Sleep and approaching Death preoccupying the poet in his final illness, and effects a radically pessimistic revocation of the otherwise celebratory discourse of motherhood.

Struck's feminist project is further developed in *Lieben* and in her 1982 novel *Kindheits Ende* (The End of Childhood). The complex system of relations that rests on the intertextual exchange is set up in these texts as a specifically female relationship that reflects and complements the fictional relationships among the characters themselves. "What is it, this erotic relationship with language?" asks Struck's Lotte (*Lieben* 71). This is a discourse that excludes the male writer: Lotte mistrusts the literary intentions of her lover, suggesting "that with your writing you distance yourself from me, that you consider me with cold eyes like a butterfly collector" (48). In *Kindheits Ende,* similarly, the protagonist declares, "As I write, I am once again symbiotically joined to you" (542), but is unwilling to concede that male authors are capable of writing anything that does not induce and sustain a distance from their text and its subjects: "being objective...like a man" (461). The feminine space that Struck seeks to open out with these programmatic statements is troubling: her texts unquestioningly embrace stereotypical models of male (cold, unemotional, distant) and female (empathetic, natural, corporeal), and the corresponding textual strategies of identification that she employs seek legitimation in the reader's sympathy with these models.

Nonetheless, Struck's early fiction remains of interest, even if more as a record of a particular period in the political development of a feminist consciousness than for its aesthetic achievement. The feminist perspective that informs these texts is, as I have suggested, problematically reductive, but through it the narrative still manages to indicate a level of cognitive awareness of how the female self is constructed, socially and linguistically. In this respect, also, the intertextual mode does facilitate the expression of a still fragile, but situated, female writing subject. The conflict between private ("writing for me") and public ("writing as a cry for help") is, as Leal suggests, never resolved, but precisely the anxiety generated within this conflict sustains an element of authenticity in the narrative voice.

"I am not presumptuous": The Intertextual Approach to Bachmann

Of all Struck's texts, it is the 1993 text *Ingeborg B. Duell mit dem Spiegelbild* (Ingeborg B. Duel with the Mirror Image) that is most evidently driven by the belief in a female literary lineage. With it, we are returned urgently to those questions raised in Struck's earlier texts by an intertextual narrative grounded in a discourse of feminine identification. *Ingeborg B.* supplies these issues with an especially solid context. Its overt homage to Bachmann engages directly with the implications of a female literary heritage, and its intertextual methodology focuses the relationship between the two authors in a dedicated manner. However, as the culmination of an intertextual project in the service of a vision of female creativity and community, the text is also evidence of an unconvincing development of the intertextual dynamic as a feminine space in her writing.

The narrator, the fictional author Vera Hauser, is entrenched in a battle on two fronts, privately, with her unsympathetic boyfriend Frank G., and publicly, with a hostile world of literary critics. The narrative line, essentially recounting Vera Hauser's aggrieved sense of isolation and of being misunderstood, is woven into and often subsumed under a complex intertextual fabric: literary and medical citations rub shoulders with religious and mythological references and with figures of authors and critics from the literary world, most importantly, as the title suggests, with Ingeborg Bachmann. Nine years after Bachmann's death from severe burns sustained in a house fire, the protagonist finds herself returning to the theme of fire after witnessing the suicide of a Green Party activist, Dietrich Bruno. Her reflections on the motivations and tribulations of this young protestor encourage her to reinvigorate her "conversation" with Bachmann, begun much earlier with a letter sent to the author on her deathbed. Gradually, the stories of these three figures, the narrator, the suicide protestor, and the author Bachmann, are woven together, the narrator finding her voice within the intertextual framework of this double death by fire.

A powerful public gesture of protest, the self-immolation of the activist, is thus read alongside what is essentially a private tragedy, and Bachmann comes to stand symbolically for the suffering of women writers as a group. Christa Wolf's critique of Bachmann, a "'wild woman'" in the face of whose "'obsessiveness...one [can] only shrug one's shoulders, not knowing what to do'" (221), is cited, along with a question—"Must a woman adopt the male gaze on the way up to the very top?" (221)—to demarcate the female literary territory occupied by this text. The male critics, with their objectivizing, dehumanizing gaze, use Bachmann "for their own ends" (36). They have taken her and her reputation captive, as "prey" (182), pillorying her and then, after her death, canonizing her.

The narrator seeks to replace what she sees as a hypocritical public discourse with her own, essentially private, conversation with the author. Her professed intention, to allow Bachmann "to be yourself" (93), is problematic since the entirely fictional dimension of her recreated character is never acknowledged as such. Bachmann, a notionally "real" figure in the text, is wholly subjected to the specific interpretation Struck chooses to construct. In dwelling on the pain of death and the sacrificial associations of the motif of fire, Struck creates a legacy for the other author that is at least as mythical and hagiographical as anything else written about her.[4] Her life is presented as a narrative of suffering linked fundamentally with her identity as a woman and a woman writer.

A central concern is to rehabilitate Bachmann from the category of madness. Struck counters what Max Frisch described as Bachmann's "madness" (33) with Bachmann's own words: "'Men are incurably sick, don't you know that?'" (15). These words are allowed to resonate with the situation of the category of women writers per se: "And then, after women die, there's the robbing of the corpse, and then the diagnosis that they were 'sick': and that's how they diagnosed I.B. 'She was sick'—that guillotine" (167). By this means the narrator sets up parallel lines between herself and the other author: "*Joie de vivre,* destruction, breaking of boundaries. My body, like hers was, is too delicate for my desire to break boundaries. Others call that madness" (182). The gender groupings are brought into play more extremely still to align the narrator with her predecessor: "They have violated you in the same way as they have me" (162).

The title of the first section, "Approaching" (*Annäherung*), represents the process whereby the narrator attempts to close the gap with the "Alter Ego Ingeborg Bachmann" (182). The first reference to the author is made in the same colloquial tone that characterizes the opening narrative sequence:

> I lost my bearings again, I had already lost them before, while I was going from the *Gänsemarkt* to my car, as we'd each gone in our own car to the bar.
>
> That must have been what it was like for Bachmann, I thought, that she always got so bewildered by men that she kept losing hold of things. And in my case I get dizzy and can hardly see any more (12).

In somewhat inelegant prose, a jarring connection is made between an iconic author and an as yet unestablished narrator figure drinking cocktails on an unremarkable date. A few lines later, Bachmann is introduced directly, by way of a rather bald, decontextualized quotation, with the words: "'There is nothing that is separate for me'" (13). Both in the case of the first, casual reference to the author and the second, clearly demarcated quotation from her, the narrative is inadequately prepared for the intertexts. This is not so much a problem of incongruity: as we have seen in the case of Jelinek, an intertext can be highly effective as a dissonant element in a narrative. Here, however, the obvious authorial intention, to align Bachmann with the narrator, clumsily removes any intertextual resonance from the narrative. These are the first of many examples where the insertion of a quotation or reference sets up an entirely inadvertent and unacknowledged tension in the text. In purely formal terms, the intertextual mode here militates against the first approach to Bachmann.

Thematically, too, Bachmann's presence accentuates the central conflict that Struck desires to overcome, namely the uneasy juxtaposition of separation and unity, the inevitable distance that evolves together with the desire to approach another. The "Duel with the Mirror Image" of the subtitle anticipates a conflict that remains essentially unaddressed by the end of the narrative. Were Struck agile enough to exploit the ironic contradictions that her "duel" posed within the body of the text, then she could develop the metaphor of the "mirror complex" as a way of exploring the complex issues surrounding the process of identification and the recognition of separateness that it entails. However, the narrator's understanding of Bachmann's role in her search for self is inconsistent. On the one hand, we are assailed by an increasingly direct and intimate voice of address that takes possession of Bachmann as "dearest," "you," "my dearest." This voice appropriates her words ("[k]eep back, I want to scream in I.B's words" [191]) and seeks emotively to place the narrator in the author's literary legacy ("I read *Malina*... and I recognize my own dreams" [100]). On the other hand, the narrator constantly betrays the anxiety concomitant with her desire to align herself with the mythical Bachmann. "Oh, you say, this being sisters, this feminist pseudo-holiness, we aren't sisters" (189), and, more explicitly still, "I am not presumptuous. I am not comparing myself with her, I am not comparing her with me. She is very distant from me. It is the distance of the *Du* (she wrote about the *Sie* and the *Du,* in *Malina*)" (182).[5]

This reference to *Malina* exemplifies the intertextual insubstantiality that so often undoes the potential effectiveness of the transferred ideas in their new context. In *Malina,* the "I" relates to Malina and Ivan in entirely different ways, yet refers to both in the *Du* form, aware as Bachmann does so that the resonances of the word in its different contexts are scarcely comparable. While her "Malina-Du" is "precise and suited to our conversations and discussions," the *Du* that she uses for Ivan is diametrically set against this in tone and implication: it is "imprecise, it can take on color, darken, lighten... there is no limit to the range of its expressions..." (127). She identifies a quality of perfection in the *Du* she uses for Ivan that is inexpressible as a form of actual address (that is, as an utterance in the conventional sense of being audible) and as yet still only a potential within herself. The *Du* remains, then, a word signifying distance and removal from the addressee, because in its perfect manifestation it forecloses absolute oneness with the "I": "[The *Du*] has still not been said with that tone, with that expression I hear within me, when I am unable to utter a word in front of Ivan. Not in front of him, but inside me, one day, I will perfect the *Du*. It will be perfection itself" (*Malina* 127). When we return to Struck's recontextualization, to the difficulty the narrator professes to have in addressing the other author as *Sie* and the distance exacerbated by the familiar *Du* form, we become aware of the discrepancy between the highly complex original idea and the rather reductive intertextual transformation it is accorded in the new text. Struck's conception of the forms of address played out in *Malina* displays an awareness only of the interrelational tensions that the *Du* provokes in the speaker and neglects the ontological crisis that it induces in the self: "Now I am saying *Du* again. Forgive me. The *Du* is the other distance. I will always waver between *Du* and *Sie*" (188). Here, the crisis appears more precisely to be a fear of admitting to the historical and literary distance and to the mentor/disciple split that is—at least for the reader—already very much in place.

Bachmann's uncompleted trilogy, *Todesarten* (Ways of Dying), is the text's most substantial intertext. At various points, the closing sequence of *Malina* is invoked, Struck appropriating the final, neutral words that remove us from Bachmann's protagonist, "[i]t was murder" (*Malina* 337). These words are reapplied to Bruno, when the narrator, questioning the medical care that the protestor has received, asks "was it murder?" (104). They are also reapplied to Bachmann herself, first with the question, "[c]ould they have saved you, dearest? Was it murder?" (120), and later with the accusatory "[i]t was a murder of the mind" (219). As with the reductive intertextual response to the *Du* address that enshrines the complex interrelationships we are presented with in *Malina,* here, with the intertext, we are asked to equate Bachmann's experience (including her death) rather too closely with that of her protagonist.

In *Malina,* the death of the "I," forced into the wall and into silence by her alter ego Malina, has to do with a complex subject positioning. The narrator's love for Ivan makes her into the other to his self. Malina demands that she give up this love to allow for her transformation into a (writing) subject. Her refusal to do so eventually silences her, literally and metaphorically, with the emergence of the neutral narrative voice at the end of the text. Ivan and Malina are in place then to confirm the split subjectivity of the narrator.

Recontextualized, the image loses this complexity altogether. Struck places Bachmann in the wall, using the intertext not to debate with Bachmann's representation of the structuring of the female intellectual psyche, but to reinforce that rather cruder image she sets up of the endlessly suffering author driven to madness by her critics: "I hear you speaking out of the wall, out of the crack, out of the cracks I hear you whispering..." (121). Moreover, the fact that the narrator can still hear the whispering of the other author suggests a continued connection with the outer world absent in the original text, where the voice is absorbed completely: "It is a very old, a very strong wall, that no one can fall out of, that no one can break open, that no sound can ever come out of again" (*Malina* 337). The intertext's function, here as throughout the text, seems to be to reinforce through a narratively quotational process the dialogic relationship that we have seen insistently put in place by the narrator of the new text. Yet this, precisely, is what Bachmann is negating in *Malina,* where finally not even an inner dialogue is allowed to remain. It is this neglect of the ongoing dynamic force of the pieces of text Struck borrows that deadens their potential effect as intertextual instances in her narrative.

Such neglect is in evidence with material taken from the second part of the *Todesarten* trilogy, *Das Buch Franza* (The Book of Franza, 1979). One of these is the notion of shedding skin (*Häutung*), which is linked to the motif of immolation, discussed above.[6] At one point, talking to her brother, Franza refers to this: "She stared at her hands, where blisters had formed, which were bursting open, I am shedding my skin, she said, don't you see, it will all get better, I am getting a new skin. It isn't infectious, I'm sure. Are you disgusted" (399). The metaphor she uses to express her desire for regeneration and escape from her sickness is alluded to several times by Struck, who at one point quotes from the passage directly:

> You have Franza travel in the train with the brother, and you have her stare at her hands, "where blisters had formed, which were bursting open, I am shedding my skin, she said, don't you see, it will all get better, I am getting a new skin." And you have her apologize to her brother, with whom she is escaping from her "Bluebeard marriage." "It isn't infectious, I'm sure. Are you disgusted."
>
> And it's the same for me as it is for you, I am shedding my skin, as I create Dietrich Bruno anew and look into the fire and my hands guide the pen over the white paper (161).

The intertext is in place here to support the narrator of the new text, yet the clumsy transferral of the words and the typically unsubtle alignment of this protagonist with her intertextual counterpart strains the text, establishing only a derivative and essentially redundant intertextual narrative position. Rehoused in this way, the citation loses its original force: the delicacy and fragility of Franza's words, the utter sense of aloneness that Bachmann's narrative hollows out for her, all this is shattered in Vera Hauser's eager claims to identification.

We see this again in the intertextual use of the Bluebeard myth, which Bachmann uses variously in different texts.[7] In *Das Buch Franza,* the "Bluebeard marriage" to which Struck makes reference in the above citation introduces an extended description of Franza's abusive husband. He is a psychiatrist who uses his wife as a case study and deliberately allows her to gain access to his notes, cultivating in her such a state of anxiety that she is led to say:

> [m]y husband, forgive this ludicrous expression that doesn't have any relation to anything, is murdering me. I am being murdered, help me. That is what I should have said, but imagine, in this society, if someone comes and says: I am being murdered (406-07).

In Struck's text, the Bluebeard myth corresponds perfectly to the picture she paints of the predatory male with his objectified and defenseless female. The Bachmann intertext is divested of the specific representative force that Franza's situation portrays, as a woman objectified and turned into a representative of sickness. Now what originates as literary intertext is reapplied in a biographical context and Max Frisch is made shorthand for the male literary establishment accused of destroying Bachmann. "Could I.B. say it any other way: Didn't you know that men are sick. And who was it she fell in with, with that MF, the educated Bluebeard?" (33).

A further example of the insubstantiality of the intertextual voice is the paring down of the figuratively compelling space that the desert lends to *The Book of Franza*. The desert forms a literal and metaphorical backdrop to the last days of Franza's life, and is where she dies, striking her head against a rock as she tries to flee from a male attacker. The Egyptian desert is not only the place of the Other, an alien environment with the signifying force of death for "the whites." For Franza it represents desire, an undefined search ("what are you searching for in this desert...what do you want here?" [438] is a question repeated at several key moments in the text), and at times even a balm to her sickness: "Either she did not like the city or she really did want to go further on from here, in or down into the desert, this wild woman, who grew lively as [Martin's] courage began to fail him" (429). The desert is on some level just as much a corresponding as an alien force:

> Ever since she had staggered out of the bus, a battle had begun in her, within her two enemies had set on each other, with a vehement resolve, saying nothing more to one another than: I or I. I and the desert. Or I and the other. And to the exclusion of everything else and tolerating no half measures, I and I begin to go at one another (418).

And in the end, the desert offers a metaphorical comment on "the Franza case," reflecting and enhancing her decline: "A few days of desert had disappointed [Martin], the ravaging went on. She was deathly sick" (434).

Struck's invocation of this space is by contrast clichéd and sentimental, employed reductively to illustrate Bachmann's putative condition: "Is the house of writing a cloister, a house of being silent, a room of waiting, a desert? In the end, I.B. went into the desert. Before being burnt, the desert" (206). Equally undeveloped is a conversation the narrator has about the desert. At some point, her interlocutor, having described its physical and mental challenges, "[t]he heat from the sky; the sunlight; the blackness; the big stones!" and "[t]he eroticism of the desert," comments: "'My friend E. thinks that women don't belong in the desert at all.... He says they are not suited to the desert'" (216–17). The narrator, somewhat obscurely, notes: "But only when you are in the desert can you write about the desert" (218). As intertextual instances, these moments add little to the new text, nor do they comment on or illuminate Bachmann's vision.

These examples serve, I hope, to illustrate the overwhelming lack of a convincing context in which to embed the Bachmann intertext. Too often, we are allowed to register the incommensurability of Struck's literary form with Bachmann's: the writing slackens, becomes wooden in the process of quotation, seeks but fails to find legitimation in remembrance. Sentences such as "[i]f I can only bear it, these hours, like Franza bears it lying on the ground..." and "[y]es, these gentlemen Jordan and Körner still exist. Yes, that's how it is, go on, laugh at me, I don't care" (190) seem more gratuitously referential than intertextually challenging. Similarly, awkward or flaccid invocations of the other author leave the new text vulnerable: "the monstrousness of some ways of dying!" (95) and an isolated, decontextualized word left hanging at the end of a section: "Ways of dying" (*Todesarten* 204), for instance, do nothing to enlighten us or make us sympathetic to the narrative.

For an author expressly seeking, as does Struck, to explore the territory of literary influence and inheritance, the intertextual dimension is eminently a hugely interesting resource. *Ingeborg B.* represents her most sustained engagement with these themes, but (or perhaps for this very reason) the text is also her least accomplished attempt at intertextual writing. Struck shows herself unable to harness the intertextual complexities that accompany her pursuit of the texts and life of the earlier author. Desiring above all to close ranks with Bachmann as a way of reasserting her own literary authority, she places faith in the narrative's capacity to absorb and control the dominating presence of the literary muse. The idealized feminist literary bond, with Bachmann modeled as the iconic pathological figure of non-belonging, of non-conformity to a male literary canon, is placed under strain in a text that does not bear comparison to its model.

What Struck fails to acknowledge is the fact that the intertextual aspect, precisely because it brings together different discourses and invites different significations into the new text, is the site where identificatory processes (and textual authority itself) are most critically held up to challenge. It is disappointing that her early work, generating substantial feminist critical response, should have faded into a more trivial aesthetic in its pursuit of a more substantial intertextual expression of a female literary heritage. It remains to be seen to what extent a discourse of connection continues to have relevance in the work of women authors identifying themselves as part of this heritage.

Notes

Unless otherwise noted, translations are my own.

[1] These reviews are reprinted in Adler and Schrimpf (251–55, 321–23, respectively). The collection of reviews and essays here gives a balanced overview of Struck's reception in Germany up until 1984.

[2] For an overview of the theoretical territory, see Worton and Still; Allen.

[3] This, essentially, is Bloom's thesis in *The Anxiety of Influence*. Bloom roots his analysis of male poets in Freud's psychosexual paradigm of the Oedipus complex, where the sons strive to usurp the past and overcome the influence of the father-poet.

[4] See Hotz for a comprehensive overview of Bachmann's reception in the media.

[5] *Du* and *Sie* are, respectively, the informal and formal second-person pronoun.

[6] This could also be an intertextual reference to Verena Stefan's canonical feminist text, *Häutungen*.

[7] Struck has drawn upon this myth elsewhere, in *Blaubarts Schatten*. Puw Davies gives an interesting reading of this text, suggesting that "Struck uses intertextuality as a means of recalling the topos of the solidarity of women's narrative communities traditionally associated with the 'Märchen'" (494).

Works Cited

Adler, Hans, and Hans Joachim Schrimpf, eds. *Karin Struck*. Frankfurt a.M.: Suhrkamp, 1984.

Albrecht, Monika, and Dirk Göttsche, eds. *Bachmann-Handbuch: Leben—Werk—Wirkung*. Stuttgart: J.B. Metzler Verlag, 2002.

Allen, Graham. *Intertextuality*. London: Routledge, 2000.

Bachmann, Ingeborg. *Werke*. Ed. Christine Koschel, Inge von Weidenbaum, and Clemens Münster. 4 vols. München: Piper, 1978. Vol. 3.

——. *Wir müssen wahre Sätze finden: Gespräche und Interviews*. Ed. Christine Koschel and Inge von Weidenbaum. München: Piper, 1983.

Bloom, Harold. *The Anxiety of Influence: A Theory of Poetry*. New York: Oxford UP, 1973.

Eberhardt, Joachim. *"Es gibt für mich keine Zitate": Intertextualität im dichterischen Werk Ingeborg Bachmanns*. Tübingen: Niemeyer, 2002.

Ezergailis, Inta. *Women Writers: the Divided Self: Analysis of Novels by Christa Wolf, Ingeborg Bachmann, Doris Lessing and Others*. Bonn: Bouvier, 1982.

Handke, Peter. "Denunziation ohne Wahrnehmung." *Der Spiegel* 17 Mar. 1975. Qtd. in Adler and Schrimpf: 251–55.

Hotz, Constance. *"Die Bachmann": das Image der Dichterin: Ingeborg Bachmann im journalistischen Diskurs*. Konstanz: Faude, 1990.

Jelinek, Elfriede. *Die Klavierspielerin*. 1983. Reinbek bei Hamburg: Rowohlt, 1986.

Jurgensen, Manfred. *Karin Struck: eine Einführung*. Bern: Peter Lang, 1985.

Kristeva, Julia. *Revolution in Poetic Language*. 1974. Trans. Margaret Waller. New York: Columbia UP, 1984.

Leal, Joanne. "The Politics of 'Innerlichkeit': Karin Struck's *Klassenliebe* and Verena Stefan's *Häutungen*." *German Life and Letters* 50.4 (1997): 508–28.

Meyer, Herman. *Das Zitat in der Erzählkunst: zur Geschichte und Poetik des europäischen Romans*. Stuttgart: Metzler, 1961.

Puw Davies, Mererid. "'In Blaubarts Schatten': Murder, Märchen and Memory." *German Life and Letters* 50.4 (1997): 491–507.

Stefan, Verena. *Häutungen*. 1975. Frankfurt a.M.: Fischer, 1994.

Struck, Karin. *Blaubarts Schatten*. München: List, 1991.

——. *Ingeborg B. Duell mit dem Spiegelbild*. München: Langen Müller, 1993.

——. *Kindheits Ende*. Frankfurt a.M.: Suhrkamp, 1982.

——. *Klassenliebe*. Frankfurt a.M.: Suhrkamp, 1973.

——. *Lieben*. Frankfurt a.M.: Suhrkamp, 1977.

―――――. *Die Mutter*. Frankfurt a.M.: Suhrkamp, 1975.
Wohmann, Gabrielle. "Lotte―ganz in Honig getaucht." *Die Welt* 21 May 1977. Qtd. in Adler and Schrimpf: 321–23.
Worton, Michael, and Judith Still, eds. *Intertextuality: Theories and Practices*. Manchester: Manchester UP, 1990.

Neither Foreigners Nor Aliens: The Interwoven Stories of Sinti and Roma and Black Germans

Nicola Lauré al-Samarai

The article undertakes a comparative investigation of the diverging histories of two communities of people of color that have been located in Germany for many generations: the Sinti and Roma and the Black Germans. My argument is made against a background of a racialist concept of nation that still exists today and that arose during the German colonial period that continues to be repressed even today—a concept that construes the categories of Germanness and whiteness to be identical. The focuses of my investigation are on both a historical locating of the rejection (*Ausgrenzung*) and persecution narratives of both communities as well as a history of resistance that is connected to these narratives and that involves the political and cultural self-identification that in recent decades has led to a significant change of perspective. (NLa-S)

To Oscar and Vinzens Rose, who survived the survival.

Some years ago, when I came upon an introductory survey on German cultural studies published in 1995 (Burns) that dealt with cultural historical developments since the 1871 founding of the German nation-state, I was surprised to discover that it contained not a single reference to German colonialism. The term "colonialism" was itself banished from the index. Although the first chapter, "Imperial Germany," covered most of the period during which the German Reich functioned as a colonial power, the authorial collective apparently did not consider this historical fact of any importance for the establishing of imperial concepts of culture and related forms of knowledge production, for it simply erased colonialism from its narration of the German nation.

Here, as in many places, it becomes clear that, despite growing scholarly attention, German colonialism, which formally lasted from 1884 to 1918, still comprises a multilayered constitutive site of forgetting. The almost complete erasure of the colonial epoch from the collective memory of German society, as well as the eradication of the significance of a colonial imagination for the emergence of a national identity and a German discourse on race, are fraught with far-reaching consequences, among others, the failure to grasp the continuity of racist concepts and their relevance for intellectual and cultural complexes of meaning (Zantop 12).[1] The uninterrupted transmission of numerous overtly colonial/racist images and related patterns of thought and perception still evident in today's united Germany contradicts neither the Federal Republic's partial discrediting of a *völkisch* conception of nation as a result of discussions about National Socialism, nor the rigidly practiced displacement of historical responsibility within the GDR that facilitated the official repression of "problematic" epochs (Behrends, Kuck, and Poutrus 2). This historical and intellectual configuration forms the backdrop for more recent controversial debates on important topics like ethnicity, racism, and migration that, by the mid-nineties, had made their way to Germany. Vis-à-vis the rapidly developing theoretical approaches of critical cultural and postcolonial studies in other European countries and the USA, comparable transnational German debates appear not only belated. Even more problematic is the apparent appropriation of theoretical models and terms in the fields of social sciences and humanities in ways that ignore specific historical and political contexts as well as subaltern perspectives. This is particularly the case, for example, with regard to the concept of hybridity, a term that has been taken up by a number of academic discourses, yet which in its German reception often is reduced to "cultural mixing." As Kien Nghi Ha rightly observes, deploying the concept of hybridity while negating its colonial/racist associations runs the risk of reifying cultural differences along racialized national boundaries (Kien, "Hybride Bastarde" 109), despite the frequent claims of an anti-essentialist approach to cultural difference. Kien maintains that such a dehistoricized (mis)reading is far from coincidental:

> The suspicion arises that a critical appropriation of the concept of hybridity in the context of its colonial history has not only been sacrificed to the political unconcious, but is also thought to be irrelevant and undesirable. At the very least, it is remarkable how this historical amnesia and the repression of colonial history in the German reception of postcolonial criticism correlates with a culturalist perspective that conceives hybridity to be above all a sign

of social modernization, expanded consumer options, and postmodern aesthetics particularly suited to cosmopolitan and aesthetically sophisticated metropolitan elites (109).

This postmodern-eurocentric misrepresentation of critical postcolonial approaches must be seen in the context of a German tradition of social consensus that can be traced back to the immediate postwar period. Most Germans, confronted with the shocking magnitude of Nazi racial and extermination policies, responded with a massive repression of racist practices in the collective memory. The result in subsequent years was a lack of even the most basic scholarly vocabulary for describing racist categories and activities (Bielefeld 56–57). A later regression, discernable even in the present, affects not only scholarly discourse. It explains, on the one hand, the continued widespread ignorance about processes of institutional and social discrimination frequently subsumed in Germany under the category of xenophobia (*Ausländer- oder Fremdenfeindlichkeit*)—a trivialization very much at odds with social reality. On the other hand, and closely related to this, the repression of German racism and its colonial past contributes to the reification of the history of migration in Germany to a postwar phenomenon that confirms the carefully cultivated myth of the new beginning, the so-called "Zero Hour" (Kien, *Ethnizität* 21). As a consequence, the realities of marginalized groups, whose contradictory and changing presences can be discerned in much earlier periods of German history, disappear once more from view. Hence, discursively interrelated processes of silencing prevent a critical, temporally and spatially located discussion of both the impact of racialized constructions of alienness/foreignness (*Fremdheitskonstruktionen*) and accompanying hegemonic social and cultural patterns of interpretation deeply rooted in imperial and colonial imaginaries (Kien, *Aspekte* 5).

These interpretive paradigms affect our understanding not only of postwar migrants in Germany who have lived in Germany for well over a half century; they also have an impact on two communities of color who have lived in Germany for generations: Sinti and Roma[2] and Black Germans. While the ancestors of contemporary Sinti and Roma emigrated from India via Turkey and Greece to German-speaking Central Europe as early as the fifteenth century (Reemtsma 27–28), the presence of Black Germans results from specific relations between Germany and its African colonies that date back to the end of the nineteenth century, during which a scarcely noticed migration from the colonies into the metropoles was initiated and so-called "colonial subjects" transferred their domicile permanently to Germany (Oguntoye 7–8).[3]

Today approximately 60,000 Sinti and Roma and 500,000 Black Germans reside in the Federal Republic.[4] In spite of the fact that both groups can lay claim to a long and continous historical presence, each is confronted with a white mainstream society that defines them as "aliens" or "foreigners," as people who "do not belong" because they are assumed to come from "elsewhere," and as individuals who not only look but essentially are different. Even today anti-ziganist and colonial/racist traditions cause massively distorted perceptions[5] as well as structural discrimination and exclusion. Both groups often disappear from contemporary debates about migration because their respective histories disrupt familiar postwar chronologies by calling them into question. Furthermore, Sinti and Roma remain largely invisible in discussions of postcoloniality due to the fact that they never experienced colonization in the "traditional" sense (Friedrichsmeyer 283). Dominant racist constructions of Sinti and Roma and Black Germans and the resulting distortion of the complexity of their everyday experiences and social relations can in this way be seen as the outcome of ongoing attempts by mainstream white German society to establish what I term a representative and structural non-relation that in powerful ways prescribes the historical and contemporary lived realities of both groups. Thus it is, I think, analytically useful in the following pages to specify and make more concrete certain significant elements of this non-relation, to interrogate its colonial origins, and, through an examination of the histories of each of these communities, to sketch out ongoing dominant practices of the social and cultural displacement of Sinti and Roma and Black Germans.

Two important points must be clarified at the outset of my discussion. Considering the very different historical periods of migration in question, we are confronted with two equally distinct communal chronologies. The following comparison treats the foundation of the German nation-state in 1871 as a crucial historical starting point that initiated a shift in discursive as well as institutional frameworks.[6] Because both histories have to date not been connected either in historical or cultural studies discourses, my necessarily abbreviated discussion will constitute a primarily descriptive synthesis and a stock-taking that for this reason entail certain substantive omissions and at times display teleological tendencies.

Itineraries of Exclusion: Two Versions of Marginalization

The founding of the German nation-state in 1871 is characterized by a development that on the one hand hastened the decline of particularist inner-German identities, but whose internal homogenizing effects produced, on the other hand, new and shifting boundaries that were necessary for the constitution of this newly formed national body's notions of inclusiveness (Gosewinkel 13-14). Intensifying discussions within this new order about the character of national identity in the highly charged context of debates on ethnic and political identification generated a national self-conception by means of which the nation was imagined not as a voluntary community of citizens, but rather as a *Volksgemeinschaft* that shared a common ancestry and a common bloodline (Wippermann 136). The dominance of an exclusive principle of descent as the underlying basis for a *völkisch* conception of the nation is the result of a development that began in the *Kaiserreich* (Gosewinkel 18) and can only be understood in the context of the 1884 accession of Germany into the ranks of the major European colonial powers. As Pascal Grosse convincingly demonstrates, for the first time in German history German colonialism established the conditions for a racialized bourgeois order, that is, a society in which anthropological criteria pervaded and structured most social, juristic, and economic aspects of public and private life (Grosse, *Kolonialismus* 10).

The powerful conceptual framework through which Germany came to be conceived as a racially homogeneous nation was premised upon a biologist model of the social body—the *Volkskörper*—which assumed an equivalence between the categories Germanness and whiteness as a mechanism for constructing a collective understanding of the nation that both secured national identity and belonging and authorized action on its behalf. This construction is of importance for two reasons. First, the equation of Germanness/whiteness with purity and supremacy provided the basis for a superior self-conception of the white German majority (Campt 62). Second, it determined both the social constructions of, as well as the everyday lived relationships to, individuals defined as "alien/foreign" and Germans of color in particular. With the discursive invocation of biopolitical concepts that since the eighteenth century were devoted to the control and regulation of "life-processes," this national discourse of national purity constantly renewed racist, anti-ziganist, anti-Semitic, and eugenic ideologies through a racialized and racializing exercise of power. It not only gave scientific authority to the control, productivity, and hierarchization of life forms but, by drawing a caesura between those who deserved to live and those who deserved to die, simultaneously legitimized political practices of exclusion, terror, and murder (Steyerl 29) that came to be implemented on a practical level in the Third Reich.

Within this framework, the categorization of Sinti and Roma and Black Germans as "of foreign race" (*fremdrassig*) is best understood with respect to the conceptual permanence of these categories and their relationality with regard to each of these populations. Gypsy stereotypes congealed around the turn of the century into an anthropology-based racial category that stigmatized Sinti and Roma as unassimilable, extra-European "aliens" whose allegedly nomadic way of life, unsteady work habits, thievery, and idleness, along with their unbridled sexual behavior, were indicators of their intrinsic asocial character. Similarly, the stereotyping of people of African descent is based on related, although distinct, concepts of primitive ethnicities that fixed the members of both groups as racialized objects. The construction of each population as "racially inferior" thus linked assumptions about a more or less nonexistent cultural capacity (*Kulturfähigkeit*) with those about their "degenerative danger" for the "community of the Volk" (*Volksgemeinschaft*).

Secondly, and closely related to this, the social construction of the "half-breed" (*Mischling*)—whether "gypsy" or Black—can also be seen to emerge from the same conceptual framework as the embodiment of this degeneration, as a particularly dangerous threat to the purity of the *Volk*. In this context, the discussions about what was seen as the urgent "question of colonial half-breeds" (*koloniale Mischlingsfrage*) arising from German colonization attracted broad public attention at the turn of the century and can be read as an important test case, in that it provoked an intensification of a racialized national and political discourse that enjoyed broad social consensus and had a lasting impact. The integration of anti-ziganist and colonial/racist concepts into the legislative actions of the *Kaiserreich*, the Weimar Republic, and the National Socialist regime in this way exemplifies the deployment of a legalized political practice that resulted in two different histories of exclusion and persecution.

Since the *Kaiserreich*, the stigma of specific forms of racialized asociality has informed the conceptualization and enactment of state "gypsy policies" with an ever-increasing reach. These policies linked racial anthropology with discourses of criminal biology and introduced state-sponsored discrimination based upon a permanent criminalization of the Sinti and Roma minority.[7] Ever-escalating bureaucratic regulations and the expansion of special racist decrees continued until the end of the Weimar Republic. While "traditional gypsy-policies" intensified at the beginning of the Third Reich and contributed to a broadening of the group of persons defined as "gypsy-asocials" (*zigeunerisch-asozialer*

Personenkreis), the reciprocal collaboration of science, state legislation, and a centralized police apparatus in 1938 eventually led to the establishment of a state directive that justified the "management of the gypsy question on the basis of race" (*Regelung der Zigeunerfrage aus dem Wesen der Rasse*)—a qualitative shift from the persecution of a way of life to the eradication of an entire population (Reemtsma 101). Based on this legal justification, Sinti and Roma were systematically deprived of rights, forced to forfeit their German citizenship, and compulsorily ghettoized in so-called "gypsy camps" that exploited them through forced labor and laid the groundwork for their deportation to concentration camps, culminating finally in the genocidal murder of a half million Sinti and Roma in Germany and other European countries.[8]

Because of the heterogeneity of their community, the situation of Blacks living in Germany turned out to be much more contradictory. Of particular relevance for Black colonial migrants was the complex interplay between an ideological conception of race, pragmatic policies directed toward maintaining power in the colonies, and an escapist colonial fantasy world that justified the social reality of colonization in the Weimar Republic and the Third Reich (Grosse, "Kolonialmigration" 92). The resulting revisionist interpretive framework significantly influenced German interactions with colonial migrants and limited the latter's working options from the interwar period to the forties. As "living capital," they were strategically positioned in ways that intended to evoke former German grandeur, for example, through their appearing as former colonial subjects in human anthropological exhibitions (*Völkerschauen*) and colonial films. Yet these public stagings of what quite literally amounted to post-colonial nostalgia meant in practical terms the intentional cultural and physical separation and isolation of the Black colonial migrants from the majority population (Grosse, "Kolonialmigration" 104). Although numerous individuals and their children also lost their rights to citizenship, until 1940 the contradictory interests of National Socialist racial and colonial policies initially justified a wait-and-see stance on the part of government officials.

However, the fate of Afro- and Asian-German children, born as a consequence of the occupation of the Rhineland by French colonial troops after the First World War, was entirely different. The smear campaign waged against them from 1919 until the mid-twenties appropriated important argumentative strategies from the debates around "colonial half-breeds" and transformed them into a degenerative discourse in the Weimar Republic. As a visible result of wartime defeat, the construction of the *Rheinlandbastard* who, in *völkisch* logic, penetrated the "innermost reaches of the body of the Volk," became a symbol of the "threat to the health of the Volk" (*Volksgesundheit*) as the epitome of the "internal racial enemy" (El-Tayeb 160–61). The names of the Rhineland children had been collected as early as the twenties, and shortly after the Nazi seizure of power, officials from various ministries and from the Office for Racial Politics of the NSDAP deliberated on a "solution to the bastard question" (*Lösung der Bastardfrage*). Despite the absence of legal authorization, party officials decided to pursue compulsory sterilization of the Rhineland children which was carried out by the Gestapo in 1937 as a secret *Nacht-und-Nebel-Aktion* (night-and-fog action).[9]

In the postwar order of both the FRG and the GDR, the end of the National Socialist dictatorship generated the myth of a new beginning. This mythology negated the extent to which both state structures were situated within the continuity of German history as successors to the Third Reich. However, the specific temporal marking (and the vehemence of its enforcement) that such a historiography instantiates must be understood as a powerful discursive component of a symbolic politics that—contrary to historical facts and circumstances—signaled the white German mainstream's need for a complete break with its incriminating history. The purported "liberation" of the German majority from its history thus represents a reductionism premised upon repression (Kien, *Koloniale Muster* 57) that, in spite of the different political systems of both postwar regimes, established a dominant selective memory with significant commonalities. Memory in both Germanies was premised upon the persistence of a *völkisch*-national interpretive framework, by means of which an imagined racial homogeneity of the national community was and is continually reconstituted. This framework consists of (and, at the same time manifests) numerous historical gaps that either discursively foreclose the multiple associations and interconnections of subaltern German histories or bury them completely. The disjunctive time/space that emerges as its consequence and within which the most varied (hi)stories of migration, emigration, expulsion, and genocide overlap, resonate with, and/or efface each other (Steyerl 39) at present only allows us access to traces of the postwar West German histories of Sinti and Roma and Black Germans. These histories show that ongoing, although shifting, forms of anti-ziganist and racist political practices not only draw on a stubborn reservoir of stereotypical imagery, they also highlight the continuity of scientific, ideological, and cultural discourses on which they rely and from which they emerge. In the final analysis, it is a continuity that is both founded upon and, at the same time, legitimizes itself through the effacement of the histories of marginalization and persecution of both Sinti and Roma and Black Germans.

In the postwar period Sinti and Roma were immediately criminalized as a threat to social order and were—for instance, in the 1953 "Vagrant Ordinance" (*Landfahrerordnung*)—again subjected to special "criminal preventive" racist legislation. Moreover, they saw themselves confronted by a white mainstream society that, until the beginning of the eighties, not only minimized or denied the genocide, but also had failed to develop any sense of injustice connected to it. On the contrary, the majority of the men and women hired by the West German government for the task of a new comprehensive registration (*Totalerfassung*) of Sinti and Roma survivors had already worked as police officials responsible for the "gypsy questions" in the Nazi administration. Furthermore, the collaboration between state authorities and anthropologists identified as "gypsy specialists" continued seamlessly in the postwar period to use documentation compiled by the Nazis. As a consequence, Sinti and Roma, who were consistently accused of an "unwillingness to integrate into industrial society" and of clinging to a "gypsy lifestyle" (Winckel 41), suffered massive structural disadvantages, extending from a lack of educational opportunities to discrimination by officials in all areas of life. That anti-ziganist thought and activity persist up until the present day and are consistently supported and legitimized by the government is proven in the following summary of a very recent study:

> In contrast to anti-Semitism, which, despite increasing transgressions of the taboo, is socially denounced, anti-ziganism goes widely unscrutinized and is taken for granted. The projection of the image of the "gypsy" onto real existing people functions without a hitch. State activities support these modes of thinking by rigorously denying any legitimacy to the claims of the minority and by reproducing anti-ziganist stereotypes more or less in the name of the state (Winckel 106-07).

In contrast, for the small group of Black German survivors of the NS-regime, the comprehensive repression of the German colonial past meant the effacement not only of their history and fate in the Third Reich, but also the erasure of their very existence. Detached from any historical connection with earlier generations, the Black German children born as "occupation babies" (*Besatzungskinder*) after 1945 captured public attention. As the German Bundestag declared in the early 1950s, these children represented "a human and racial problem of a special sort" that should provoke considerable reflection (Lemke 45). The perception of these Afro-German children as "aliens" was the defining criterion that guided their treatment by officials and by private and public institutions. Analogously, social, scientific, and pedagogical studies on "race" and "miscegenation" revived discourses that examined their special "problematic nature" (Wollrad 20). Thus, for example, between 1952 and 1960 a significant number of Afro-German boys and girls—primarily children residing in public and private institutions in Germany—again became the objects of anthropological investigation whose approaches and research interests drew explicitly on studies of "racial science" written in the first half of the twentieth century (Lemke 55–72). The construction of a racial concept that emphasized the "stain" of "miscegenation" and reproduced "racial distinctiveness" (Campt and Grosse 64) enabled the continued biologization of the social in various areas of society. Lemke concludes:

> Even fifteen years after the end of the war "miscegenation" was seen as something exclusively negative, even threatening, since it continued to be founded upon the pseudo-biological assumption that it was always the negative qualities of both "races" that were inherited, such that Afro-German children were necessarily psychically and physically less talented (Lemke 186).

Strategies for the socio-cultural displacement of Sinti and Roma and Black Germans both historically and in the present signify distinct discursive practices that can be read as acts of collective ideological expulsion.[10] While the current attempts to situate both groups outside the white German mainstream in the case of Sinti and Roma have come to be articulated in terms of a "cultural difference" that constitutes an insurmountable contradiction to bourgeois society, this reference is not applicable in the Black German context. What remains is an "optical divergence" that materializes, or, more precisely, instantiates their alleged "alienness/foreignness" (Wollrad 22). In this way, both cultural anti-ziganism and biological racism function as a way of coding ontological difference that reasserts a familiar claim: namely, the ideological fiction that in "earlier times" a space existed in which culture developed "undisturbed" by external influences (Wollrad 22). In other words, in order to sustain a position that denies the real existence of Germans of color by postulating their unchanging, genetically determined, meta-cultural "alienness/foreignness," it is repeatedly necessary to contest ideologically the real facts and the heterogeneous composition of the German people (El-Tayeb 141). This process of creating non-histories as a means of exercising power and securing domination generates a neocolonial cartography with a multitude of new sites in which various silenced presences are interwined through the perpetuation of colonial gestures. A critical scrutiny of this multilayered, oppressive, interpretive framework reveals the impossibility of an additive approach to the histories of Sinti and Roma and Black Germans, whereby dominant history is expanded through the "supplement" of "minority histories." Rather it requires us to acknowledge not only a relationality that emphasizes the colonial roots and references of corresponding discourses but—by making visible the persistence of the untold and the repressed—re-creates the interconnections between a dominant and two subjugated German historicities and thus provides the decisive link between both communal histories as well as between the present and the past.

Claiming Space: The Struggle for Political and Cultural Self-Determination

The exclusion of subaltern voices and histories from the dominant public sphere in Germany does not mean they do not exist. Rather, the contestatory political and cultural practices of self-empowerment reveal the existence of numerous spaces of subaltern activity in which specific intersubjective experiences of national identity, community interest, and cultural values are negotiated (Bhabha 2). The multiple intermediary positionalities and diverging experiences of shifting boundaries call hegemonic constructions and representations into question and also produce complex and fragmentary counter-narratives that—as tentative expressions of a transgressive culture of hybridity—can be located within autonomous subaltern systems of meaning (Kien, *Ethnizität* 137). To return to my opening comments, these systems of meaning should in no way be understood as the consequence of a harmonious "cultural mixing," for they are the hard-won products of profoundly unequal power relations. These contradictory and deeply historical subject positionings are grounded in specific empirical knowledge formations that contribute decisively to the development of strategies of individual and communal selfhood that are shaped and articulated in and through these subaltern frameworks.

Against this backdrop, it is possible to locate the distinct positionings of Sinti and Roma and Black Germans in their struggles for political and cultural self-determination. Although both groups are situated within diametrally opposed communal circumstances—Sinti and Roma can rely upon firmly established community structures, while Black Germans are most often isolated from one another and must use considerable effort to create their own forms of community—they share a fundamental experience of oppression. This derives from the crucial contradiction between dominant perceptions of them as "aliens/foreigners" on the one hand, and, on the other, their subjective experience "of being internal to and to some extent an acknowledged member of this society... and yet also throroughly marginalized by and within it" (Campt 102). In this connection the provocative question posed by Michelle Wright with respect to Afro-Germans can also be applied to Sinti and Roma: specifically, "[h]ow one, as an Other-from-Within, should respond to a discourse that posits one as an Other-from-Without?" (Wright, qtd. in Campt 103).

Even if this question cannot yet be answered, addressing the histories of political resistance of Sinti and Roma and Black Germans seems to me an important prerequisite for moving in that direction. In this concluding section, I will sketch out the paths of the Sinti and Roma Civil Rights Movement and the Black German movement in an attempt to counter the frequent omission of the politically organized practices of resistance of each group as part of their respective efforts to create their own path into history. The challenges and shifting perspectives initiated by each of these movements have created the conditions for self-defined social spaces of articulation that made possible both the representation of their own experiences, standpoints, and visions, and also the difficult task of inscribing their historical and current presence into the social record.

As early as the 1950s, Sinti and Roma undertook the first efforts to articulate their political interests. In 1956, Oskar and Vinzens Rose founded the Association of Racially Persecuted People of Non-Jewish Belief (*Verband rassisch Verfolgter nicht-jüdischen Glaubens*), whose main objective was directed toward obtaining reparations for survivors of the National Socialist persecution. The Nazi genocide not only severely affected this population; the government's refusal to pay compensation also led to the collapse of the entire social and vocational structure of the community. Because state officials transferred numerous Sinti and Roma to crowded ghettos made up of barracks and trailers at the urban periphery near garbage dumps, sewage disposal plants, and super highways (Rose, *Bürgerrechte* 13), their continuing demands for educational, vocational, and geographical integration are more than understandable. In subsequent years, civil rights groups were founded in various localities. These groups eventually merged in 1982 into the Central Council of German Sinti and Roma, which has since then represented nationally and internationally the interests of Sinti and Roma living in Germany.[11]

The Civil Rights Movement achieved its first significant successes in the 1970s by drawing attention to the situation of Sinti and Roma through targeted public relations campaigns, cooperation with domestic and international organizations, and spectacular acts of resistance. In

1980, civil rights activists undertook a week-long hunger strike at the memorial of the Dachau concentration camp in Bavaria to effect the cancellation of the racist registration practices by police and judicial authorities that had continued to make use of Nazi records. In 1981, the occupation of the university archive in Tübingen compelled the release of the documents of the Research Center for Racial Hygiene (*Rassenhygienische Forschungsstelle*), which were still employed for dubious anthropological purposes (Peritore, "Geschichte" 4). As part of its tenaciously fought battle for public recognition of the Nazi genocide by the West German government, the Central Council demanded the official condemnation of the persecutors in 1982. The direct result of the efforts of the Central Council was the investigation and criminal prosecution of crimes perpetrated against Sinti and Roma (Winckel 66–69).

The current recognition of Sinti and Roma as a national minority was a major achievement of the Civil Rights Movement and brought about comprehensive structural changes of basic conditions. Of particular significance was the founding of the Documentation and Cultural Center of German Sinti and Roma in 1997 in Heidelberg. The establishment of this independent, specialized institution after many years of preliminary work transformed the character and the direction of civil rights activities, because it opened up the possibility of defining a self-determined representational space that enabled the recognition of the historical experiences and the cultural and intellectual accomplishments of Sinti and Roma. Recordings of interviews with Holocaust survivors, collections of family photographs and personal possessions, archives of source materials, and an increasing number of scholarly publications, instructional material, and compilations of life stories (Rose, *Dokumentationszentrum* 69–71) comprise some of the different elements of memory work through which the center safeguards cultural and historical traces and makes visible the diversity of different communal perspectives. These multiple forms of re-membering increasingly involve self-referential networks within which new and very different forms of cultural and intellectual articulations are developing.

Although in recent years Sinti and Roma have begun to present their own perspectives on the past to those outside their community, because of a reluctance to speak publicly that has been practiced by many generations, this new path is neither straightforward nor self-evident. The fact that the community was required to hide its experiences and social relations from the outside world made it necessary to develop close-knit family and communal structures that resulted in a refinement of informal, mainly oral techniques of transmitting history and cultural traditions. The contents of this intergenerational inheritance were intended to remain inaccessible to the external world, protected by the community's own spoken language, *Romanes,* as well as specific cultural codes. In this regard, a comment by Daniel Strauss at the beginning of the 1990s points to an important internal debate:

> For our part, we will have to discuss whether it is now necessary more than ever before in our history for us to express ourselves and to initiate and assertively and self-confidently conduct discussions with the majority German population (Wurr and Träbing-Butzmann 84).

Concretely, this means opening up a restricted area that has hitherto been necessary for the survival of Sinti and Roma—not only as a space for cultural retreat, but also as the only place that sheltered their collective memory and historicity.

In contrast to Sinti and Roma, the history of the Black German political movement is significantly shorter. Its beginnings coincided with the publication of the seminal work *Showing Our Colors: Afro-German Women Speak Out* (*Farbe bekennen: Afro-deutsche Frauen auf den Spuren ihrer Geschichte*), arguably the most important milestone for the Black German movement. The painstaking research of activist May Ayim contained in this text advanced for the first time a framework for the critical periodization of Black German history by focusing attention on the continuing presence of Black people in Germany from the colonial period into the Federal Republic of the mid-eighties, thus laying the foundation for an autonomous Black German historiography. With the assistance of the African-American poet and activist Audre Lorde, resident in Berlin at the time of the book's preparation, the neologism *Afro-German* was created. This self-designation exploded the historical axiom of the irreconcilability of Germanness and Blackness, and even today offers an appropriate alternative to discriminatory dominant terms still in use (Oguntoye, *Farbe bekennen* 10). For many men and women who until then had lived in complete isolation, this intervention served as an invitation to meet and address their history and current situation both individually and collectively.

With the founding of the Initiative of Black Germans (*Initiative Schwarze Deutsche/ISD*) and the Black women's organization *ADEFRA* almost twenty years ago, a nation-wide infrastructure developed shortly thereafter with branch networks and regular publications that introduced and established Black German perspectives on a national and international level. Unlike Sinti and Roma, at the outset of their political work Black Germans were not able to draw on a communal structure or a collective memory. What existed instead were numerous isolated individual experiences that had to be patiently assembled and through which a collective dimension eventually emerged (Lauré al-Samarai 207). The initial grassroots work of the ISD and ADEFRA can therefore be understood as an internal consciousness-raising and empowerment effort in the face of an invisibility that derived from individual isolation. Over the years, these efforts have reached thousands of Black Germans and formed the basis for a communal practice whose importance derives from the communal permanence it has succeeded in establishing.

Although the individual isolation of Black Germans is still a determining condition that often hinders self-organization, many successes have been achieved in recent years. Along with educational efforts aimed at sensitizing the white German mainstream population, these include internal discussions about increasing the visibility and accessibility of Black German culture and history. In the complicated process of the re-possession and re-appropriation of that which has been forgotten, repressed, and unsaid, Black social scientists, cultural studies scholars, and historians play an important role, since they reassemble the scattered puzzle of community history, gather together evidence about Black German lived experiences, and elaborate theoretical positions. The fact that the first steps toward a temporally and spatially located Black German self-conception were taken by women, who made their critical Black and feminist perspectives and approaches a starting point for thinking and conceptualizing their realities, is consistently reflected in the small canon of cultural and intellectual traditions that has been assembled over the last twenty years. Moreover, in the artistic and literary productions of women and men, multiple and ambivalent positionings are to be found that often no longer deal solely with the experiences of Othering, but rather emphasize an individual and collective normality (Piesche 199). Despite all these successes, May Ayim pointed out presciently in the mid-nineties that

> racism and repression...will remain a topical issue in Germany in the foreseeable future. That is revealing and alarming and yet...not a reason for resignation, but instead a demand for increased political activism, which also means, for example, that we have to create more and better strategies and coalitions at the national and international level (Ayim 138).

It is thus all the more important that the beginnings of an exchange between Sinti and Roma and Black Germans have emerged, despite the fact that this dialogue was initiated in an unlikely context: a 2002 exhibition that grossly misrepresented the fate of Black people during National Socialism.[12] The solidarity with which the Central Council supported the Black community protests was not limited to the duration of the exhibit, but led to discussions about further cooperation, in which the diverging experiences of the two communities and above all their different structural access to political participation are of great importance. While Black Germans still undertake their political work on an informal level and particular institutions and bodies therefore remain closed to them, Sinti and Roma are able to access these as a consequence of the Civil Rights Movement.

This example of a possible future coalition demonstrates the necessity for both communities to communicate about commonalities and differences in their history and present-day experiences of racist exclusion, as well as emphasizing the gravity of the crucial lack of knowledge among and between each of these communities. The historical and current erasure of both groups is so profound that in many ways it impedes attempts for them to relate to one another, and hence complicates the elaboration of inter- and transcultural strategies of resistance. Thus, there remains an urgent need for dialogue between different and diverse German subalterns—for example, discussions situated within the counter-discourses of Sinti and Roma and Black Germans that confront the connections, contradictions, and discontinuities in cultural and knowledge production; conversations that examine how subaltern voices are (mis)placed and/or coopted in the service of state and social techniques of Othering; dialogues that draw upon the experiences of men and women for an analysis of diverging gendered subjectivities, which include queer perspectives, challenge heteronormative concepts, and identify hegemonic mechanisms of exclusion within subaltern contexts; and/or productive exchanges that ponder conflicted or hyphenated identities. Sadly, these discussions for the most part have not yet begun in Germany, but they remain the hope and aspiration of many for the future.

Translated by Sara Lennox

Notes

I would like to thank the Central Council of German Sinti and Roma in Heidelberg for the permission to use their internal papers, Kien Nghi Ha for an unpublished manuscript and his precise critique, and Eske Wollrad and Tina Campt for their helpful comments. I am indebted to Sara Lennox for her careful translation and to Tina Campt and Junot Diaz who gave it voice.

[1] Susanne Zantop identifies three factors characterizing a Germany-specific "postcolonial situation" that explain the hesitant interrogation of colonial conceptual frameworks and discourses: the brevity of the colonial period, the absence of a vocal colonial minority (that is, former "colonial subjects"), and the central role played by the Holocaust discussion in the postwar period (Zantop 12).

[2] The terms Sinti and Roma are self-designations. The negative connotations of the German word "Zigeuner," which has analogues in other European languages, are comparable with those that the English term "gypsy" evokes. The majority of German Sinti and Roma reject the word "Zigeuner."

[3] The precolonial presence of people of African descent is of secondary importance in this context. For it was not until the advent of colonial migration that Black people appeared as a migrant group and, hence, could develop their own metropolitan communality.

[4] In the following I will not be addressing the situation of men and women of Romani or African descent who currently live in Germany but were not socialized in German contexts.

[5] As a 1998 study shows, dominant perceptions of Sinti and Roma are still primarily limited to gypsy stereotypes (Wurr and Träbing-Butzmann 99; 101). I would assert that a comparable public opinion poll on Black Germans (notwithstanding deeply-rooted clichés about people of African descent) would probably reveal that there is no public recognition of the existence of Black Germans as a group. This is, however, a speculative observation on my part since at present no adequate empirical evidence is available.

[6] It should not be forgotten that the massive marginalization of Sinti Germans began at the point of their immigration in the fifteenth century and, until the nineteenth century, entailed a legally institutionalized discrimination by special regulations that were used to prohibit their mobile way of life by confining it to particular social niches, or—if possible—by destroying it (Wurr and Träbing-Butzmann 75–76).

[7] In her detailed study, Bonillo answers the question of whether Sinti and Roma encountered race-based discrimination already in the *Kaiserreich* with a decisive yes (Bonillo 223–24). Her conclusion is important because, up until the 1990s, numerous scholarly studies remained committed to a criminal biological paradigm that minimized the practices of racist exclusion in the *Kaiserreich,* as well as the Nazi genocide, as measures aimed at the prevention of criminal acts.

[8] Since the mid-nineties an increasing number of studies have focused on the National Socialist persecution of Sinti and Roma, concentrating in

particular on different local experiences. General surveys include König; Riechert; and Rose and Weiss.

[9] For historical facts about the persecution see Pommerin.

[10] That both groups are conceived of as not belonging in Germany is shown by practical considerations flaring up repeatedly from the turn of the century into the 1960s about their permanent resettlement (Wippermann 13; Pommerin 74) or an encouragement toward "voluntary" emigration (Lemke 188).

[11] In addition to the Central Council, various other interest groups exist, e.g., Rom e.V. Köln, Rom Union Frankfurt, or the Cinti Union Roma National Congress in Hamburg, which are primarily concerned with the difficult situation of Roma who have migrated from Eastern Europe, and which offer assistance to refugees (Reemtsma 143-44).

[12] The exhibition, entitled *Besondere Kennzeichen: Neger. Schwarze im NS,* took place from November 2002 to February 2003 in the NS-Dokumentationszentrum El-De-Haus in Cologne. The organizers were Peter Martin, Horst Mazerath, and Christine Alonzo.

Works Cited

Ayim, May. "Rassismus und Verdrängung im vereinten Deutschland." *Grenzenlos und unverschämt.* Berlin: Orlanda, 1997. 133-38.

Behrends, Jan C., Dennis Kuck, and Patrice Poutrus. *Historische Ursachen der Fremdenfeindlichkeit in den neuen Bundesländern.* Thesenpapier der Projektgruppe *Herrschaft und Eigen-Sinn* des ZZF Potsdam. 2001 <http://www.zzf-pdm.de/papers/fremde/thesp>.

Bhabha, Homi K. *Die Verortung der Kultur.* Tübingen: Stauffenburg, 2000.

Bielefeld, Ulrich. "Selbstverständnis und Rassismus: Die Krise des Antirassismus als Krise seiner Theorie und Praxis." *Politik der Multikultur: Vergleichende Perspektiven zu Einwanderung und Integration.* Ed. Mechthild Jansen and Sigrid Baringhorst. Baden-Baden: Nomos, 1994. 47-68.

Bonillo, Marion. *"Zigeunerpolitik" im Deutschen Kaiserreich 1871-1918.* Frankfurt a.M.: Peter Lang, 2000.

Burns, Rob, ed. *German Cultural Studies: An Introduction.* Oxford: Oxford UP, 1995.

Campt, Tina. *Other Germans: Black Germans and the Politics of Race, Gender, and Memory in the Third Reich.* Ann Arbor: U of Michigan P, 2004.

Campt, Tina, and Pascal Grosse. "'Mischlingskinder' im Nachkriegsdeutschland: Zum Verhältnis von Psychologie, Anthropologie und Gesellschaftspolitik." *Psychologie und Geschichte* 6.1/2 (1994): 48-78.

El-Tayeb, Fatima. *Schwarze Deutsche: Der Diskurs um "Rasse" und nationale Identität 1890-1933*. Frankfurt a.M.: Campus, 2001.

Friedrichsmeyer, Sara. "Christoph Hein's *Horns Ende*: Gypsy Essences and German Community." *The Imperialist Imagination: German Colonialism and Its Legacy*. Ed. Sara Friedrichsmeyer, Sara Lennox, and Susanne Zantop. Michigan: U of Michigan P, 1998. 281-93.

Gosewinkel, Dieter. *Einbürgern und Ausschließen: Die Nationalisierung der Staatsangehörigkeit vom Deutschen Bund bis zur Bundesrepublik Deutschland*. Göttingen: Vandenhoeck & Ruprecht, 2001.

Grosse, Pascal. *Kolonialismus, Eugenik und bürgerliche Gesellschaft in Deutschland 1850-1918*. Frankfurt a.M.: Campus, 2000.

———. "Zwischen Privatheit und Öffentlichkeit: Kolonialmigration in Deutschland 1900-1940." *Phantasiereiche. Zur Kulturgeschichte des deutschen Kolonialismus*. Ed. Birthe Kundrus. Frankfurt a.M.: Campus, 2003. 91-109.

Kien, Ha Nghi. "Die kolonialen Muster deutscher Arbeitsmigrationspolitik." *Spricht die Subalterne deutsch? Migration und postkoloniale Kritik*. Ed. Hito Steyerl and Encarnación Gutiérrez Rodriguez. Münster: Unrast, 2004. 56-107.

———. *Ethnizität und Migration*. Münster: Westfälisches Dampfboot, 1999.

———. "Hybride Bastarde: Identitätskonstruktionen in kolonial-rassistischen Wissenschaftskontexten." *Kulturelle Identität: Konstruktionen und Krisen*. Ed. Eva Kimminich. Frankfurt a.M.: Peter Lang, 2003. 107-60.

———. "Problematische Aspekte der deutschsprachigen Rezeption von Hybridität." *Hybridität und ihre deutschsprachige Rezeption. Zur diskursiven Einverleibung des Anderen*. Ed. Karl Hörning, Julia Reuter. Bielefeld, forthcoming (transcript).

König, Ulrich. *Sinti und Roma unter dem Nationalsozialismus: Verfolgung und Widerstand*. Bochum: Studien-Verlag Dr. N. Brockmeyer, 1989.

Lauré al-Samarai, Nicola. "Unwegsame Erinnerungen: Auto/biographische Zeugnisse von Schwarzen Deutschen aus der BRD und der DDR." *AfrikanerInnen in Deutschland und Schwarze Deutsche—Geschichte und Gegenwart*. Ed. Marianne Bechhaus-Gerst and Reinhardt Klein-Arendt. Münster: LIT, 2004. 197-210.

Lemke Muniz de Faria, Yara-Colette. *Zwischen Fürsorge und Ausgrenzung: Afrodeutsche "Besatzungskinder" im Nachkriegsdeutschland*. Berlin: Metropol, 2002.

Oguntoye, Katharina. *Eine afrodeutsche Geschichte: Zur Lebenssituation von Afrikanern und Afrodeutschen in Deutschland von 1884–1950*. Berlin: Hoho, 1997.

Oguntoye, Katharina, May Opitz, and Dagmar Schultz, ed. *Farbe bekennen: Afrodeutsche Frauen auf den Spuren ihrer Geschichte*. Berlin: Orlanda, 1986.

Peritore, Silvio. "Geschichte nach 1945/Bürgerrechtsbewegung (Stand Sept. 01)." Internes Papier des Dokumentationszentrums deutscher Sinti und Roma. Heidelberg, 2001.

———. "Der Völkermord an den Sinti und Roma in der Gedenkstättenarbeit: Politischer und gesellschaftlicher Umgang/kritische Bestandsaufnahme." Internes Papier des Dokumentationszentrums deutscher Sinti und Roma. Heidelberg, n.d.

Piesche, Peggy. "Identität und Wahrnehmung in literarischen Texten Schwarzer deutscher Autorinnen der 90er Jahre." *AufBrüche: Kulturelle Produktionen von Migrantinnen, Schwarzen und jüdischen Frauen in Deutschland*. Ed. Cathy S. Gelbin, Kader Konuk, and Peggy Piesche. Königstein/Taunus: Ulrike Helmer, 1999. 195–205.

Pommerin, Reiner. *Sterilisierung der Rheinlandbastarde: Das Schicksal einer farbigen deutschen Minderheit, 1918–1937*. Düsseldorf: Droste Verlag, 1979.

Reemtsma, Karin. *Sinti und Roma: Geschichte, Gegenwart, Kultur*. München: Beck, 1996.

Riechert, Hansjörg. *Im Schatten von Auschwitz: Die nationalsozialistische Sterilisationspolitik gegenüber Sinti und Roma*. Münster: Waxmann, 1995.

Rose, Romani. *Das Dokumentationszentrum deutscher Sinti und Roma*. Heidelberg: Dokumentationszentrum, 1997.

———. *Wir wollen Bürgerrechte und keinen Rassismus*. Broschüre des Zentralrates deutscher Sinti und Roma. Heidelberg: Dokumentationszentrum, 1985.

Rose, Romani, and Walter Weiss. *Sinti und Roma im "Dritten Reich": Das Programm der Vernichtung durch Arbeit*. Göttingen: Lamuv, 1991.

Steyerl, Hito. "Postkolonialismus und Biopolitik: Probleme der Übertragung postkolonialer Ansätze in den deutschen Kontext." *Spricht die Subalterne deutsch? Migration und postkoloniale Kritik*. Ed. Hito Steyerl and Encarnación Gutiérrez Rodriguez. Münster: Unrast, 2003. 38–55.

Wigger, Iris. "Ein eigenartiges Volk: Die Ethnisierung des Zigeunerstereotyps im Spiegel von Enzyklopädien und Lexika." *Stichwort: Zigeuner. Zur Stigmatisierung von Sinti und Roma in Lexika und Enzyklopädien*. Ed. Anita Awosusi. Heidelberg: Wunderhorn, 1998. 13–43.

Winckel, Änneke. *Antiziganismus: Rassismus gegen Sinti und Roma im vereinigten Deutschland*. Münster: Unrast, 2003.

Wippermann, Wolfgang. "Das 'ius sanguinis' und die Minderheiten im deutschen Kaiserreich." *Nationale Minderheiten und staatliche Minderheitenpolitik in Deutschland im 19. Jahrhundert*. Ed. Hans Henning Hahn and Peter Kunze. Berlin: Akademie, 1999. 133-43.

Wollrad, Eske. "Deutschland den Deutschen, Indien den Indianern! Zum Verhältnis von Kultur, Hybriditätsdiskursen und Rassismus." *Der Sprung in der Schüssel. Künstlerinnen und Theologinnen im Austausch*. Ed. Kirsten Beuth, et al. Herbolzheim: Centaurus, 2002. 7-25.

Wurr, Rüdiger, and Sylvia Träbing-Butzmann. *Schattenkämpfe: Widerstände und Perspektiven der schulischen Emanzipation deutscher Sinti*. Kiel: Agimos, 1998.

Zantop, Susanne M. *Kolonialphantasien im vorkolonialen Deutschland (1770-1870)*. Berlin: Erich Schmidt, 1999.

Feminist Theories on the Separation of the Private and the Public: Looking Back, Looking Forward

Ulla Wischermann

This article discusses the development of feminist theories concerning the separation of public and private spheres. It reconstructs the critique of a dichotomization of both concepts and applies newer problematizations, for example the concept of experience, to the earlier dictum of the women's movement that the private/personal is political. This analysis of discourses concerning private life and the public sphere is devoted not only to a historical reconstruction but it also casts a glance into the future, into a transformed cultural and media landscape, and poses questions as to the role of the private in the public sphere and beyond, as to whether the public sphere would have to protect privacy. (UW)

The topic of "private/public" has been actively debated in various scholarly discourses for many years. Since Habermas's *Structural Transformation of the Public Sphere* and even prior to it, this debate has intensely preoccupied the women's movement and feminist research. In this essay I shall try to present the focal points of the discussion that has been going on for more than three decades and has emerged from various disciplines and theoretical traditions, and to relate these points to each other. What I have in mind is not only a historical reconstruction, but at the same time an attempt to develop a feminist concept of the public and private sphere that integrates more recent and older studies.

The critique of dichotomies continues to be of fundamental importance to this issue. A look into the past will show that we are by no means talking about a new invention of postmodern theory. On the contrary: the disintegration and crossing of boundaries have always been central themes, particularly of feminist discourse concerning the private and public sphere. Whether the debate was about characterizing the private as the political, creating alternative public spheres, or the disintegration of the private sphere under the influence of the mass media and the resulting need to protect the private sphere, the central question was always how boundaries could be dissolved. These debates are not only extremely productive for research, but also continue to represent an important point of departure for linking feminist theory and political practice.

By deconstructing the dichotomization of private and public, feminist theory critiques an understanding of politics that holds on to a separation of the two spheres, assigns gender-specific connotations to them (male or female), and by implication orders them hierarchically. By being assigned to the private sphere—so claims the analysis—women's lives and work are, to a large degree, made invisible, while their experiences, interests, forms of organization, and action are excluded as not worthy of politics.

This exclusion of women from the political public sphere, which is coded as male, was one of the first central themes examined by feminist historians in the 1970s and 1980s. They pursued a double perspective: on the one hand, they forcefully tackled the problem of naturalizing and polarizing gender roles in bourgeois society (Hausen), critiqued the resulting marking of the private sphere as "woman's realm," in which work is performed out of love (Bock/Duden), and reflected on the way boundaries between the private and public are drawn in the context of patriarchal power structures (Lerner). On the other hand, this historiography reconstructed many instances where women had crossed boundaries, and it was able to illustrate by numerous examples that the exclusion of women from the public sphere was by no means a general fact, although, to be sure—and this needs to be emphasized—it was a constant component of the aims and objectives of male power.

Another very fundamental critique of dichotomizations was developed at a later point within feminist debates about the disintegration of the category of gender (Butler; Landweer and Rumpf). If the sex/gender distinction is dissolved into gender, and if even the body's materiality is declared to be a fiction that is created only by the gaze that constitutes meaning, is controlled by, and controls discourse (so the arguments go), then both the system of two sexes and the categories of private and public lose their relevance in the end. Thus feminist postmodern thought, beyond discourses of equality and/or difference, introduces new positions and ways of thinking.

As long ago as 1985, when her "Cyborg Manifesto" was first published, Donna Haraway ventured a look into the future and asserted the following: traditional dichotomies lose their validity due to both new gene and reproductive technologies and new communication and information technologies. As a result of these technologies, binary oppositions that are considered to be stable, such as that between "mind and body, animals and human beings, organism and machine" and, therefore, also that between men and women, as well as between public and private, are dissolved (Haraway 48f.). She views the fact that these boundaries have become fluid with ambivalence: on the one hand, the "information technology of power" can be sealed and strengthened by it; on the other hand, new possibilities open up as well to unmask the fragility of dichotomies and to begin new processes of negotiation. She emphasizes that to interfere in these developments and negotiations is not an end in itself, but must be seen as a political task. For Haraway, the cyborg metaphor is fiction and theory, comprising irony and resistance. As the creature of a postgender world, it stands for dissolving the boundaries between subjects, their bodies, and the outside world.

Postmodern and postcolonial discourses as well as the contributions of queer theory continue to characterize Haraway's critique of dichotomies. They make us more keenly aware of differences, exclusions, and hierarchical relationships, and politicize them (Dingler 137). At the same time, they point to the central problem: the fact that the production of discourse, for instance about differences, helps to increase these very differences. They thus direct our attention to the complexity of construction and deconstruction, of "gendering" processes and "doing gender," which are also relevant for describing the private and public spheres.

The Characterization of the Private as (also) Political and the Category of Experience

In spite of their critique of dichotomous concepts, many feminist theorists try to retain the categories of private/public. The intention here is by no means to rehabilitate them, but rather to reinterpret them. The categories are not meant to remain in force as separate from each other and underlaid with a gender subtext, but rather to be characterized and analyzed in a process-related perspective as relational.

A first stage on this road was to characterize the private as also political. Linked to this was the demand that the private be brought into the public sphere and made part of the political debate. Such a reinterpretation of the private had programmatic relevance for women's movements on a national and international, a current but also historical level. A look at the history of women's movements shows that "[a]ll political actions, central issues, and scandals of feminists aimed at shifting the gender-specifically drawn boundaries between the private sphere and the public sphere, to the latter of which only men had access" (Gerhard, *Atempause* 18). The allegedly private sphere was regarded as a point of departure for political demands: the debate around housework, in which the gender-specific division of labor was brought up as the most important reason for practical and social discrimination; the protest against the control of female sexuality and childbearing ability; and lastly the exposure of violence/rape in marriage and intimate relationships.

A central point in the demand that the private be politicized became the category of experience. The personal experiences of oppressed and/or marginalized groups that originate in societal ostracism or social conflicts, as experiences of injustice, must be articulated and politically generalized in order to influence political and social transformation. It was the authors Oskar Negt and Alexander Kluge who, ten years after Jürgen Habermas, with their category of experience brought new impetus to the debate about the private and the public spheres. They opposed the then-prevailing model of the bourgeois public sphere as *the* political public sphere and countered it with a "living" proletarian public sphere (Negt and Kluge; Negt). For secondary school and university students and particularly for the women's movement in the 1970s, the concept of experience became the focus of their theory and practice. Experience was considered to be the unifying and politicizing resource that must be mobilized and used in the battle for social change. The articulation and generalizing of the experience of those who were oppressed and marginalized, as well as the expressions of left-wing lives, were supposed to find themselves again in a process-related production of the public sphere that moves "from the private to the political" (Negt 34f.).

As a result, in this model, activities that are supposedly unpolitical—because they have been classified as private—such as childraising, the founding of women's shelters, or the activities of the peace movement and environmentalism, gain special political importance: "By emancipating the private sphere and developing specific human needs, these movements offer the subjective basis—and form the 'place of production,' as it were—for politics" (Hohendahl 13).

This was to be put in practice, for instance, in and through women's encounter groups that followed a program of feminist consciousness-raising work (see, for instance, Schenk; *Frauenjahrbuch*; Dackweiler). These consciousness-raising groups were at the same time "a technique for analysis, an organizational structure, a practical method, and a specific production process of a feminist public sphere" (Dackweiler and Holland-Cunz 108f.) and represented an attempt to organize autonomously women's life experiences that were considered private, to politicize them and make them public.

It became clear both in the practice of the consciousness-raising groups and in the subsequent development of theory that the wish behind this attempt, "Sisterhood is powerful," could not be seamlessly implemented, and contained many contradictions. It rapidly emerged that making the personal a central issue by no means led straight to a politicization of the private, but could also get bogged down in the publication of intimate matters. At the same time, commonly held concepts of the collective feeling of belonging (*"Wir"-Gefühl*), being essentialistic, moved more and more into the center of feminist critique and cast doubt on a politics of identity and representation that had hitherto been considered valid (see, for instance, hooks; Rodriguez; Spivak).

Parallel to these developments, the realization that experience can by no means be regarded as real and authentic or used as a "proof of truth" (Gerhard and Wunder 10) gained acceptance. As early as the beginning of the 1990s, the US historian Joan Scott substantiated the significance, but above all the problematic nature, of the category of experience from a deconstructivist perspective, using history as an example, and showed how difficult it is to study experience. The author emphasizes the discursive character of experience and the fact that it is socially constructed. She concludes that there is no straight line from authentic experience by way of the dawning of social consciousness to, let's say, a shared class identity (Scott).

Such reflections suggest, perhaps, the corollary that the category of experience has become too problematic to still be useful for speculations on the relationship between private and public. However, even if there are many contradictions and problems, we should not give up the concept of experience precipitously. Experience continues to be an important dimension that enables us to focus on issues that are excluded from predominant public spheres and place them on the agenda of the political public sphere (Gerhard and Wunder 10).

Oppositional Public Spheres as a "Hinge" between the Private and the Public?

If the public sphere is to be transformed by including experience and politicizing the private, the question arises as to what the negotiation between private and public might look like.

Looking back, we can see that early concepts of a counter-public sphere imagined the possibility of and the need for such a negotiation. These concepts, which, again, the authors Negt and Kluge promoted and developed further in critical media theory, assumed that the production of alternative public spheres is politically necessary for delimiting, but also influencing the dominant public sphere (Negt and Kluge; Enzensberger). Here, according to the authors, the "counter-public sphere" comprises both the place of political identity formation and alternative life plans, and the space for critiquing power and for creating oppositional, democratically organized media.

Karl-Heinz Stamm analyzes how motivating and relevant to practice concepts of counter-public spheres were for the secondary school and university student movement. He describes the variety of movement media and countercultural projects, and shows how closely interwoven the "production of experience in new social movements" and the formation of an oppositional public sphere were. The public spheres of the movement and the counter-public spheres are empirically reconstructed in the ecology and the peace movements, but (surprisingly) not in the autonomous women's movement—a shortcoming that Regina Dackweiler and Barbara Holland-Cunz (1991) tried to make up for with an essay in which they discuss the development of consciousness-raising and ecofeminism groups, interpreting this development as a "structural transformation of the feminist public sphere." Both studies share one (conspicuous) feature: while, in their understanding of public sphere, they do go beyond the classic model of the public sphere and critique its dichotomies and exclusion mechanisms, they nevertheless continue to take its assessments as a point of departure and extrapolate from it by working, on the analogy of Habermas's model, with the interpretative model of "structural transformation" and "disintegration"—this time, of an alternative public sphere.

It is likely that such perspectives have contributed to the opinion that the efforts of social movements and the production of an alternative public sphere have failed and have directed researchers' interest more toward influencing public opinion and toward producing a political public sphere in the media. However, the US feminist theoretician Nancy Fraser has succeeded in summarizing concepts of oppositional public spheres that ended up on the academic scrap heap some time ago, a way that gives them new momentum (Fraser, "Öffentlichkeit neu denken"; Fraser, "Was ist kritisch?"). She gives new value to the alternative public sphere as an indisputable contribution to democratic communication structures, and tries not only to discuss its relevance in the context of research on social movements but also to develop it further from a feminist perspective.

Unlike Habermas, Fraser takes the view that the "ideal of participatory equality...can be attained more easily when there is a large number of public spheres than when there is a single one" (Fraser,

"Was ist kritisch?" 136). Adding to the number of such heterogeneous "competing public spheres," she adds, is not separatist: on the contrary, it is desirable, for this is the way to expand the discursive space in which political processes of negotiation that are necessary in a civil society take place. The public sphere, she believes, is constituted by conflicts. Strengthening oppositional public spheres, then, means allowing diverging opinions and, since this involves conflict, questioning the hegemonic public sphere. The author emphasizes that through these "subaltern counter-public spheres" inequalities and exclusions come to light, and groups that are marginalized on the basis of class, ethnicity, or gender can get a hearing. In this way, for instance, it becomes possible to include interests and problems that are "labeled 'private' by middle-class, masculinized ideology and thus treated as inadmissible" (Fraser, "Was ist kritisch?" 149). On the whole, according to Fraser, these public spheres are indispensable arenas for the forming of opinion through discourse, and "underrated places where social identities are constructed, deconstructed, and reconstructed" (132 f.). Also, because counter-public spheres can take on not only separating, but also bridging functions between oppositional and institutionalized political discourses (see also Fraser, "Öffentlichkeit neu denken"), they can be credited with potentials for democracy that are worth considering.

Viewed superficially, concepts of alternative public spheres now seem out-of-date and too dependent upon the terminology and the political conditions of the past. In view of their productive development from the perspective of democratic theory and in view of new oppositional public spheres, however—for instance, the movements that critique globalization being formed and articulated in the New Media—these concepts should not be shelved too hastily.

New Questions: Privacy as Protection from the Public Sphere? Or: Must the Public Sphere Protect Privacy?

The book *Über den Wert des Privaten* (On the Value of the Private) by Beate Rössler is a notable attempt to revive the debate around privacy and the public sphere. The author intentionally takes a stand opposing mainstream theories about the public sphere by declaring without hesitation that the public sphere is a residual category and by making the private her focus. Her attempt to develop a normative theory of the private addresses the question: "Why do we value privacy, and why should we value it?" (10). And she gives the following reason for its rehabilitation: "What I am trying to show is that we protect privacy for the sake of our autonomy. In liberal societies, the function of privacy is to make possible and to protect an autonomous life" (10). It is protected from unwanted incursions by others because one is personally in control of access to the private sphere (23).

Rössler deliberately wants to avoid the debates of former feminist theories, which mostly returned to a quasi-natural notion of privacy that was clearly coded according to gender type. She profiles a legal, conventional concept of what is private that references subjective civil rights and liberties (45). By giving prominence to the indispensability of the private for the sphere of "equal liberties" (54), the blueprint becomes a reinterpretation. Privacy, according to her thesis, protects equal liberties and thus makes possible individual autonomy and self-determination. This, Rössler concludes, requires a different model of society that needs to discard the connotation—still in effect—of the private as a female sphere.

The no doubt theoretically attractive idea of emancipating the private sphere is, in this context, closely connected with holding on to the systematic idea of the distinction between private and public (48). Obviously Rössler does not intend simply to return to the old dichotomous models, but we need to ask whether—in spite of new definitions—old boundaries are not being redrawn here, boundaries that perhaps may not be relevant from Rössler's "perspective of justice" (48), but are in any event suspect from a perspective more critical of power and control issues. Weak points in this work, in my opinion, are the fact that the arguments are mainly drawn from US, that is, [non-German] contexts of legal theory, as well as the perceptible distance of the author from radical feminist and deconstructivist ideas, and a particular fixation on the traditional family in the context of privacy.

No one can claim, on the other hand, that the American political scientist and legal philosopher Jean Cohen continues to advocate traditional forms of the family as Rössler has done. On the contrary, in her recently published book *Regulating Intimacy: A New Legal Paradigm* (Cohen 2002), she returns to the very societal changes in the private sphere that caused the model of the nuclear family to collapse, such as the development of reproductive medicine (22) and the great variety of lifestyles and forms of sexual orientation (77). Already in her earlier essays, Cohen linked the right to privacy with the legal protection of privacy. Even if she goes about investigating the traps and ambiguities of legally regulating the private sphere and private relationships in subtly differentiated ways, she considers protected privacy, in the end, to be a guarantee for "decision-making autonomy, bodily integrity, inviolability of personal rights, each individual's 'territories of selfhood'" (Cohen, "Das Öffentliche" 325). Cohen's theorizing about the private sphere undoubtedly contains impulses and suggestions that are worth considering, but would need to be modified for other contexts. Because it makes US liberal freedoms the pivot and a key issue of its argumentation, this legal-philosophical approach cannot be automatically applied to other legal systems, such as the German one.

The discourse I have just described about a "democratization of the private sphere" (Giddens), in which equal freedoms create the basis for a lived experience of self-determination, relationships, and feelings, represents an important challenge in the conversation about privacy and the public sphere. But it should be more solidly framed by almost diametrically opposed discourses according to which public and private have long since dissolved—namely, under the influence of new and old mass media.

The Private in the Public Sphere

The social scientist Richard Sennett was one of the first to lament vociferously that the societally necessary equilibrium between private and public had been thrown completely off balance. He bemoaned the fact that the private had caused the decline of the public sphere and projected bleak scenarios of a "tyranny of intimacy." According to Sennett, there are attempts to make "privacy—being by oneself, with the family, with friends—an end in itself." "For each one of us," he goes on, "our own self has become our chief burden." In his opinion, this would mean that "[l]ooking at society can no longer be separated from looking at the self; public things are debated by applying them to one's own self" (38). Ever since it became obvious that the media are increasingly focusing on private and intimate matters, or that political matters are being personalized, Sennett's explanation for "society's intimate way of seeing" (Schneider 17) has been readily used as an analytical framework. Looked at from this angle, talk-show confessions, Big Brother productions, and embarrassing revelations from the private lives of politicians can be seen, in the final analysis, merely as decline, particularly as the decline of the political function of the media and the public sphere.

However, it is traditional in women's and gender studies always also to look at the "other side of the coin," and to question perspectives and ways of drawing boundaries that have previously been understood as firm. Thus, there is also the opportunity not merely to critique the utilization and exhibition of the private in the media as an expression of tabloid mentality and commercialization, but also to consider it as the potential for reformulating the categories of privacy and public sphere

(Herrmann and Lünenborg; Herrmann). For instance, when in talk shows today feelings and private experience are made public, this has little to do on the surface with the feminist demand that the private sphere be politicized. Nevertheless, female media researchers feel it is productive to go against mainstream research and not to judge these media presentations that reveal private things only from a negative standpoint. For instance, they ask: can such publications of personal experiences in the media initiate or intensify discourse that would otherwise not take place or be excluded? Or: are personalized models of representation by which no group identity is constructed also possibly an opportunity to present difference? (Herrmann 152 ff.). Or: does the entertaining presentation of politics that is increasingly practiced today bring about only depoliticization, or can it perhaps draw people's attention to politics and give politics greater social significance? (Hofmann).

Such against-the-grain approaches are important, in any case, but I must emphasize that we need many more empirical studies and more theoretical reflection in order to arrive at complex and plausible statements as to whether and, if so, how "looking at private circumstances in the media can expand one's understanding and perspectives of politics" (Herrmann and Lünenborg 7). It will be of central importance to name criteria that are relevant for defining the political in the private sphere, such as generalizability, social significance, respect for the intimate, and self-determination of the individual. And if the premise "What is relevant for the public sphere is that which is of public interest" remains valid, there needs to be a guarantee that this public sphere is pluralistic and no longer male-dominated or characterized by exclusion.

A further development that, however, I can mention only briefly at the end of this article, and that again sheds a different light on shifts in the relationship between private and public in the media, is the development of new media such as the Internet. At present the Internet is radically altering the communication media: it is decentralized, open-ended, and, above all, interactive, with the established roles of users and producers no longer in effect, and these features are seen as the basis for uncontrollability, openness, and non-hierarchic communication across national and cultural boundaries, for instance, as a framework for uncensored spaces and counter-public spheres. In these new spaces of communication and action, new public spheres and worldwide Net communities are formed. But at the same time a display of the private that is difficult to comprehend is taking place here as well (Wischermann 2004). Moreover—in a reverse conclusion, so to speak—there are now debates about the fact that the private sphere is about to disappear in a network world, because everything that is done on the Net can be reconstructed electronically (Castells).

At this point, if not before, we must realize that for a long time now, concepts of public and private have no longer been able to rely on prevalent dichotomies and polarities. And in view of the way reality is constructed in the media, these concepts cannot continue to refer to old patterns of evaluation and theories of decline. Recent critical lines of research in the area of Anglo-American cultural studies emphasize the relevance of media for the social structure, and locate media within the framework of the existing balance of power and the cultural production of meaning. In their analysis of the media and society, they critique an understanding of the public sphere that simply ignores or condemns the mass media. Discursive models of the public sphere that do not see that sphere as being "contaminated" by media culture are described as illusionary and counterproductive (Dahlgren and Sparks 17). Accordingly, my recommendation is not to insist on theories of decline, but to bring the analysis and the theoretical framework more realistically in tune with the present-day situation and to develop them further.

Outlook

The description of various discourses located within a number of different theoretical approaches and disciplines should make clear the extent to which the private is operative in the public sphere and, vice versa, the public is operative in the private sphere (cf. Klaus; Wischermann, "Der Kommunikationsraum Internet"). Feminist theories on the separation of private and public have clearly shown how this pair of concepts is constantly undermined when dichotomies disintegrate. Consequently, academic models and analyses need to stop using customary polarizations and dichotomizations. This is possible only if the relationship private/public is seen in principle as a relational one, as one about which we need to engage in constantly new processes of communication and negotiation. Or, as Regina Becker-Schmidt once suggested, they can be regarded as salient points on a continuum. Only if researchers devote their attention specifically to the transitions, reciprocal relationships, and interconnections between them are up-to-date descriptions and new insights possible.

Translated by Ilze Klavina Mueller

Works Cited

Becker-Schmidt, Regina. "Zum feministischen Umgang mit Dichotomien." *Kurskorrekturen: Feminismus zwischen Kritischer Theorie und Postmoderne*. Ed. G.-A. Knapp. Frankfurt a.M.: Campus, 1998. 84–125.

Bock, Gisela, and Barbara Duden. "Arbeit aus Liebe—Liebe als Arbeit. Zur Entstehung der Hausarbeit im Kapitalismus." *Frauen und Wissenschaft* (1976): 118–39.

Butler, Judith. *Das Unbehagen der Geschlechter*. Frankfurt a.M.: Suhrkamp, 1991. English title: *Gender Trouble: Feminism and the Subversion of Identity*. Thinking Gender. Ed. Linda J. Nicholson. New York: Routledge, 1990.

Castells, Manuel. "Internet, Netzgesellschaft: Das World Wide Web als neues technisch-soziales Paradigma." *Lettre International* 54.3 (2001): 38–44.

Cohen, Jean. *Regulating Intimacy: A New Legal Paradigm*. New York: Sage, 2002.

Cohen, Jean L. "Das Öffentliche und Private neu denken." *Die sichtbare Frau: Die Aneignung der gesellschaftlichen Räume*. Ed. M. Brückner and B. Meyer. Freiburg: Kore, 1994. 300–26.

Dackweiler, Regina. *Ausgegrenzt und eingemeindet: Die neue Frauenbewegung im Blick der Sozialwissenschaften*. Münster: Westfälisches Dampfboot, 1995.

Dackweiler, Regina, and Barbara Holland-Cunz. "Strukturwandel feministischer Öffentlichkeit." *beiträge zur feministischen theorie und praxis* 14.30/31 (1991): 105–22.

Dahlgren, Peter, and Colin Sparks, eds. *Communication and Citizenship: Journalism and the Public Sphere in the New Media Age*. London: Routledge, 1991.

Dingler, Johannes, et al. "Dimensionen postmoderner Feminismen: Plädoyer für die Mehrstimmigkeit im feministischen Theoriekanon." *Feministische Studien* 18.1 (2000): 129–44.

Enzensberger, Hans Magnus. "Baukasten zu einer Theorie der Medien." *Kursbuch 20* (1970): 159–86.

Fraser, Nancy. "Was ist kritisch an der Kritischen Theorie? Habermas und die Geschlechterfrage." *Widerspenstige Praktiken: Macht, Diskurs, Geschlecht*. Ed. N. Fraser. Frankfurt a.M.: Suhrkamp, 1994. 173–221.

———. "Öffentlichkeit neu denken. Ein Beitrag zur Kritik real existierender Demokratie." *Vermittelte Weiblichkeit: feministische Wissenschafts- und Gesellschaftstheorie*. Ed. E. Scheich. Hamburg: Brosch, 1996. 151–82.

―――. *Die halbierte Gerechtigkeit. Schlüsselbegriffe des postindustriellen Sozialstaats.* Frankfurt a.M.: Suhrkamp, 2001.

Frauenjahrbuch 75. Frankfurt a.M.: Roter Stern, 1975.

Gerhard, Ute. "'Illegitime Töchter': Das komplizierte Verhältnis zwischen Feminismus und Soziologie." *Die Diagnosefähigkeit der Soziologie.* Ed. J. Friedrichs et al. Opladen: Westdeutscher Verlag, 1998. 343-82.

―――. *Atempause: Feminismus als demokratisches Projekt.* Frankfurt a.M.: Fischer, 1999.

Gerhard, Ute, Heide Wunder, et al. *Öffentlichkeiten und Geschlechterverhältnisse: Dimensionen von Erfahrung.* Antrag auf Einrichtung eines Graduiertenkollegs an der Johann Wolfgang Goethe-Universität Frankfurt/Main und der Universität Gesamthochschule Kassel. Frankfurt a.M./Kassel, unpubl. ms., 1998.

Giddens, Anthony. *Wandel der Intimität: Sexualität, Liebe und Ethik in modernen Gesellschaften.* Frankfurt a.M.: Fischer, 1993.

Habermas, Jürgen. *Strukturwandel der Öffentlichkeit: Untersuchungen zu einer Kategorie der bürgerlichen Gesellschaft.* Frankfurt a.M.: Suhrkamp, 1962.

Haraway, Donna. *Die Neuerfindung der Natur: Primaten, Cyborgs und Frauen.* Frankfurt a.M.: Campus, 1995.

Hausen, Karin. "Die Polarisierung der 'Geschlechtscharaktere'—Eine Spiegelung der Dissoziation von Erwerbs- und Familienleben." *Seminar: Familie und Gesellschaftsstruktur: Materialien zu den sozioökonomischen Bedingungen von Familienformen.* Ed. H. Rosenbaum. Frankfurt a.M.: Suhrkamp, 1978. 161-91.

Herrmann, Friederike. *Privatheit, Medien und Geschlecht: Bisexualität in Daily Talks.* Opladen: Leske + Budrich, 2002.

Herrmann, Friederike, and Margret Lünenborg, eds. *Tabubruch als Programm. Privates und Intimes in den Medien.* Opladen: Leske + Budrich, 2001.

Hofmann, Gunter. "Helden des Ungefähren." *Die Zeit* 27 June 2002: 4.

Hohendahl, Peter Uwe, ed. *Öffentlichkeit—Geschichte eines kritischen Begriffs.* Stuttgart: Metzler, 2000.

hooks, bell. *Black Looks: Popkultur—Medien—Rassismus.* München: Orlanda, 1994.

Klaus, Elisabeth. "Das Öffentliche im Privaten—Das Private im Öffentlichen. Ein kommunikationstheoretischer Ansatz." *Tabubruch als Programm. Privates und Intimes in den Medien.* Ed. F. Herrmann and M. Lünenborg. Opladen: Leske + Budrich, 2001. 15-35.

Landweer, Hilge, and Mechthild Rumpf, eds. *Kritik der Kategorie "Geschlecht." Feministische Studien* 11.2 (1993).

Lerner, Gerda. *Die Entstehung des Patriarchats*. Frankfurt a.M.: Campus, 1991.
Negt, Oskar. "Gegenöffentlichkeit und Erfahrung: Über die Krisis in der Arbeitsweise linker Medien heute." *Medien und Öffentlichkeit: Positionierungen, Symptome, Simulationsbrüche*. N.p., 1996. 33–40.
Negt, Oskar, and Alexander Kluge. *Öffentlichkeit und Erfahrung: Zur Organisationsanalyse von bürgerlicher und proletarischer Öffentlichkeit*. Frankfurt a.M.: Suhrkamp, 1972.
Rodriguez, Encarnacion Gutierrez. "Migrationspolitik jenseits des Differenz- und Identitätsdiskurses." *beiträge zur feministischen theorie und praxis* 42 (1996): 99–111.
Rössler, Beate. *Der Wert des Privaten*. Frankfurt a.M.: Suhrkamp, 2001.
Schenk, Herrad. *Die feministische Herausforderung: 150 Jahre Frauenbewegung in Deutschland*. München: C.H.Beck, 1980.
Schneider, Irmela. "Theorien des Intimen und Privaten: Überlegungen im Anschluss an Richard Sennett und Anthony Giddens." *Tabubruch als Programm: Privates und Intimes in den Medien*. Ed. F. Herrmann and M. Lünenborg. Opladen: Leske + Budrich, 2001. 37–48.
Scott, Joan W. "Experience." *Feminists Theorize the Political*. Ed. J. Butler and J. W. Scott. New York: Routledge, 1992. 22–40.
Sennett, Richard. *Verfall und Ende des öffentlichen Lebens: Die Tyrannei der Intimität*. Frankfurt a.M.: Fischer, 1986.
Spivak, Gayatri Chakravorty. "Can the Subaltern Speak?" *Marxism and the Interpretation of Culture*. Ed. C. Nelson and L. Grosberg. Chicago: U of Illinois P, 1988. 271–313.
Stamm, Karl-Heinz. *Alternative Öffentlichkeit: Die Erfahrungsproduktion neuer sozialer Bewegungen*. Frankfurt a.M.: Campus, 1988.
Wischermann, Ulla. "Der Kommunikationsraum Internet als Gendered Space." *Medien & Kommunikationswissenschaft* 52.2 (2004). 214–29.
―――. *Frauenbewegungen und Öffentlichkeiten um 1900: Netzwerke—Gegenöffentlichkeiten—Protestinszenierungen*. Königstein: Ulrike Helmer, 2003.

Did Women Really Read Differently? A Historical-Empirical Contribution to Gender-Oriented Reading Research

Silke Schlichtmann

Do women read differently? My article pursues this question from a historical perspective for the period around 1800. On the one hand, in a reflection that is methodical and source-based, it attempts to explain which requirements should be fulfilled by a reading research approach that is historically and empirically gender-oriented. On the other, it offers an exemplary implementation of the suggested research approach. In the process, what becomes clear is that an investigation that takes into account primarily the self-utterances of readers and proceeds in gender-comparative fashion will emerge with different results than previous work that was based on the reading craze around 1800 and ignored a firmly established gender-comparative approach. Instead of striking gender polarities, a picture emerges in which other factors, for example poetological concepts, appear as more influential than the category of gender. (SS)

"Women read differently." This thesis, which Ruth Klüger first published in 1994 in the feature pages of *Die Zeit* (1994a) and has subsequently advocated in at least four other publications (Klüger 1994b, 1996a, 1996b, 2000), assumes, without offering proof, the effect not only of social, but also of biological gender; in other words, it clearly contains a strand of essentialistic reasoning that uses ahistorical arguments. Astonishingly, in spite of concurrent debates about the category of gender in gender-oriented reading research, Klüger's view has in the meantime become almost a commonplace—perhaps not least because it is so seductively catchy and also because of its inherent "feministically correct ethos" (Dieckmann). Do/did women actually read differently, as she asserts, and if so, to what extent? So far, at least from a historical perspective, this question has hardly been examined; similarly, the methodological presuppositions for postulating gender-differentiating theses in this context have rarely been explicitly discussed.

It is precisely this dual epistemological interest that I intend to pursue: have women read differently, and how can one find out? I plan to focus on the turn of the eighteenth century—that historical phase, in other words, during which, it is widely assumed, a first consolidation of the so-called two-gender model took place. The model posits a sociocultural distinction between a masculine and a feminine gender character based on contradictory opposites (see, for example, Hausen; Honegger; Laqueur). In shaping this model of polarity, literature played an important role. First, the development of gender characters, particularly of the female gender character, was, implicitly, and often explicitly as well, a central literary theme. Second, reading itself is supposed to have been both the means of practicing, and the expression of enforcing, distinct gender characters. Accordingly, women read emotionally, with identification, and focusing on content, while male reading was rational and distanced, and prioritized the formal, aesthetic dimension—that, at any rate, is the tenor of the research.

State and Critique of the Research

This consensus is surprising in that studies of the history of readers for the above period that take into account ways of reading from the perspective of gender have been rare up to now. It is true that there has been analysis based on empirical material (books from lending libraries, letters, diaries, preparatory instruction in reading, etc.), dealing with gender-specific reading preferences and recommendations, that is, preferred or requested reading material (for instance, Martens; Raabe; Becher).[1] But with this focus on what was being read, the question of how reading was taking place, from a perspective that compared the genders—which is certainly harder to answer—has been, to a large extent, not considered.

Erich Schön and Friedrich A. Kittler are among the few who have directly addressed this topic. Of course, they give priority to feminine reading, and by this special treatment already present woman as a deviation from the norm (= man), as did the arguments used around 1800. Something else that is problematic about Schön's article is that his reconstruction of ways of reading is based solely on material that documents the debates on the reading craze and gender characteristics during the period in question. He thus chooses a genre of source material that includes primarily programmatic statements penned almost exclusively by men. The information contained in them regarding reading practices at that point in history should at least be viewed with the utmost caution. Thus, one will look in vain in his article for texts documenting the reading habits of real male and female readers that will corroborate the conclusions he draws based on this material: compared to men, he claims, women have less literary competence, read more atavistically, and satisfy their needs for fantasy more openly through reading. In my opinion, Schön's approach runs the risk of uncritically reproducing the contemporary discourse around the reading craze and gender, whose effectiveness for the social practice of reading first needs to be examined.

Kittler, who analyzes discourse in his history of the media, assigns to women around the turn of the nineteenth century the function of reader, characterized by receptivity, while, according to him, men, by productive rereading, assume the complementary function of author (that is, yet another confirmation of gender polarity based on the opposition of active versus passive). While he does include first-person testimonies by male and female readers in his study, he utilizes them in a disturbingly selective manner; besides, the base of his sources is clearly too narrow to posit theses that have a claim to general validity, although that is what he does.

Thus, three issues in current research appear problematic to me: 1) a lack of reflection on whether the sources selected are capable of supporting the stated goal of the study—that is, no critique of the sources; 2) a certain methodological carelessness in statements about the gender specificity of certain ways of reading, without a clear-cut comparison of male and female reading, and 3) a lack of openness with respect to the possible results of the study, and consequently a selective awareness and evaluation of sources and, combined with this, a lack of awareness of the researchers' own assumptions, which give direction to the analysis. The latter must be assumed to be the reason for bracketing out, in text analyses, passages in the sources that do not fit the picture.

A Gender-Critical Attempt to Reconstruct Historical Reading Practices

In this article I should like to present a model of what a historical-empirical, gender-oriented study of reading that tries to avoid these flaws might look like. I shall make reference to my study of gender difference in the contemporary reader response to Goethe's novels (Schlichtmann). As a preface, what follows are a few comments on my method and selection of sources. In order to be able to reconstruct historical ways of reading appropriately, I believe it is necessary to study as large a body of evidence of ways of reading as possible, and this is found in first-person documents. In the analysis, when bringing out possible gender-specific reading practices documented in this evidence, statements by male readers need to be systematically compared with those made by female readers.

Of course, such a historical-empirical study focused on gender difference and based on readers' first-person evidence can run into problems. Particularly problematic are the sources on which the study is based. I concentrated on sources documenting the reading of Goethe's novels (especially *Wilhelm Meisters Lehrjahre* [*Wilhelm Meister's Years of Apprenticeship*] and *Die Wahlverwandtschaften* [*Elective Affinities*]), found largely in contemporary letters by women and men from the upper-middle class. I need to explain why I chose these. Focusing on middle-class readers seems meaningful in the context of a widely held view in historical gender research that in this social group the new polar gender hierarchy was not only most intensively advocated discursively, but also, for the first time, translated into practice.[2] Concentrating on the readings of Goethe's novels is historically justified in view of the genre of the novel, inasmuch as it is this genre specifically that always became the object of violent polemics in the discourse on the reading craze because of its harmful effects.[3] As for Goethe, this selection of sources stands to reason, since in the case of the central author of *Germanistik*, it is easiest to put together a wide-ranging body of texts in a carefully designed procedure to form the sound basis of a study.

The reason for my decision to choose first-person accounts as my source material is my conviction that in order to reconstruct ways of reading that were really practiced, it makes more sense to look at what readers themselves write about their reading than to rely solely on examining programmatic texts. For only in this way is it possible to discern whether women readers may be reporting on completely different ways of reading from those ascribed to them in publicistic discussions. Also, only here is it possible to discern whether male readers, too, may read in a way that they ascribe solely to women in the programmatic texts. Of course, this does not imply the naive belief that first-person documents offer a direct and undistorted view of historical reading practice. It is always necessary to remember the way the sources were formed, which is contingent on the historical context.

For the text category of the letter—which, because of the large number of texts available, was given priority over the other genre that suggested itself, the diary—the implication is above all as follows: around the year 1800, the letter is in transition from being a predominantly public form of writing to a predominantly private one, which implies that there is, at least to some extent, still uncertainty in regard to its actual circle of recipients. Moreover, every letter is composed in a specific way depending on the addressee; there are self-stylizations as well as third-person stylizations; the sender and recipient assign mutually determined roles to each other; construct hierarchies; reinforce or undermine them. It is necessary to keep all of this in mind when reconstructing the acts of reading, as well as the fact that there are period- and group-specific rules for writing in effect. This is why it is also important not to look at acts of reading in isolation, but in the context of entire correspondences, as this is most likely to ensure that letters will be appropriately categorized and interpreted. Nevertheless, it must also be emphasized that in the end, strictly speaking, it is possible to reconstruct only how the reading experiences of real women and men are articulated within the specific communication situations of different correspondences. The refractions that occur in the process may be kept in mind and thus, to a certain degree, be included in the analysis. Still, a number of uncertainties continue to exist in every historical reconstruction. An answer to the question of gender difference in reading around 1800 must always be sought with an awareness of these limitations.

In order to avoid to the greatest possible extent merely reproducing the period's notions of gender as well as projecting one's own gender stereotypes onto the historical subjects in the analysis of the text, and in order to make the process comprehensible, it is necessary to establish before beginning the study what one wants to know and to determine exactly how to get there. My goal is to find out whether women used to read differently than men, and I am particularly interested in finding out whether—as both contemporaries and modern reading researchers claim—the idea of a polar order of the genders is reflected in the reading practices of men and women around 1800 and, if so, in what way and where. Therefore, in the study, we must be on the lookout both for reading practices that indicate agreement with the notions of a polarity model and for those that contradict this model. We must keep our eyes open both for commonalities and differences between the genders and, over and above that, for those things that connect and separate individuals within the groups of male and female readers themselves; that implies considering additional categories beside that of gender. Opening up the perspective of the study makes it possible to avert a risk that may otherwise be inherent in the method of comparison: the risk that the very fact of such a comparison will produce or reinforce the binary order.

Exemplary Implementation

To model my comparative study of the evidence regarding reading practices,[4] I have selected three instances of assumptions about gender-specific ways of reading contained in the polarity model:

1. The contrast of activity vs. passivity in the form advocated by Kittler, with his postulate that women assume the function of reader.

2. The opposition of rationality and emotionality, according to which only the male readers practice reading guided by reason and capable of judgment, while female readers remain at the level of emotion-driven reading acts capable only of simple opinions.

3. The contrasting of subject matter and form, according to which female reading is established as having a content- and ethics-oriented perspective, while only male reading practice is characterized by the consideration of formal aesthetic aspects.

"A woman's function is to be a reader" (Kittler)?

"As they reread their own writing, men move up to the function of authorship, while women describing their own reading assume the complementary function of reader" (Kittler 135): this, according to Kittler, is how simple, clear, and gender-complementary the division of the production and consumption of literature looks around 1800. Male authorship is grounded in female reading, coupled with desire and love: "Female readers and [male] author are embraced by a hermeneutically erotic circle that controls both reading and love" (137). The principal witness of Kittler's argument is Bettina Brentano, who takes "the function of female reader to its extreme" (136) by referentializing, in her readings of Goethe, the male hero of the novel and the author, female figures and herself, and then readdressing these readings directly to the central author.

In what follows I would like to point out a few weak points in this thesis. In my opinion, they are caused by Kittler's one-sided analysis of his sources and by the fact that he does not differentiate among his sources. In his remarks about the reader Bettina Brentano, Kittler quotes constantly from her book of letters, *Goethes Briefwechsel mit einem Kinde* (Goethe's Correspondence with a Child), published in 1835, but speaks of it as though these were the letters Brentano sent to Goethe between 1807 and 1811—although the very passages on which he primarily bases his arguments are partly missing in the original correspondence and must be regarded to a large extent as later interpolations. Now, a separation between the original letters and the book of letters may appear fairly unimportant strictly from the point of view of discourse analysis. But such an action becomes problematic, especially if an examination of each body of text leads to different results, and when, in a different case where it is helpful to his argumentation, the same author definitely points to possible differences between the original and the adaptation (135).

It is true that there really is much talk of love in Bettina Brentano's letters to Goethe. But we need to ask whether there is nothing beyond this function of the loving reader in her writing to the author. If we look at the original letters that have been passed down to us, we are forced to realize that in addition to the clearly hierarchizing positionings that function according to the model of loving woman reader and the God-author, Brentano also uses formulations that call this hierarchy into question—for instance, when she addresses Goethe as her "twin brother" (GBK [see list of abbreviations] 591), seeing a sort of spiritual affinity between them, or when she, who so often portrays herself as a child, addresses Goethe, too, as "HerzensKind" (heart's child, darling; GBK 696). Above all, however, we need to point out that in the original correspondence "instances of equating the hero and the author, and fictional and reading women" (Kittler 137) are by no means the structures that define the reading. In fact, a direct comparison with a literary figure is found only in its absence, when Brentano declares why an identification with Ottilie in the *Wahlverwandtschaften* is out of the question for her (GBK 672). And the author himself is also not perceived primarily in the light of his literary figures, just as Goethe's works actually play a comparatively minor role in these letters.

This does not change until *Goethes Briefwechsel mit einem Kinde,* that is, the text in which Bettina Brentano, who in the meantime has long since become Bettina von Arnim, at the same time abandons the part of the woman who is merely a devoted, loving reader, gives up for good the position of pure consumption, for the book of letters is the result of several years of creative process. The re-reading, which according to Kittler is coded as male, has without a doubt taken place. Goethe's literary work now occupies more space, with *Wilhelm Meisters Lehrjahre* occupying a special position, inasmuch as the Goethe-Brentano relationship is now given form in light of the Meister-Mignon constellation. In other words, it is not until this point that Bettina Brentano or, to be more precise, the figure of Bettine sketched by Brentano, finds during her reading of *Wilhelm Meister* "her own image in its protagonist's child/beloved [*Kindgeliebte*]" (Kittler 135).

It is true that this identification with the character Mignon does not function in the form of a plain equation, but contains a modification of the purported model. That also means that the work not only conveys an enthusiastic love for the author, but at the same time criticizes Goethe and his work (see GBK 98-99). It is also necessary to emphasize that Mignon is the only one of Goethe's figures in which (the literary character) Bettine recognizes herself in broad terms. Bettine rejects all his other female characters—that is, if we even want to count the threshold figure of Mignon as a female character. "To write to an author that, first, he himself loves the women whom the protagonists of his novels love, and that, secondly, the undersigned is like these women" (Kittler 136)—might perhaps indeed describe the function of female reader in its most extreme form, but, as far as the second half of the statement is concerned, it is by no means what Bettina Brentano is doing. Rather, she expressly dissociates herself from Goethe's female characters. Even Lotte in *Werther,* she says, "never edified" her and in *Wilhelm Meister* she "loathes all the women" (GBK 297). Brentano writes that her hope for the author's love is grounded in the very fact that she is *not* like his female characters: "and I had counted on your growing fond of me as soon as you got to know me, because I am better and more charming than the entire female cast of your novels..." (GBK 297).

At this point I shall break off my examination of Bettina Brentano's love for and reading of Goethe. Although brief, my remarks should have made it clear that Kittler's analysis of this source exhibits a problematic one-sidedness that serves to support a catchy thesis that can be seamlessly made to fit the polarized system of the two-gender model. It is true that Bettina Brentano's writing is imbued with love and admiration for Goethe, and her idolization of the author, while at the same time casting that authority figure in an erotic role, sometimes reaches extreme proportions (which, to be sure, is also the product of stage management on her part). But, and this is important, this is only part of the truth—first, because Brentano's letters also include opposing currents, and for a series of Kittler's theses, particularly those that concern identificatory reading, there are more negative than positive illustrations; and secondly, because the idolization of authors is part of a contemporary phenomenon in which not only women participate.

All we have to do is to compare the letters of the reader Bettina Brentano and those of master builder, composer, and friend of Goethe Carl Friedrich Zelter, and we shall see that the male expressions of love, which address formulations to Goethe such as "divine friend" (Z 110, 156, 214, 225), "sweetly beloved friendly heart" (351), and "most beautiful one" (380), "sweetest one" (562), are in every way the equal of the female ones. Zelter also tells the author that he intensively reread the Goethe texts (for instance, 120-21, 172, 235, 258); the declaration that he has already read something "[m]any, many times" (192) or "countless times" (176) recurs again and again. Zelter thus proves to be a responding reader who fulfills a function complementary to authorship—that of being a reader—in a virtually exemplary manner.

And he is by no means the only one on the male side. For instance, the diplomat Karl Friedrich von Reinhard also rereads *Die Wahlverwandtschaften* for the second time just a few months after the novel's publication (R 110–11), the writer Moritz August von Thümmel even reads the first volume of the *Lehrjahre* twice within a few weeks (GSA 28/913/I), and the Viennese cathedral preacher and composer Jakob Rudolf Khünl notes that he "actually read [the *Lehrjahre*] eight times within a period of 8 years" (GÖ 2, 85). Love for the author coupled with veneration for his work is also a component of the letters of male readers. The tutor Karl Johann Braun von Braunthal, for instance, writes to the poet of his "boldness in clinging to you like a caterpillar" (GÖ 2, 329), and the romantic writer and convert Zacharias Werner speaks to Goethe of the "ardor of my grateful devotion" (GR 2, 15) and refers to him as the man "for whom my heart burns in a way unfathomable to me" (GR 2, 59). Of interest for the question of gender, though, is the fact that a number of the male readers, in depicting their devotion to the author, use ways of speaking that are inscribed more or less clearly with gender categories. The quoted readers take what tends to be a "feminine" stance. This accords with the phenomenon that the literary public around 1800 is frequently thought of as "feminine." But as for the socio-historical *practice* of reading, associated with an author-stabilizing love, it must be noted that this represents a phenomenon that crosses gender boundaries.

Such findings, admittedly, can be obtained only as the result of a deliberately comparative procedure where one's view is not constricted from the outset by assuming that the two-gender model still has an undiminished power.

Female Emotionality versus Male Rationality?

Emma Körner, Christian Gottfried Körner's 21-year-old daughter, in a letter dated November 1809 to Friedrich Benedict Weber, fourteen years her senior, a professor of cameralistics and her father's cousin, tells about her reading of *Die Wahlverwandtschaften*. Right at the outset, she says that she would "consider it very arrogant for a girl my age to judge a work of this type," but since her addressee has asked for her opinion, "I shall try to satisfy you as best I can, only I ask you not to forget that in everything that might have struck me about this work I am only speaking of my individual feeling, for I might have missed a lot of things I am incapable of judging or appreciating" (DR 16, 116). The picture this female reader draws of herself is an almost ideal portrait of feminine modesty, combined with her emphasis on the subjectivity and inadequacy of her reading.

A similar reaction, though, can be found on the male side as well. The 25-year-old archeologist and classical philologist Friedrich Gottlieb Welcker also expresses reservations when, in December 1809, a few hours after reading *Die Wahlverwandtschaften,* he wants to share his "idea" of it with his friend Caroline von Humboldt, eighteen years older than he: "Perhaps it's not the right one; for it's still too new for me to be more certain" (HW 69).

Thus both Körner and Welcker begin with a qualifying remark regarding the general validity of their ways of reading. To a certain degree, this must be attributed to a writing convention prevalent at the time that is common to both genders. To be sure, the models for justifying the qualification are clearly different for the male and female reader. While for Welcker it boils down to the time factor, that is, a fault that can be remedied relatively easily, in Körner's case we first have a reference to an age- and gender-specific code of conduct whose rules she seems to be willing to follow, but also the consideration that she indeed lacks discernment, a general deficit. Körner's statements contradict the fact that in the remarks about Goethe's novel that follow, she is by no means expressing a noncommittal opinion based merely on her own feelings and subjective views, but definitely pronouncing a well-founded judgment. Thus, for instance, she represents her criticism of the character Ottilie not simply as mere displeasure, but explains the premises that underlie her assessment. As a high positive standard, she introduces the requirement that the work be interesting, then mentions the related requirement, namely, the condition the character Ottilie would need to meet for her to appear interesting ("if she had loved Eduard unbeknownst to herself" [DR 16, 116]) and thus also implies the negative attributive value she discovers in Goethe's *Wahlverwandtschaften* (Ottilie's attribute of loving Eduard intentionally). In this way—a crucial characteristic of a well-founded judgment, as opposed to a simple expression of opinion—Körner makes sure that her explanations can be reproduced intersubjectively and thus understood even by those who do not agree with her. It is true that we could fault the lack of a priori reasons in Körner's argumentation (she names the conditions under which the character Ottilie would be interesting, but does not explain why under precisely these conditions), yet this would be a criticism that—as the comparison with Welcker's reading shows—would apply equally well to male readers. Thus, of far greater importance, it seems to me—and this could be substantiated by further examples—is that in her comments on Goethe's novel, the reader Emma Körner, on the one hand, by being explicitly self-deprecating and by qualifying the relevance of her remarks, acts in accordance with a contemporary code of behavior of feminine modesty, subjectivity, and focus on emotion; on the other hand, however, she actually undermines the rules of this code in her statements, in a judgment she firmly articulates.

At this point it becomes clear how important it is during analysis to methodically differentiate levels of articulating the experience of reading: while the polarity model is maintained on the level of self-characterization, it may be undermined on the level of reading practice. We have noted that in Körner's case there is a doubling of the explicit labeling of her own reading, which is in agreement with the gender-specific characteristics of the polarity model, while she demonstrates a way of reading that contradicts this model. The same kind of doubling is found in the case of other female readers; what is more, it can be observed on other levels as well.[5]

However—and this, too, is a result of an investigation of a broader range of source material—the data I have just presented should not be misunderstood as a general gender difference that is independent of additional factors. Not all female readers state that their own ability to judge is limited, and of those who do, not all attribute this to the fact that they are women. In addition to completely individual factors, those that are more generally decisive here are, for instance, the degree to which these woman identify with the character traits of the female gender, and the addressee to whom the woman reader sends her readings. To be sure—and this is the point where a gender difference is articulated—if there is a reference to gender as the reason for self-deprecation, this only happens in the case of female readers. Masculinity clearly uses other characteristics as its reasons.

Female Ethics versus Male Aesthetics?

In a letter by Charlotte von Stein to her son Friedrich dated October 1796, the following lines appear in a comment about *Wilhelm Meisters Lehrjahre*: "Moreover, the behavior of all his women in the novel is unseemly, and when he has occasionally brought noble human feelings to our attention, he has spattered them with a bit of filth to make quite sure he has left nothing divine in human nature" (St 54). Here, Stein concentrates entirely on the content of the novel, especially on its characters, and her judgment of the female characters is clearly based on moral standards.

On the other hand, a remark regarding Goethe's novel by Christian Gottfried Körner in a letter to Friedrich Schiller dated November of the same year takes a completely different tone: "I imagine the unity of the whole as the representation of a beautiful human character, which is gradually developed as its inner predispositions and external conditions act in combination. The aim of this development is perfect *equilibrium*—harmony with freedom" (NA 36.1, 370). Körner's reading, which has a primarily formal, aesthetic orientation, refers to central values of classical aesthetics ("unity of the whole," "*equilibrium*," and "harmony"), which he reads into, or rather, gathers from, *Wilhelm Meister*; the novel thus proves to be a graphic demonstration of the autonomy of classical art.

When we compare Stein's and Körner's ways of reading in the matter of gender difference, the validity of the two-gender reading model actually seems to be borne out here: we have the female reader, with her interest in subject matter and her ethical orientation, while, on the other hand, the male reader's way of reading has a strongly formal, aesthetic orientation. But such a conclusion immediately becomes shaky as soon as we undertake the necessary expansion of source material. For that is when we find, for instance, the following criticism of Goethe's novel in a 1795 letter by Johann Gottfried Herder: "I cannot bear it either in art or in life that true existence—particularly moral existence—is sacrificed to what is called talent, and that is supposed to be everything. Characters like Marianne and Philine—I loathe that whole business" (H 152-53). In other words, Herder reads—and this is also confirmed by his additional remarks, which are not quoted here—with an interest that is primarily content-focused, heteronomous, and that demands in particular that the characters and their behavior be morally exemplary. That is, the male reader Herder responds to the novel with value expectations that are comparable to those of the female reader Stein, and he is by no means the only male to do so. In this respect Goethe's "oldest friend" [*Urfreund*], Carl Ludwig von Knebel, is also painfully struck by "several radical evils" as he reads; "Wilhelm's straying [*Umwandern*] to Natalie" in particular is something he finds "extremely objectionable" (HN 100). And Goethe's brother-in-law Johann Georg Schlosser even describes the novel as a "bordello" (GvBZ 2, 145). If, among male readers, there are not only people like Körner, whose orientation in reading is primarily formal and aesthetic, but also like Herder, whose attention is mainly focused on the content level and the moral implications of the literary work, we need to ask at this point (if we have not done so already) whether, in addition to or instead of gender, additional influences are fundamental and central in the readers' system of assumptions for the way they read.

Both Herder and Körner are professional readers. But an important difference between the two is that Körner subscribes to classical aesthetics, while Herder rejects the aesthetic autonomy of art and adheres to the kind of moral, pragmatic values of art that were characteristic of the Enlightenment. This also explains the difference between those ways of reading whose orientation tends to be more formal and aesthetic and those whose orientation tends to be focused on content and morality. Not gender, but the internalized concept of literature seems to be primarily responsible for the premises under which reading takes place, and for the aspects focused on in the reading.[6] Evidence from women readers about their reading also suggests this, inasmuch as they by no means leave the aesthetics of Goethe's novel out of consideration. Let me quote just one more example, Charlotte von Kalb's admiring words: "Welche Demant Schrift—welche Mäsigung und welcher Reichthum—wie viele Schönheiten habe ich schon erblickt...diese Volendung im einzelnen—und die Verbindung die in einer so schönen Volendung glänzt" (GJb 13, 65; "What adamantine writing—what moderation and what abundance—how many beauties I've already glimpsed...this perfection in each detail—and the combination that shines in such beautiful perfection"). Kalb, quite familiar with the positions of classical aesthetics, takes its central categories—harmony, unity, and equilibrium—as the criteria for her examination of Goethe's novel while completely neglecting the novel's concrete subject matter level here and in later statements.

Conclusion

Women read differently. This catchy thesis, with its inherent assumption that there is a distinct catalogue of features that supposedly characterizes a specifically female way of reading, is not tenable for the historical phase of radical change around the turn of the nineteenth century. In any case, that is what the study of first-person utterances by male and female readers who were Goethe's contemporaries suggests. True, the discourse around reading conducted in programmatic writings may be understood as part of the dichotomizing gender discourse, but it is methodologically inadmissible to claim, solely on the basis of texts relating to the reading-craze debate or first-person statements by female readers, that this polarity discourse clearly corresponds with the cultural practice of reading. We need to question any thesis arrived at in this manner—the type of thesis that has been predominant in our discipline so far—and ask whether it is not merely reproducing two-hundred-year-old gender stereotypes.

Since not every type of source material is equally fruitful for every type of inquiry, critical reflection regarding sources and methodology is indispensable before beginning an investigation into possible gender differences. Regarding the question as to gender differences in reading practices around the turn of the nineteenth century, this means, in my opinion, that without an empirical approach that compares men and women and includes first-person utterances by readers in the analysis, results cannot but remain purely speculative and consequently are not really worth discussing. In practice, this significance of the selection of sources and methods becomes evident, if not before, then at the moment when we actually examine 1) not only theoretical texts but also first-person statements, and 2) not only statements provided by women but also those provided by men. As we select this new type of source material, the gender polarities that were once so striking begin to dissolve. And the comparative method can show that much that appeared to be typically female when only the reading practices of women readers were studied, since it so aptly fulfills the relevant characteristics of the polarity model, needs to be qualified in the context of gender specificity if it can also be documented for male readers. True, the two-gender model is partly maintained when readers self-label the way they read, but hardly in the reconstructible reading practices themselves.

The methodological demand that a study of the relevance of the category of gender should always be comparative is by no means a complete novelty in gender research; for instance, it has long been practiced in linguistics or sociology. This is why the fact that it is absent in historical research on reading is all the more astonishing. One reason might be the status of the sources. In historical perspective, it is not possible for researchers themselves to produce a body of study material following standardized rules, and the assembling of meaningful sources that are capable of being compared is an immensely costly undertaking for which—even with an author as widely and well researched as Goethe—a visit to the archives is indispensable.

One desideratum for future gender-oriented research on reading is a broad reappraisal of archival first-person documents, including readers' responses to other, less lionized authors. In this way, it might be possible to work out to what extent the subject of the reading influences reading practice—just as it would be important to take a closer look at how the structure of the act of reading is dependent on many factors. That means that various levels of articulating difference have to be considered, inasmuch as the category of gender is only one possible influencing factor, which can be eclipsed, or canceled out, by others.

Translated by Ilze Klavina Mueller

Notes

[1] To be sure, we need to criticize the fact that the focus of these studies is largely on female readers, and therefore no true gender comparison is carried out.

[2] Of fundamental importance for this view, no doubt, was Karin Hausen's view—which she, however, expressly called a hypothesis—that the polarization of gender characteristics corresponds with the historical reality in the educated middle class (Hausen 383). Anne-Charlott Trepp distinctly opposes the tendency to equate ideology and reality.

[3] While Goethe's novels were not exactly the focus of this criticism, it did not bypass them either.

[4] In the context of this article I cannot offer any detailed analyses and will sometimes present only results, while always disclosing how I obtained them. For a differentiated examination that also addresses the readings discussed in this paper, see my above-mentioned study.

[5] For instance, as far as the articulation of curiosity is concerned, it is coded as female and focused on subject matter. Women readers expressly claim this attribute as their own, while male readers avoid such a self-characterization, but nevertheless show an intense desire to find out how the plot develops.

[6] In Herder's case, the vehemence with which he expresses his criticism (but not his criteria) may also have something to do with the fact that he and Goethe had broken off their friendship; this factor—a troubled relationship with the author—would also need to be considered in the case of Stein.

Works Cited

Becher, Ursula A.J. "Lektürepräferenzen und Lesepraktiken von Frauen im 18. Jahrhundert." *Lesekulturen im 18. Jahrhundert*. Ed. Hans Erich Bödeker. Hamburg: Felix Meiner Verlag, 1992. 27–42.

Dieckmann, Dorothea. "Lesen Frauen anders? Wider die Vereinfachungen einer 'feministisch korrekten' Moral." *Neue Zürcher Zeitung* 4 (1996): 49.

Hausen, Karin. "Die Polarisierung der 'Geschlechtscharaktere'—Eine Spiegelung der Dissoziation von Erwerbs- und Familienleben." *Sozialgeschichte der Familie in der Neuzeit Europas*. Ed. Werner Conze. Stuttgart: Ernst Klett Verlag, 1976. 363-93.

Honegger, Claudia. *Die Ordnung der Geschlechter: Die Wissenschaften vom Menschen und das Weib. 1750-1850*. Frankfurt a.M.: Campus, 1991.

Kittler, Friedrich A. *Aufschreibesysteme 1800/1900*. 2nd ed. München: Wilhelm Fink, 1987.

Klüger, Ruth. "Frauen lesen anders." *Die Zeit* 48 (1994a): 54.

———. *Lesen Frauen anders?* Heidelberg: C.F. Müller, 1994b.

———. "Frauen lesen anders." *Emma* 5 (1996a): 68-71.

———. "Frauen lesen anders." *Frauen lesen anders. Essays*. München: Deutscher Taschenbuch Verlag, 1996b. 83-104.

———. "Frauen lesen anders." *Das Literaturquartett*. Ed. Brigitte Ebersbach. Dortmund: Edition Ebersbach, 2000. 77-105.

Laqueur, Thomas. *Auf den Leib geschrieben: Die Inszenierung der Geschlechter von der Antike bis Freud*. Frankfurt a.M.: Campus, 1992.

Martens, Wolfgang. "Leserezepte fürs Frauenzimmer: Die Frauenzimmerbibliotheken der deutschen Moralischen Wochenschriften." *Archiv für Geschichte des Buchwesens* 15 (1975): col. 1143-1200.

Raabe, Mechthild. *Leser und Lektüre im 18. Jahrhundert: Die Ausleihbücher der Herzog August Bibliothek Wolfenbüttel 1714-1799*. 4 vols. München: Saur, 1989.

Schlichtmann, Silke. *Geschlechterdifferenz in der Literaturrezeption um 1800? Zu zeitgenössischen Goethe-Lektüren*. Tübingen: Max Niemeyer, 2001.

Schön, Erich. "Weibliches Lesen: Romanleserinnen im späten 18. Jahrhundert." *Untersuchungen zum Roman von Frauen um 1800*. Ed. Helga Gallas and Magdalene Heuser. Tübingen: Max Niemeyer, 1990. 20-40.

Trepp, Anne-Charlott. *Sanfte Männlichkeit und selbständige Weiblichkeit: Frauen und Männer im Hamburger Bürgertum zwischen 1770 und 1840*. Göttingen: Vandenhoeck & Ruprecht, 1996.

Quoted Sources with Abbreviations

DR: *Briefe der Familie Körner (1804-1815)*. Ed. Albrecht Weber. *Deutsche Rundschau* 15 (1878): 461-79 and *Deutsche Rundschau* 16 (1878): 115-36.

GBK: *Bettina von Arnim: Werke und Briefe in vier Bänden*. Ed. Walter Schmitz and Sibylle von Steinsdorff. Vol. 2: *Goethe's Briefwechsel*

mit einem Kinde. Frankfurt a.M.: Deutscher Klassiker Verlag, 1992.
GJb: *Briefe von Charlotte von Kalb an Goethe*. Ed. Eduard von der Hellen. *Goethe-Jahrbuch* 13 (1892): 41-79.
GÖ: *Goethe und Österreich: Briefe mit Erläuterungen*. 2 vols. Ed. August Sauer. Weimar: Verlag der Goethe-Gesellschaft, 1902/04.
GR: *Goethe und die Romantik. Briefe mit Erläuterungen*. 2 vols. Ed. Carl Schüddekopf and Oskar Walzel. Weimar: Verlag der Goethe-Gesellschaft, 1898/99.
GSA: Goethe- und Schiller-Archiv Weimar.
GvBZ: *Goethe in vertraulichen Briefen seiner Zeitgenossen*. Compiled by Wilhelm Bode. New ed. by Regine Otto and Paul-Gerhard Wenzlaff. 3 vols. Berlin: Aufbau, 1979.
H: *Johann Gottfried Herder: Briefe. Gesamtausgabe. 1763-1803*. Ed. Karl-Heinz Hahn et al. Vol. 7: Jan. 1793-Dec. 1798. Revised by Wilhelm Dobbek and Günter Arnold. Weimar: Hermann Böhlaus Nachfolger, 1982.
HN: *Von und an Herder: Ungedruckte Briefe aus Herders Nachlaß*. Ed. Heinrich Düntzer and Ferdinand Gottfried von Herder. 3rd vol. Leipzig: Dyk'sche Buchhandlung, 1862.
HW: *Karoline von Humboldt und Friedrich Gottlieb Welcker: Briefwechsel 1807-1826*. Ed. Erna Sander Rindtorff. Bonn: Ludwig Röhrscheid, 1936.
NA: *Schillers Werke: Nationalausgabe*. Ed. Julius Petersen et al. Weimar: Hermann Böhlaus Nachfolger, 1943 ff. Vols. 33-40: *Briefe an Schiller*.
R: *Goethe und Reinhard: Briefwechsel in den Jahren 1807-1832*. Ed. Otto Heuschele. Wiesbaden: Insel-Verlag, 1957.
St: *Heinrich Düntzer: Charlotte von Stein, Goethes Freundin. Ein Lebensbild mit Benutzung der Familienpapiere entworfen*. Vol. 2: 1794-1827. Stuttgart: J.G. Cotta, 1874.
Z: *Briefwechsel zwischen Goethe und Zelter in den Jahren 1799 bis 1832*. Ed. Hans-Günther Ottenberg and Edith Zehm. München: Carl Hanser, 1991.

Musing Together at Year Twenty

Ruth-Ellen Boetcher Joeres and Marjorie Gelus

The two editors pool their reflections at Year 20 of the *Yearbook,* addressing, variously, questions of: Who am I to be editing the *Yearbook*? How does one go about co-writing an essay? What can a glance at the twenty volumes tell us about how the *Yearbook* started and what it has become? What is its job? How well is it doing its job? What ideas might we entertain to make it more responsive to our needs in this new century? The editors' questions and answers diverge and come together, but both heartily endorse these sentiments: happy birthday, *Yearbook! L'chaim,* Women in German! (R-EBJ and MG)

Marjorie: I have often wondered what, exactly, lies behind the finished product of a piece of writing with multiple authors: too often, nobody is saying who wrote what. The preface to last year's *Yearbook,* for instance, by "The Coeditors," was actually written entirely by Ruth-Ellen. For that matter, so was this year's preface. When she and I first began talking about writing a piece together for this year's volume, I began to wonder again how that would work. And as we started running ideas past each other, I became uneasy, because they weren't meshing well. Ruth-Ellen was looking toward where the *Yearbook* lies in the grand scheme of things, and I was inclined toward a modest close-up. If we couldn't find a topic that both of us could endorse enthusiastically, the chances that the piece would end up being genuinely co-written were poor. But also the ways that each of us writes did not look easy to yoke together: her leaping from peak to peak of abstraction, me sniffing at the wildflowers on the valley floor. Over the years, though, I have absorbed enough of the spirit of Women in German to understand that whatever the nature of the gifts that we bring to the table, we should bring them and lay them out there, which is to say: this piece needed two distinct voices. And so our plan was hatched, with Ruth-Ellen offering her thoughts in her voice, me doing the same, and then together weaving a frame for the two. An important influence on our plan was our recent memory of the lovely work that Elizabeth R. Baer and Hester Baer did in the piece that they wrote together for the last volume of the *Yearbook,* "Postmemory Envy?" (19: 75–98). First we will offer my reflections, then Ruth-Ellen's, on the *Yearbook* at twenty. That will be followed by her response to my thoughts, and mine to hers, and then a concluding paragraph by Ruth-Ellen.

My career trajectory began in my graduate training in Berkeley at a time (1966–71—major culture wars) when, if anybody knew that critical theory was soon about to hit hard on how we conducted our discipline, nobody there mentioned it—unlike, say, Stanford in the same era and the same place. I do remember one lone class in the "theory" of tragedy, by one Professor David George, but he decided to leave the academy in about the second week of the semester, just after we had all signed on for our seminar projects (mine on Schopenhauer). The path he broke was reclaimed by the seeds of entrenchment. So it was that I managed to receive a Doctor of Philosophy degree in German from the University of California at Berkeley in 1975 without knowing even that I was practicing New Criticism, much less that there were other options. I think it goes without saying that there was also no mentoring there for me.

In 1971, I went to Queens College of the City University of New York as an ABD Instructor, and in the eleven years that I spent teaching there, I got wind of the changing discipline. I was busy, and hoped that I could ignore it. But as it became more difficult to place the articles that I was writing, I reconsidered (still, of course, without mentoring: at Queens College, one of my colleagues referred to my abject ABD self as "the highest-paid graduate student in the country"; I was later denied tenure, and later than that, the entire City University of New York lost a class-action suit on behalf of women, amounting to some $7 million). Very belatedly, I realized that I could not ignore what was happening in my discipline, and (revelation) across disciplines, and even to the concept of discipline, and so I began to try to teach myself, embarking on an ambitious reading project. It started with Jonathan Culler on structuralist poetics and then on deconstruction, and proceeded through such stalwarts as Terry Eagleton, Gerald Graff, and Robert Scholes, with anthologies and textbooks by Vincent Leitch, Toril Moi, Rick Rylance, Naomi Schor, Elaine Showalter, Jane Tompkins, etc. My project later became collaborative, with monthly meetings of "The Smart Ladies"—a reading group of four or five of my feminist colleagues (at my next, and clearly final, place of employment, the California State University at Sacramento, where I began teaching in 1983, and where, again, no mentoring was available for new faculty). We Smart

Ladies delved into whatever struck our fancy over the dozen years of our collaboration: Butler, Case, Cixous, Derrida, Ebert, Foucault, Freud, Gallop, Gayle Greene, Elizabeth Grosz, Donna Haraway, Katherine Hayles, Marianne Hirsch, Irigaray, Kristeva, Lacan, Lévi-Strauss, McClintock, Modleski, Phelan, Rubin, Sedgwick, Spivak, Michael Warner, among many others.

Early on in this new theory venture of mine, I declared it time for me to try my hand at writing a new kind of article, one incorporating theory in some yet-to-be specified way. After much sifting through my assembled materials, I settled on feminist theory, and set out as if on a lab experiment to figure out how to apply some principles of feminist theory to the practice of criticism, with Heinrich von Kleist's "The Earthquake in Chile" ("Das Erdbeben in Chili") as the guinea pig. Readers, it worked. When it came time to circulate the resulting article, "Birth as Metaphor in Kleist's 'Das Erdbeben in Chili,'" for publication, I continued to venture into new territory, deciding to submit it to a venue that I had been only vaguely aware of, the *Women in German Yearbook*—and to attend their annual conference for the first time.

Both ventures were a new experience. I was encouraged ever so warmly by then-editors Jeanette Clausen and Sara Friedrichsmeyer to revise and resubmit my article. Since I was accustomed to either rejection or acceptance, this gray area made me uneasy and somewhat testy: why should I spend great energy revising an article that still might not be accepted, when I might place it as is with another publication? When I met the editors shortly thereafter at the 1991 conference in Great Barrington, MA, I broached with them the subject of possibly reconsidering their policies. They were polite, but did not change their policies. I grudgingly revised and resubmitted, and the article appeared in volume 8 of the *Yearbook*. Now, thirteen years later, I embrace those policies as at the heart of the whole Women in German undertaking—and the slumber-party-like conferences as embodying the same ethos. I have not missed one conference since.

The *Yearbook* is now celebrating its twentieth birthday, and Ruth-Ellen and I want to pool our reflections on the occasion. I have begun with a sketch of my own early career because it exemplifies what is so valuable about the entire Women in German enterprise, and that is the lively and supportive community that it creates for its members across a spectrum of age, expertise, interests, and institutional affiliations (or lack of them). In my own case, I have found a home in my discipline that I would otherwise not likely have found. Both the *Yearbook* and the organization have played important roles in that, and to limit my focus to just the *Yearbook* would be to narrow it artificially.

The *Yearbook* is famous for the close critique it gives to submissions, offering (usually) gentle but cogent criticism from two readers and two editors, and encouraging resubmission. The care taken with all manuscripts submitted was probably designed with newer writers in mind, with an eye to helping them—in a way that the terse acceptance/rejection model couldn't manage—join the conversation of the discipline. The editors and others of the membership actively scout conferences for likely articles, and I was approached twice with requests for submission. For someone like me, with a late start and a leisurely pace in participating in our conversation, such requests and such helpful editing were beyond encouraging, they were heartwarming. That I am now an editor only underscores the vision of inclusiveness that shapes Women in German. There is a valued place even in the editorship for representatives of smaller colleges and state teaching colleges, not just of elite research universities.

But the *Yearbook* and the organization emerge from the same impulse, one that permeates the annual conferences. While bringing along the *Nachwuchs* (next generation) is clearly of paramount importance, no less vital for all of us, I think, is the sustaining of a diverse and humane community of scholars. The conference papers range from good to inspiring, but it is the discussion afterwards that shows what we are about, and we always leave generous time for it: instead of passively and anonymously consuming ideas and information, we respond, argue, question, engage, expand, recast, recontextualize, and problematize, making of a presentation a conversation that brings to bear what each of us has to offer. Graduate students and new professors are given central roles to play in running the conference and the organization, and work closely and freely with more senior professors. Attendance ranges from novice to very grey eminence, liberally sprinkled with heavy-hitters (from across that whole spectrum). In the absence of pomp and circumstance, we get more of a sense of the whole complexity of one another than is possible at a typical conference: we carpool together, room together (some of us), eat together, dress badly together, attend the same set of (non-competing) panels together, take excursions together, and, most famously and hilariously, plan and perform Saturday-night cabarets together, spoofing the whole conference.

When I attended my first Women in German conference in 1991 (twenty years into my teaching career), I knew a small handful of Germanists, few of them well. I wrote in a vacuum, and to a vacuum (it has always been extremely rare for me to receive feedback on my work). I was blundering my way through my developing career by a spottily effective series of private guesses. The feminism that had been creeping up on me slowly since the early 1970s still had almost no place in my teaching or my writing. Thirteen years later, much has changed for the better. I credit many things for that—increased conference attendance on all fronts, especially GSA and MLA; the *Wende* (fall of the Berlin Wall); advancing age; better meds—but without a doubt, Women in German has been at the heart of it.

We end up where and as we do for a big mix of reasons. Big ponds, little ponds, big fish, little fish, energetic fish, challenged fish. By living with Women in German for thirteen years, I have settled into a soothing awareness of the dignity of all our roles. Elite expertise is thrilling to watch, but there is a huge array of types of work to be done (and ways of doing it) to keep the academic enterprise vital, and you don't personally have to be breaking the paths to be doing something important and interesting. It's easy to take too much to heart the labels and grades and fears of mediocrity that may attach to us and inhibit us. But in a community like Women in German, you can watch what happens when we are all thrown into a common enterprise together, and expected to do our share to keep it afloat. People rise to the occasion. They find nerve that they weren't sure they had—to run business meetings, or make announcements, or perform in the cabaret. They perform tasks that they may not have expected to be called upon to perform—to organize panels, or design websites, or serve on the Steering Committee, or as *Newsletter* editor, or on the Editorial Board of the *Yearbook,* or as coeditor of same. They venture beyond whatever inhibits them to respond to the call simply to step forward and make themselves known, and to occupy a position, however hesitant or tentative, in the common endeavor. They glimpse the mercy of knowing that their limiting labels are not immutable. All these beginnings are the richest gift that Women in German can provide.

Whatever we may or may not be doing on the cutting edge of feminist theory, we are certainly offering transformative support for feminist Germanists to pursue their chosen paths. We are a checkered group that pays attention to how to live well together, and there are places for all of us at this table. If our *Yearbook* has not (yet) made the transition to a periodical, if it is not as widely visible as we might like, maybe we can change that. But maybe, too, it has something to do with how we envision and shape our enterprise, namely: making room for all of us to participate in the project.

My career could have been spared much desultoriness by the kind of vigorous and ongoing mentoring and collaboration that Women in German offers. What occurs to me on the occasion of this twentieth year of our *Yearbook* is to pay tribute and give thanks to the organization that created it. Happy birthday, *Yearbook. L'chaim,* Women in German.

Ruth-Ellen: When I think about the *Yearbook* at twenty, I remember the review I undertook in the year when I applied to be coeditor. Such a year it was: my original understanding, that the new coeditor would be replacing Pat Herminghouse and working with Susanne Zantop, who was just about to complete her first term, was shattered by the terrible events of January 2001. But when I did my review of all the *Yearbooks,* it was before that awful time. And it was, once again, a lesson for me in the facile nature of viewing the passage of time, as the nineteenth century did, as a steady and progressive move forward. It is true that the *Yearbook* has moved on from a fairly slim and dull-green volume into one that has a much brighter and shinier cover in addition to considerably greater heft and a larger format. And a font that looks more professional, less produced by a typewriter. In a sense, it is as if the *Yearbook* has "arrived," now that it is published by a reputable academic press that does what it can to publicize it to counter the "physical inaccessibility" that Jeanette Clausen mentions in the piece that opens this twentieth volume.

But Jeanette Clausen is also the author of the very first piece in volume 1, her "interpretive history" of WiG, that presciently presents many of the topics that have marked the contents of the *Yearbook* as well as of the annual WiG meetings themselves ever since: the connections between WiG and Women's Studies, not to mention feminism in general; WiG's relationship with other academic units and with the university itself; and, inherent within her piece, the carrying out of the feminist goal of theory put into practice, often via practice itself, the role of experience, the need for connections between thought and action—themes that, in other words, have to do with how feminist German Studies defines itself in contrast to comparable academic sub-disciplines. Jeanette ends that piece with an incisive phrase that sees the WiG goal as that of "radically transforming scholarship and teaching in our field" (17). And that phrase reflects the rest of the articles in volume 1, everything from Jeannine Blackwell's eloquent attack on the difficulties placed in the way of those doing research on German women's literature, to Barbara Wright's account of the "feminist transformation" in foreign language teaching, to Richard Johnson's argument that the men in the peace movement need to heed the feminist women who are also there.

Maybe what struck me most in the early volumes is a clear mix of thought and practice. At that point in the development of feminist inquiry, an emphasis on experience was a political move, an acknowledgment most often of those who had not been heard before, a sense that we feminists were augmenting the larger field of knowledge by focusing on ourselves via a blending of the personal and the political. In that way, the *Yearbook* reflected its times. But maybe the argument can be made differently: just as those early years acknowledged the politics and practice of feminism while at the same time expanding and distinguishing the ways in which we, as opposed to other academics, thought about scholarship, the volumes of the current decade—or, for that matter, the 1990s—reflect the revisions and transformations within feminist work itself. In other words, I don't see a qualitative difference between the earlier and later volumes. I mostly see changes in focus. I would not expect, for example, a concern in the editorial prefaces of the early years like that expressed by the editors in volumes 18 and 19 that there is too little attention addressed to issues of race and ethnicity in the manuscripts submitted to the *Yearbook*. In the 1980s, at least within the purview of German feminist scholarship, race and ethnicity had not yet become compelling issues of interest. Problems focusing on the very pursuit of feminist work in the field were far more central. (At the same time, in the spirit of progression and daring that marked the early volumes, even that very first volume presented a piece on Vera Kamenko's *Unter uns war Krieg*. Its author was, again, Jeanette Clausen, whose focus on "language as experience" offers a linguistic social analysis that emphasizes the analytical category of ethnicity.)

The comments made by Clausen and Jeannine Blackwell in the piece beginning this volume about the missing theory in the early years of the *Yearbook* are appropriate: at least in our particular area of feminist inquiry, Germanists were somewhat behind the Americans in engaging in the basic work of re-discovery that feminist literary criticism practiced, because they recognized their need to address issues of loss, reception, research difficulties, etc., before moving on. But now we are in another era altogether, and the *Yearbook* has, to my mind, moved right along, expanding its areas of focus, showing evidence of a revision in feminist scholarship but also revising the ways in which feminist scholarship is conducted, moving out from the necessary work of rediscovering and re-introducing German women writers, as well as extending the areas of interest and the methodological and theoretical ways in which we examine and talk about what we examine. Certainly the fact that the *Yearbook* editorial board now has several non-Germanists among its members is a case in point.

The main thing is, here we are now. With a yearbook that has reached its twentieth volume. It is significant to mention at this point, I think, that the assembling of this particular volume was difficult. There are many reasons, some of them having to do only with the circumstances of Marjorie's life and mine this year and therefore not pertinent to a larger discussion—but I think I am not reading too much into our difficulties when I say that the *Yearbook*—academic feminism itself—feminist *Germanistik*—seem to be in a state of transformative crisis. As a matter of fact, it is not only feminism in its various forms but in our specific case German Studies itself that seems to be in the throes of change.

Jeannine and Jeanette also mention the growing costs of producing the *Yearbook.* Yes, there are those, but I suspect the problems go beyond the financial. I am quite frankly not sure what it is this yearbook—or any other yearbook, as genre—represents. I have said for quite some time that the yearbook format, an annual publication that therefore is highly restricted in what it can and cannot present, is perhaps inappropriate, too limiting, even archaic. It is in the very nature of a yearbook that it also directs itself to what can best be described as a subsection of a group—a yearbook most often emerges as the voice of a particular group like the Schiller-Gesellschaft or the Droste-Gesellschaft or the Malwida von Meysenbug-Gesellschaft. I have argued for pursuing another course altogether and finding a press that would be willing to take on a quarterly of feminist work in German Studies. (With a catchy title, of course: when the editorial board was discussing the issue of a title for the quarterly, GAGS [Gender and German Studies], GIGS [Gender in...], and FIGS [Feminists...] were suggested.) With a quarterly, of course, there would be all the possibilities open to that larger format: letters to the editors, special issues, book reviews, responses to previous articles. There would also be the possibility of expanding what it is we mean by German Studies: gender would remain the primary category of analysis, but, as is also becoming evident in recent years in the *Yearbook,* more attention could be paid to race, ethnicity, sexuality, national identity, etc. And perhaps we could expand the editorial board, including more historians, sociologists, geographers, art historians, and anthropologists, among others, whose work either centers or is often focused on German-speaking countries.

It is an exciting prospect for me. It also embodies some of the feistiness I always felt in those early years of the *Yearbook*: in this case, a challenge to a now widespread belief that publishers simply cannot afford to underwrite any more journals. After all, three publishers expressed interest in this quarterly idea a couple of years ago when it was originally broached.

Perhaps the difficulties we experienced with the *Yearbook* this year are reflecting what is going on in general: the continuing uncertainties about feminist German scholarship but also about the field of German

Studies itself, its parameters, its purposes, its aims. I should add "US" to the field designation, because the *Yearbook* has also been the primary representative of our particular branch of German Studies, namely that which, in most cases, occurs in this country. (Although if we were a quarterly, another group I would encourage to join the editorial board would be Germanists from non-US locations; we have always had one or two, but why not more, and not just from German-speaking countries? I think of the IVG meetings in which I participated in Göttingen and Tokyo, and how many Germanists and Germanist feminists I met from non-German countries.) It is not that the field has evaporated, or been co-opted by modern language departments that, by necessity, lessen the stronger presence and influence of a (single language or language group) German department. But foreign languages in general are of decreasing interest to Americans, especially in this hyper-patriotic time in which we live. And the developing field of German Studies is obviously making serious inroads into challenging traditional forms of pedagogy and canonical scholarship. In fact, feminists have been at least partially responsible for that particular move away from the narrowness of conventional critical and pedagogical approaches.

The volume that we are now presenting is indeed full of variety, with everything from more historically based articles that nevertheless are marked by current methods of analysis, to a piece by a historian who stresses above all the analytical examination of the category of ethnicity, to a richly argued film analysis. There is no problem with that. There is also clear attention being paid to issues of cultural studies. But I have felt a tentativeness in the process this year, and whether it is simply a blip in the journal's history or something more disturbing, it is a sign for me. Again, I long for the format of a quarterly: I want a special issue on Whither German Studies, this time specifically in terms of feminist Germanist work and our role in the larger field. I want the opportunity for a sense of the ongoing, not the—admittedly artificial—way in which the *Yearbook* has come to stand for a summation of at least the last twelve months. I want the journal to take on a larger role in the field, as a place for provocative arguments to be raised (such as: does feminism itself have a future, or have we reached some point where those who should be carrying it on and developing it further will claim that women no longer need to occupy a "special" position? Keeping in mind, of course, that my very use of "women" is meant ironically, because even if white academic women, on the whole, are seen as having arrived, certainly women of color, working-class women, and women from countless other nations across the world have not, in the academy or elsewhere).

I also long for the possibility of different styles. Jeanette and Jeannine speak of the wonderful varieties of writing that the *Yearbook* has accommodated, and I agree with them, but I want more. As I proposed during my stint as a *Signs* editor, I am eager to see flexibility and diversity in style as well as content. I pushed then—and could imagine pushing now—for the use of the real essay form, product of Montaigne and Bacon and Virginia Woolf and E.B. White and Audre Lorde and Susan Sontag and Cynthia Ozick and Adrienne Rich, but also Barbara Sichtermann and Christina Thürmer-Rohr and Rosa Mayreder, and so many others, the combination of the personal and the political and the intellectual that I find eloquent and enormously effective. In *Signs* I was arguing for attention to be paid to style—and along with that, I saw the essay then, and see it now, as a perfect form for feminist scholarship. Many feminist philosophers already use it—think of the work of Marilyn Frye or Naomi Scheman or Maria Lugones, for example—and why shouldn't we?

In any case, I would like to see the *Yearbook* as a location for innovation and change in addition to having it reflect the ongoing work in our field. That innovation should penetrate all the way to style. And, I say wistfully, if the journal could appear on a quarterly basis rather than annually, I would like to see every issue marked not only by all kinds of different scholarship but all kinds of ways of presenting it. And also by more evidence of creative work, a new short story or a poem by a German-language woman writer from who knows where. Or, as we do in this volume 20, translations of current feminist *Germanist* work done in Germany or elsewhere. I long, in other words, for all sorts of diversity. We need to see ourselves as the many-sided academics most of us already are.

Maybe there is something that needs to be said here about the role of feminist inquiry in the academy today. We seem to have gone from being on the fringes, or being viewed as derivative, to being ensconced/established, to being a part of the larger crisis encompassing German Studies, feminism, the teaching and analysis of foreign languages and cultures, and, indeed, the academy in general. Not to mention the humanities, which, in times of national trouble, tend almost to disappear. Pessimist that I am, I cannot see ahead far enough to envision a "greater good" emerging out of the current mess that is the academic world, not to mention the United States. But even though I have spent a lot of time questioning the possibilities of interdisciplinarity over the years, my work in feminist inquiry benefited especially from my editor time at *Signs,* largely because I was thrown willy-nilly into working with non-German Studies types, not to mention mostly non-humanities types.

Working with a sociologist as the other *Signs* editor meant that we spent a lot of time trying to understand each other; participating in the monthly editorial board meetings was often startling, since I think the majority of us absolutely benefited from learning to understand each other and to represent ourselves so that we could be understood, but in the process we were constantly in a state of agitated frustration. Still, I would not have missed that experience for the world. It shaped how I was then and how I am now as an academic. It made me learn to listen differently, for one thing, but also to express myself differently as well.

So, what I would wish for the *Yearbook*'s future would be some of that excitement that, to my mind, is hard to find if one is, so to speak, still incestuously bound up with similar others. I would hope for a much stronger attempt to appeal to larger audiences beyond the confines of our immediate field. I would hope for larger matters to be addressed, if not in special issues, then in clusters of pieces like those in volume 19 on feminist scholarship and the Holocaust, the majority of whose authors were not strictly defined Germanists. I would try out some of the methods that worked at *Signs* and in modified form also in the *Yearbook*: forums, perhaps, taking on some touchy issue such as the still-thorny place of feminism in German Studies; regularly appearing critical overviews of subfields within feminist German Studies. I would encourage contributions concerning issues that are both field-specific (nothing wrong with placing ourselves out there as scholars who should be more present in the larger fields of German Studies and feminism) and border-crossing: what about encouraging a historian and a literary scholar to submit a jointly written piece to which they both contribute equally on a subject of interest—albeit from different vantage points—to both of them? Or what about reflecting the occasional practice of the WiG annual meetings and presenting dialogues between, say, a feminist geographer and a feminist literary scholar examining a particular topic?

In a way, nothing that I am saying here is ground-breaking: the *Yearbook* has tried a lot of these things before. But if the journal could become known as a forum, above all, for interesting questions concerning feminist German Studies (with "German Studies" being understood in its greatly broadened parameters)—if it could be more daring and provocative both in the matter of what it discusses and how it discusses it—I suspect even non-Germanists might sit up and take notice.

And of course I am back to format. I doubt that any of this can take place if we remain an annual produced primarily for members of the association after which the publication is named. We need, for one thing, to be visible more than once a year. We need to have our journal serve the role of a place for ongoing debates. And even though I, a lover of the material aspects of reading, someone who needs to hold a book or a journal in my hands to feel at home, flinch a bit at the idea of having such a publication on line, well, if that's what it takes, then maybe we should plunge in.

One thing to be said about a year in which the editors are more present than usual, as we are in this volume: by asking Jeannine and Jeanette to contribute their thoughts about WiG and its journal, and by making our piece related, if different—a piece that also is, at least in part, relating to that first piece—we are, in a way, evidencing something more ongoing and more immediate than is usually the case in an annual publication. So think of this as not only two sets of memories and thoughts about basically the same topic, but also as a conversation of sorts among four people closely connected and committed to WiG and its journal. Perhaps the conversation will indeed be continued in volume 21, and carried on well beyond that. I think that would be a good thing.

As Marjorie and I read and talked about each other's thought pieces, obviously we were struck by places and issues where we had a lot in common and other places and issues where we didn't. Since one of the frustrating things about a yearbook is the lack of response from year to year—each yearbook is a discrete item unto itself, and by the time the next one appears, everything is new and disconnected in general from that which came before—we decided that it might be useful to introduce a response here. Accordingly, each of us has written a short reaction/response to the other. As we did with the thought pieces, we have composed our responses pretty much on our own, but they nevertheless are intended to pick up on some of the issues each of us has raised.

The point of departure that we shared was the enormously important role of the personal in what we chose to write about. The personal is still present in what follows, but each of us has also made the effort to move beyond it: to incorporate the personal as significant to what we are saying about our own takes on WiG and its *Yearbook*—but also to carry the conversation further by reacting, synthesizing, commenting on our thoughts and ideas.

My first reaction upon reading Marjorie's wonderful description of the relationship between herself and WiG (*Yearbook* and organization) was: how different we are. For Marjorie, WiG has become a home; a place where the mentorlessness of the outside world does not penetrate, where the key word has something to do with likeness, with the recognition of others and of self and how the two relate, rather than with difference. And probably most of all, where the isolation inherent in so much of her professional life can finally be done away with. WiG is both home and haven, and what Marjorie feels toward it is a combination of gratitude, relief, release, and pleasure. WiG is, I think, also at least somewhat synonymous with feminism for her, probably because the feminist experiences that she has had are centered largely around this organization. WiG, as she says, is her "home in [her] discipline."

I am reminded of that Minnesota conference in the middle year of the long-ago Minnesota WiG meetings, when we had decided not to have an outside guest but instead to spend time learning about ourselves and of what we as a group were composed, and also about our particular relationship to WiG. We called it something like the constituencies of WiG; we sat in a large circle that more or less encompassed all of us, and certain of us agreed to speak up and identify ourselves in one way or another—as graduate student, new faculty, older faculty, yes, but also as Jewish, as lesbian, as working-class, as a person of color, as a male, etc. As urban or rural, as American or European or whatever. I think we all benefited from that round, because we were able to see what WiG actually consists of, the great variety of identities we encompass, the border-crossings represented by all of us with our multiple allegiances or alliances. It was that multiplicity that I most vividly remember. It was also another example for me of WiG's being way ahead of the game—because what we were doing in that discussion was establishing, above all, how complex we are as individuals, something that was far less common a subject among feminists then than it is now.

Having said that, I have to return to my original impression upon reading Marjorie's words. She and I are different, despite the fact that we share a great deal (our training at prestigious institutions, our closeness in age, our common literary interests, our love of writing, etc.—in fact, we both had pieces in that volume 8 of the *Yearbook*: Marjorie's Kleist piece began that volume, and my piece on the incompatibility of feminism and German Studies ended it). But it is our differences that interest me right now, because those differences demonstrate to me the fact that we can be different, and yet share our love and respect for and loyalty to Women in German.

One difference is the very nature of what each of us has written in our thought pieces. For one, given all my involvement with personal narratives, I seem to have left much of the personal history aside in my commentary, have given no description of how I started, how I got to WiG, etc. I am not sure why. But where the difference struck me more is in Marjorie's repeated emphasis on her isolation and how it has marked much of her academic career. I certainly suffered an initial isolation, especially in the years when I could not find an academic job. But what characterizes my career trajectory are the growing—

blossoming—exploding connections, less because of my field than because of my going out of my department and establishing connections above all with Women's Studies, but also with what was earlier called Humanities at Minnesota and then became Cultural Studies. And because of the interdisciplinary make-up of Women's Studies, with colleagues in many disciplines from History to American Studies to English to Anthropology to Sociology to Political Science, and on and on, whose paths suddenly began to cross my own. What is significant here is the fact that I saw myself not moving about in a circle called German, but rather in a world of disciplines that was joined together by our common interest in feminist inquiry. Women in German, then, became a part of that picture, one of several homes that I cherished. The questions that Jeanette raised in her initial *Yearbook* piece were also raised in those surroundings and contacts, but always within the context of multidisciplinary concerns. And so, when Marjorie labels various experiences as being WiG-typical, I recognize in them something else because of my experience: they are WiG-typical, but they are also feminism-typical.

The practice of having a category called revise-and-resubmit, for example, for submissions to a journal is something I have been familiar with for a very long time, before my introduction to Women in German. I was lucky enough not to live in that bleak world of acceptance or rejection that Marjorie was exposed to. Early on, for example, I had the pleasure and the luck of sending a manuscript to the *German Quarterly*, whose editor at that point was Ruth Klüger (Angress): she did for me what Sara and Jeanette did for Marjorie in terms of mentoring and encouragement. Marjorie's comment on the central role played by the interaction of and cooperation between graduate students and faculty at a WiG meeting also made me think of my own experiences: it was very much the same at the two interdisciplinary feminist conferences with which I was involved at Minnesota just as it is at the yearly meetings of the Society of Women in Philosophy that I have also attended on occasion. These, to my mind, constitute feminist practice. And WiG is a part of that practice. Just as I got reminded of my own experiences when I read Marjorie's important words about the "soothing awareness of the dignity of all our roles" that she feels at WiG—just as I appreciate her saying that we are all in "a common enterprise"—I cannot help but let my mind leap to similar experiences not only in the work of Women's Studies, but even at the Women's Music Festival in Michigan, where everybody has a job that is meant to contribute to the enjoyment and well-being of the whole. Feminism, in other words, that in my own experience has always been both in and outside of the academy.

These are the important accomplishments of a feminist way of working and thinking. And WiG is a vital part of that way. I find it comforting and wonderful to add to that thought that WiG is located in the context of such ways of thinking and working: that as an organization, a collection of feminist scholars, it is itself not isolated either from other feminist scholars or from its own members with their own multiple interests and identities. Marjorie and I share the delight in the diversity of our organization. What I want to add to that is the diversity of feminism itself that, to my mind, has become increasingly evident as time has gone on. I know that I am enormously grateful that my years in the academy have been marked by such helpful, indeed loving connections. And maybe Marjorie and I are not all that different after all, since WiG has given both of us these connections. As it gives them to many, many others, wherever they come from.

Marjorie: My responses to Ruth-Ellen's piece are predictable, given who we are. I watch with admiration as she wrestles the twenty years of the *Yearbook* into a coherent story, with discernible patterns, starting with a collection of pieces in volume 1 that "reflect" Jeanette Clausen's hope of "radically transforming scholarship and teaching in our field," moving on to how the early volumes evince "a clear mix of thought and practice" (220) that bespeaks their times, and how the more recent volumes exemplify "the revisions and transformation within feminist work itself" (221), and ending with discussion of the possibilities for feminist inquiry in the academy today that factors in "the larger crisis encompassing German Studies, feminism, the teaching and analysis of foreign languages and cultures, and, indeed, the academy in general. Not to mention the humanities..." (224). On the one hand, this engages in a global level of speculation that my particular career trajectory has left me not readily equipped to take part in. My work has very rarely been with graduate students, and never with dissertations, and the pace at which I have participated in the common conversation has been genteel. On the other hand, though, I have a native affinity for the particular that lets me venture anywhere near the vicinity of grand speculation only after a tedious sorting of data so mountainous that by the time I come up with something, my audience will long since have gone home. It is those wildflowers on the valley floor (215) that draw me and detain me. So, my skittishness about the big picture is a product not only of lack of practice but also of disinclination. I am grateful that there are people in the world to do important work that I cannot or will not do. And while I am grateful for the facility with which someone like Ruth-Ellen can discern patterns in teeming data and draw conclusions from them, my wariness about the stability of those patterns keeps me lingering by preference among the data.

Do twenty volumes of the *Yearbook* offer evidence of something? Undoubtedly. But before I could offer my suggestions on what that something might be, I would have to pore over each article and editorial in the twenty volumes, formulate a working idea of what they offer, then investigate what other, similar and dissimilar, venues have offered during the same period, then probe the conversations over time among circles like feminist theorists, feminist activists, traditional Germanists, scholars of German Studies, scholars of the humanities, scholars of interdisciplinarity, scholars of the academy—maybe I could pause at this point and assess my booty. Assessing could take several years. Finally, I could formulate an opinion on where the *Yearbook* stands relative to such contexts. And it would likely be a magnificent opinion. Alas, I do not have the time for that right now. I am happy and grateful to endorse Ruth-Ellen's thoughtful speculations on it all.

The concrete possibilities that both Ruth-Ellen and the team of Jeannine Blackwell and Jeanette Clausen envision for the *Yearbook*, though, seem more manageable to me. We all share concerns about its future. At their least aggressive, its stewards could just continue soliciting manuscripts and hope for the best—although Ruth-Ellen is already wondering if the difficulties of assembling the current volume should be viewed merely as a blip, or (more ominously) as a trend. At their most aggressive, the stewards could try to transform it into a periodical, online or off. The conversation about whether we could morph the *Yearbook* into a periodical has been ongoing (desultorily) at least since Ruth-Ellen began her coeditorship, and she takes it up again here enthusiastically, with exciting visions of what that new format would allow us to offer, both in terms of diversified content and style, and of expanded readership. And, contrary to her self-announced pessimism, she even hopes to challenge the entrenched belief that publishers cannot afford to underwrite any new periodicals. The conversation about morphing the *Yearbook* into an online periodical begins, to my knowledge, with Jeannine's and Jeanette's piece here. Like Ruth-Ellen (and as someone who has barely made my peace with the twentieth, let alone the twenty-first, century), I flinch slightly at that prospect, but I welcome serious consideration of what we are and what we wish to become. As current coeditor, I felt suddenly exposed by Jeanette's comment that "what we haven't had is a plan, beyond just getting the next volume together" (10). Both she and Jeannine call for a vision and a plan, cobbled together at our conferences and online. Our guiding vision, I think, must be the one articulated by Jeannine: "People hold their breath, waiting to see what intellectual pronouncements will emerge from the bad girls (and boys) at Women in German" (10).

Ruth-Ellen: We come to the end of this mix of the personal and the public, this sort of exchange between the current coeditors of the *WiG Yearbook*. We also come to the end of this twentieth volume: an end, perhaps, but we hope that it will also mark an encouragement to keep communicating. There is no way to sum it all up—that would be an artificial step in any case. This effort on our part to put together a piece that presents at least some of our ruminations on the *Yearbook* at twenty is, by the nature of its very format, meant to look ahead as much as back. To emphasize not only the individual thoughts each of us has had, but also the possibility for dialogue/conversation/interaction between us. Words communicate. Individuals communicate in words. And perhaps the best thing about communication is the implication of community that is embedded even within the two words themselves: a community of differences and commonalities that, we think, is the best way to describe Women in German. By presenting our own thoughts and ideas, we are fully aware that we are only two—that we are only a small part of a large group of constituencies that Women in German represents. We hope and trust that the communication between all of us will continue and flourish over at least the next twenty years of the yearbook, or the quarterly, or the on-line journal that may yet emerge.

Works Cited

Baer, Elizabeth R., and Hester Baer. "Postmemory Envy?" *Women in German Yearbook 19*. Ed. Ruth-Ellen Boetcher Joeres and Marjorie Gelus. Lincoln: U of Nebraska P, 2003. 75-98.

Clausen, Jeanette. "The Coalition of Women in German: An Interpretive History and Celebration." *Women in German Yearbook 1*. Ed. Marianne Burkhard and Edith Waldstein. Lanham, NH: UP of America, 1985. 1-27.

———. "Broken but not Silent: Language as Experience in Vera Kamenko's *Unter uns war Krieg*." *Women in German Yearbook 1*. Ed. Marianne Burkhard and Edith Waldstein. Lanham, NH: UP of America, 1985. 115-34.

ABOUT THE CONTRIBUTORS

Katja Altpeter-Jones is Assistant Professor of German at Lewis and Clark College. She received her PhD in German Studies, with graduate certificates in Women's Studies and Medieval and Renaissance Studies, from Duke University in 2003. Her dissertation, "Trafficking in Goods and Women," explores the confluence of the discourses of love, gender, and economics in the medieval German "Flôre und Blanscheflûr" tradition. Her research interests focus on women and gender in medieval and early modern literature and culture.

Claire Baldwin is Associate Professor of German at Colgate University. She is the author of *The Emergence of the Modern German Novel: Wieland, La Roche and Sagar* (Camden House 2002), as well as articles on eighteenth-century and twentieth-century topics. Research interests include gender and aesthetic theory in the eighteenth century, relations between art and literature, Jewish-German literature and culture, and post-war German culture.

Jeannine Blackwell served as President of Women in German from 2000 to 2004. She is Dean of the Graduate School and Professor of German at the University of Kentucky, and is affiliated faculty in Women's Studies. She just finished a term as chair of the MLA Publications Committee. Among her writings are *Bitter Healing: Anthology of German Women Writers in English 1700–1840,* co-edited with Susanne Zantop, and *The Queen's Mirror: Fairy Tales by German Women Writers 1780–1900*, co-edited with Shawn Jarvis. She is currently writing on German Pietist women's deathbed narratives, comparing religious autobiographical writings to deathbed scenes in novels.

Jeanette Clausen is Associate Vice Chancellor for Faculty Affairs and Professor of German at Indiana University Purdue University Fort Wayne. She received her doctorate in Germanic linguistics from Indiana University in 1975. Her current administrative responsibilities include assessment of campus diversity initiatives, chair/dean orientation and development, faculty orientation and development, and other uphill battles. Her translation of Irmtraud Morgner's novel *The Life and Adventures of Trobadora Beatrice as Chronicled by Her Minstrel Laura* was published by the University of Nebraska Press in 2000. She is looking forward to her term as president of WiG with optimism and trepidation.

Marjorie Gelus is Professor of German in, and Chair of, the Department of Foreign Languages at California State University, Sacramento. She has taught almost everything, but her research centers on work of the *Goethezeit,* especially on the works of Heinrich von Kleist, which she has subjected to increasingly eccentric feminist interrogation over the decades. She has been active in *Women in German* for the past fourteen years, and now, in her dotage, is enjoying a new-found extroversion in odd roles in that beloved institution of the annual *Women in German Conference,* the closing cabaret.

Carol Parrish Jamison is Associate Professor of English at Armstrong Atlantic State University in Savannah, Georgia. She teaches courses including Early English Literature, Chaucer, History of the English Language, and Advanced Grammar. All of these courses are web enhanced and can be visited at < http://www.llp.armstrong.edu/5800/index.html >. She has presented and published papers on such topics as women in Old English literature, social satire in Old French and Middle English fabliaux, Arthurian literature, and the use of websites as pedagogical tools for medieval and linguistic courses.

Ruth-Ellen Boetcher Joeres is Professor of German and Women's Studies in the Department of German, Scandinavian, and Dutch at the University of Minnesota. Her research has focused on the social and literary history of German women from the eighteenth to twentieth centuries, on feminist theorizing, and on the role of personal narratives and the personal in academic writing. Her most recent book is *Respectability and Deviance: Nineteenth-Century German Women Writers and the Ambiguity of Representation.* She is presently at work on a volume of autobiographical essays entitled *Commuting: Ambivalent Identification and the Shaping of an Academic Life.* In 2004, she was given the Distinguished University Professor for the Humanities, Arts, and Social Sciences award at the University of Minnesota.

Eva Kuttenberg received her PhD from New York University (1998) and is an Assistant Professor of German and Humanities at Penn State Erie, where she teaches language, literature, and culture of the

German-speaking countries. Her research focuses on twentieth-century literary and cinematographic texts by Austrian and German authors who adopt suicide as an aesthetic strategy. She has published on Arthur Schnitzler's fictional suicide plots and is currently investigating Thomas Bernhard's suicide scenario. Her most recent film reviews focus on Michael Haneke's *The Seventh Continent*, Lukas Stepanik and Robert Schindel's *Gebürtig*, and Andreas Troeger's short film *911*.

Nicola Lauré al-Samarai is a historian and cultural theorist who is at present completing her doctoral degree at the Center for Anti-Semitism Research at the Technical University of Berlin. She is writing her dissertation on Black Germans in the former GDR. Her publications include *Die Macht der Darstellung: Gender, sozialer Status, historiographische Re-Präsentation. Zwei Frauenbiographien aus der frühen Abbasidenzeit* (2001), and "Unwegsame Erinnerungen: Auto/biographische Zeugnisse von Schwarzen Deutschen aus der BRD und der DDR," in *AfrikanerInnen in Deutschland und Schwarze Deutsche—Geschichte und Gegenwart* (2004).

Sara Lennox is Professor of Germanic Languages and Literatures and Director of the Social Thought and Political Economy Program at the University of Massachusetts, Amherst. Her recent books include *The Imperialist Imagination: German Colonialism and Its Legacy* (1998, co-edited with Sara Friedrichsmeyer and Susanne Zantop), *Feminist Movements in a Globalizing World* (2002, co-edited with Silke Roth), and *Cemetery of the Murdered Daughters: Feminism, History, and Ingeborg Bachmann* (forthcoming). She is vice-president of the German Studies Association and has received grants from the Volkswagen Foundation and the Alexander von Humboldt Foundation for collaborative projects on Black Germans and Black Europeans.

Ilze Klavina Mueller lives in Minneapolis. A former teacher of German, she has a PhD in German language and literature and has been translating from German and Latvian for many years. Her published translations include the poetry of Christa Reinig (*Idleness Is the Root of All Love*) and Vizma Belsevica; contemporary Latvian fiction (in *Latvian Literature* and other journals); and books on twentieth-century German film (*Margarethe von Trotta: Filmmaking as Liberation*; *Metropolis: A Cinematic Laboratory for Modern Architecture*) and modern architecture (*Haus eines Kunstfreundes*; *The Ulm School of Design; Debordering Space*).

Silke Schlichtmann is an independent scholar. She studied Germanistik, English, and history at the universities of Kiel, Munich, and Trier and received her doctorate in 1999 with a dissertation on gender difference in reading around 1800. In addition to her particular focus on the Goethe era, she has published on literary modernity and recent literature. Her principal areas of interest are located in the relationship between gender and intercultural research as well as German-Jewish cultural history. At present she is preparing a biography of the Berlin Jewish writer Marianne von Eybenberg (1770–1812) and is working together with Barbara Hahn on an edition of the writings and correspondence of von Eybenberg and Sophie von Grotthuß.

Carol Strauss Sotiropoulos completed her PhD in comparative literary and cultural studies in 2001 at the University of Connecticut and was appointed Assistant Professor of German at Northern Michigan University in the same year. She was awarded a Woodrow Wilson Foundation Dissertation Grant in Women's Studies for her genre study of German, British, and French documents pertaining to late eighteenth- and early nineteenth-century women's education. Her articles on Sophie von La Roche and Maria Edgeworth have appeared in *Colloquia Germanica* and *Children's Literature in Education,* respectively. A survey essay, "Educating Women: Thinking New Forms," co-written with Margaret Higonnet, appears in the volume *Expanding Borders* (2004), sponsored by the International Comparative Literature Association.

Morwenna Symons is a graduate of Trinity Hall College Cambridge and University College London. Her PhD thesis, on the role of intertextuality in works by Elfriede Jelinek, Günter Grass, and Herta Müller, is being published in the Bithell Series of Dissertations. Her research interests include narrative techniques in modern prose, feminist theory, and film. She is currently working on a project about textual and filmic representations of violence in Jelinck and Michael Haneke.

Ulla Wischermann, DrPhil, is a lecturer in sociology in the Fachbereich Gesellschaftswissenschaften at the Johann Wolfgang Goethe-Universität Frankfurt am Main. She also serves as a scholarly coordinator at the Cornelia Goethe Centrum für Frauenstudien and as the university's representative for women's concerns. The focuses of her research are media sociology, research on social movements, theories of the public sphere, and gender studies.

NOTICE TO CONTRIBUTORS

The *Women in German Yearbook* is a refereed journal. Its publication is supported by the Coalition of Women in German. Contributions to the *Women in German Yearbook* are welcome at any time. The editors are interested in feminist approaches to all aspects of German literary, cultural, and language studies, including pedagogy, as well as in topics that involve the study of gender in different contexts: for example, work on colonialism and postcolonial theory, performance and performance theory, film and film theory, or on the contemporary cultural and political scene in German-speaking countries.

While the *Yearbook* accepts manuscripts for anonymous review in either English or German, binding commitment to publish will be contingent on submission of a final manuscript in English. The editors prefer that manuscripts not exceed 25 pages (typed, double-spaced), including notes. Please prepare manuscripts for anonymous review and follow the sixth edition (2003) of the *MLA Handbook* (separate notes from works cited). Send one paper copy of the manuscript (no e-mail attachments, please) to each editor:

Helga Kraft
Department of Germanic
  Studies
(M/C 189) 601 Morgan Street
University of Illinois
Chicago, IL 60607-7115

Phone: 312-996-3205
Fax: 312-413-2377
E-mail: kraft@uic.edu

Marjorie Gelus
Department of Foreign
  Languages
6000 J Street
California State University
Sacramento, CA 95819-6087

Phone: 916-278-5510
Fax: 916-278-5502
E-mail: gelus@csus.edu

For membership/subscription information, contact Vibs Petersen, (Studies of Culture and Society, Howard Hall, Drake University, Des Moines, IA 50311; e-mail: vibs.petersen@drake.edu).